The postwar Canadian housing and residential mortgage markets and the role of government

LAWRENCE BERK SMITH

The Postwar Canadian Housing and Residential Mortgage Markets and the Role of Government

UNIVERSITY OF TORONTO PRESS

© University of Toronto Press 1974
Toronto and Buffalo
Printed in Canada
Reprinted in 2018
ISBN 0-8020-1901-3
ISBN 978-1-4875-7313-3 (paper)
LC 72-83386

To Marilyn, Cynthia, Ilyse, and Natalie

Acknowledgments

This study was partially financed by the Canada Council, grant 570-0582. This work has been published with the help of a grant from the Social Science Research Council of Canada using funds provided by the Canada Council.

Contents

ACKNOWLEDGMENTS vi

TABLES ix

FIGURES xi

A   Introduction   1

1 / Introduction to the Postwar Housing and Mortgage Markets   3

B   The housing market   15

2 / An Integrated Stock-Flow Model of the Housing Market   17

3 / Demand and Supply Factors in the Housing Market   27

4 / Econometric and Empirical Analysis of the Canadian Housing Market   45

C   The mortgage market   71

5 / The Structure and Basic Trends in the Postwar Residential Mortgage Market   73

6 / Private Financial Institution Mortgage Investment Behaviour   90

7 / Econometric Analysis of the Mortgage Market   105

D   Housing and Government Policy   129

8 / Impacts of Monetary and Fiscal Policy upon Residential Construction   131

9 / Impacts of Government Direct Housing Programmes   140

APPENDIX   154

NOTES   159

Tables

I Canadian Dollar Debt Issues Outstanding, and Canadian Housing Starts, 1946–69 4
II Percentage of Occupied Housing by Structural Type, 1966 5
III Relative Importance of Institutionally Initiated Mortgages by Categories, 1948–69 8
IV Comparison of NHA and Conventional Mortgage Characteristics 9
V Single and Multiple Dwelling Starts, and Percentage Change in Housing Prices and Rents, 1951–70 23
VI Frequency and Size of Total Mortgage Debt of Families by Net Worth Groups, 1962 36
VII Monthly Level Payments required to Amortize $1000 at Various Interest Rates and Amortization Periods 38
VIII Components of Single Family Housing Costs, in per cent 41
IX Measures of Housing Conditions, 1951–70 59
X Selected Price and Income Average Annual Rates of Increase, 1957–70 60
XI Percentage Share of Outstanding Mortgage Debt by Principal Sectors, 1936–69 86
XII Percentage Distribution of Institutionally Held Mortgage Debt, 1950–69 87
XIII Percentage Distribution of New Institutional Mortgage Initiations, 1950–69 87
XIV Percentage Distribution of Institutional Conventional and NHA Mortgage Initiations, 1935–69 88
XV Annual Average Rate of Growth of Financial Institutions, 1935–69 88
XVI Hypothetical Mortgage and Bond Interest Rates, in per cent 94
XVII Percentage Distribution of Selected Assets held by All Life Insurance Companies as at December 31, 1935–69 99
XVIII Percentage Distribution of Selected Assets held by Trust Companies as at December 31, 1946–69 101
XIX Percentage Distribution of Selected Assets held by Mortgage Loan Companies as at December 31, 1946–69 103

xx	Percentage Distribution of Selected Assets held by Chartered Banks as at December 31, 1946–69	104
xxi	Total Mortgage Approval Regression Results (MA)	109
xxii	Residential Mortgage Approval Regression Results (MA)	110
xxiii	Conventional Residential Mortgage Approval Regressions (CRMA)	114
xxiv	NHA Mortgage Approval Regressions (NHAMA)	115
xxv	Ratio of Conventional Residential to NHA Mortgage Approval Regressions (CRMA/NHAMA)	117
xxvi	Financial Institution Net Inflow Regression Results	119
xxvii	Assumed and Derived Interest Rate Adjustments for Simulation Experiments	122
xxviii	Financial Institution Mortgage Stock Adjustment Regressions (Dependent Variable M)	123
xxix	Mortgage Approval Simulation Results, Quarter to Quarter Changes	126
xxx	Proportion of Mortgage Approval Changes from Base Year arising from Changing Investment Yields	127
xxxi	Simulated Mortgage Approval Elasticities Over Time with Respect to Various Interest Rates	128
xxxii	Housing Model Simulation Results, Quarter to Quarter Changes	134
xxxiii	Mortgage Holdings of Non-Bank Financial Institutions as a Percentage of Total Assets, 1946–70	142
xxxiv	Non-Farm Family Incomes and Incomes of NHA Borrowers for New Housing, 1970	147

Figures

1. Graphic analysis of the stock-flow relationship in the housing market 19
2. Selected interest rates, monthly series, 1951–70 20
3. Flow chart of housing and mortgage markets 21
4. Time flows of funds according to various mortgage amortization terms associated with a hypothetical investment – 100 per cent loan to value ratio 34
5. Quarterly housing starts seasonally adjusted at annual rates, 1948–70 61
6. Housing starts, mortgage yields and mortgage-bond yield differential, 1953–70 63
7. Investment opportunity frontier and institution's indifference map 91
8. Portfolio selection choice between two assets 93
9. Percentage distribution of selected assets of non-bank financial institutions, 1946–69 96
10. Flow diagram of mortgage market model 124
11. Total housing starts, privately financed housing starts, and the unemployment rate, four quarter moving sum, 1948–70 132

A
Introduction

1
Introduction to the Postwar Housing and Mortgage Markets

A. THE SIGNIFICANCE OF NEW RESIDENTIAL CONSTRUCTION AND THE MORTGAGE MARKET

During the postwar period new residential construction has occupied a major position in the Canadian economy. First, the new residential construction sector is the sector of the economy that generated the substantial improvement in the nation's housing standards. This improvement may be seen in the decline in the percentage of dwelling units without basic facilities[1] from 37.2 per cent in 1951 to 8.2 per cent of all dwellings in 1968. Second, new residential construction has played an important role in the generation of income and employment in Canada. Between 1950 and 1969 new residential construction accounted for 41.1 per cent of total private new construction expenditure, 25.2 per cent of business gross fixed capital formation and 4.8 per cent of gross national expenditure, and directly provided employment for approximately 4 per cent of the Canadian civilian non-agricultural labour force. Moreover, this activity was further enhanced by an estimated 40–50 per cent through the residential service investment it induces in the form of electric, gas, telephone, sewer and water facilities, sidewalks, and some portion of schools, hospitals, and churches;[2] and by the demand it generates for new consumer durables such as refrigerators, stoves, carpets, drapes, and other new furnishings and appliances. Third, because of its general pervasiveness, short response lag, and sensitivity to government monetary and direct lending policies, the residential construction sector has been an important medium for the transmission of government stabilization policy.

Concurrent with and facilitating the development of the housing sector during this period has been the growth of the residential mortgage market. Because of the very high value per unit nature of a house purchase or rental housing development the reliance on borrowed funds is considerable and the proportion of debt to equity finance in residential real estate is higher than for most other forms of capital formation (excluding consumer durables).[3] For example, in 1969, 81.1 per cent of all dwelling starts were financed by institutional or public mortgage funds, and these funds accounted for 83.9 per cent of the total expenditures on new housing.[4] Consequently, the ample availability of mortgage credit at a reasonable cost is a necessary condition for large scale new residential construction.

The mortgage market is also an important determinant of the cyclical behaviour of new residential construction because of the high sensitivity of the cost and availability of mortgage credit to general economic and monetary conditions. The importance of mortgage credit in the construction decision together with the interrelationship between the mortgage market and other financial markets has meant not only that the majority of fluctuations in the volume of new residential construction in the postwar period is attributable to fluctuations in the availability and cost of mortgage credit,[5] but also that many government policies designed to influence residential construction activity have operated via the mortgage market.

Throughout the postwar period Canada experienced a rapid growth in the volume of new residential construction and this growth was facilitated by an impressive rise in the volume and importance of mortgage finance in the financial markets, as is indicated in Table I. Between 1946 and 1970 Canadian housing stock is estimated to have doubled, from approximately 3,030,000 units[6] to approximately 6,085,000 units.[7] Concurrent with this, mortgage debt rose from a relatively small 7 per cent of Canadian dollar debt issues outstanding in 1946 to become by the mid-sixties the largest single outstanding form of debt in Canada and to account for approximately 36.4 per cent of Canadian dollar debt outstanding in 1969. From 1946 to 1969 the value of mortgage debt outstanding rose by 28.5 billion dollars compared to 6.8 billion dollars for government of Canada debt (including Canada Savings Bonds), 10.9 billion dollars for provincial debt, 4.1 billion dollars for municipal debt, 8.6 billion dollars for corporate debt, and 6.7 billion dollars in net new sales of corporate stock.

TABLE I
CANADIAN DOLLAR DEBT ISSUES OUTSTANDING*, AND CANADIAN HOUSING STARTS, 1946-69 ($ millions)

	1946	1950	1956	1960	1965	1968	1969
Canada Savings Bonds	1,237	1,218	2,541	3,594	5,866	6,359	6,683
Government bonds (incl. Treasury bills)	15,011	13,307	12,109	13,941	14,437	16,864	16,765
Provincial bonds	2,010	2,830	3,510	5,270	9,093	12,886	13,965
Municipal bonds	860	1,200	1,920	2,800	4,263	4,978	5,191
Corporate bonds	800	1,600	4,200	5,620	7,601	9,403	9,950
Total	19,918	20,155	24,280	31,225	41,260	50,490	52,554
Mortgages: institutional	833	1,800	4,701	8,169	15,654	21,183	23,201
total (estimated)†	1,501	3,130	8,010	11,349	20,716	27,409	30,031
Total: A	20,751	21,955	28,981	39,394	56,914	71,673	75,755
B	21,419	23,285	32,290	42,574	61,976	77,899	82,585
Mortgages as percentage of total: A	4.0	8.2	16.2	20.7	27.5	29.6	30.6
B	7.0	13.4	24.8	26.7	33.4	35.2	36.4
Housing starts (units)	64,400	92.531	127.311	108,858	166.565	196,878	210,415

*Includes holdings of government agencies.
†Totals required estimates of "personal sector" holdings and are therefore subject to the possibility of large errors. The total figures do, however, reflect reasonably well the basic trend.

Source: Bank of Canada, *Statistical Summary*; Central Mortgage and Housing Corporation, *Canadian Housing Statistics;* Central Mortgage and Housing Corporation, *Economic Research Bulletin*, no. 77 (R) (Ottawa 1971).

B. THE GENERAL STRUCTURE OF THE HOUSING MARKET

The most distinctive feature of the housing market compared to other commodity and goods markets is its diversity. Shelter space is not a homogeneous commodity and the housing market is not really a single market in the classical sense, but a series of overlapping submarkets differentiated by location, type of dwelling, type of tenure, age, quality, and financing.[8] Although the dwellings in one submarket are in some sense substitutes for dwellings in other submarkets the differences between a small one-bedroom apartment in an older downtown core building and a new five-bedroom luxury home in the suburbs are enormous. If regional location differences are added, the oversimplifications involved in discussing a single housing market are apparent. Yet, despite their differences, the institutional arrangements, the behaviour of the participants, and the forces operating upon all forms of housing are sufficiently similar to allow a substantial degree of aggregation.

Three of the major distinctions that should be made are the differences between owner-occupied and rental accommodation, between single-unit and multiple-unit dwellings, and between family and non-family household formation.[9] The relative importance of each class may be seen in Table II, the percentage of the major structural classifications of occupied housing according to the 1966 census both for all of Canada and metropolitan and major urban areas. Because the vast majority of single and semi-detached dwellings are owner-occupied and row and apartment dwellings are rented, throughout most of this study the simplifying assumption that single-unit dwellings are owner-occupied and multiple dwellings are renter-occupied will be made for exposition purposes.[10]

TABLE II
PERCENTAGE OF OCCUPIED HOUSING BY STRUCTURAL TYPE, 1966

Type of dwelling	Canada	Metropolitan and major urban areas
Single-detached	62.4	49.8
Semi-detached and duplex	11.2	13.5
Row	3.1	3.5
Apartment	22.7	33.0
Mobile	0.5	0.2
Total	99.9	100.0

Source: Central Mortgage and Housing Corporation, *Canadian Housing Statistics* (1969), p. 74.

During the postwar period a number of major developments occurred in the Canadian housing market. The most dramatic development was the substantial improvement that occurred in the nation's housing standards. In 1951, despite a very strong housing programme in the second half of the forties, 9.8 per cent of all Canadian families and 13.0 per cent of Canadian families in metropolitan areas did not have separate dwelling accommodations of their own. Moreover, many of the dwelling units that existed were of inferior or substandard quality, as the 1951 Census indicated that 13.4 per cent of all dwellings and 8.6 per cent of metropolitan and major urban dwellings were in need of major repair. By 1966 the housing situation had improved dramatically since only 4.0 per cent of all Canadian families and 4.5 per cent of Canadian families in metropolitan areas did not maintain their own households; and the 1961 Census indicated that the proportion of dwellings in need of major repair had fallen to 5.6 per cent in all of Canada and 3.5 per cent in metropolitan and major urban areas.[11] Consequently, the strong need for new residential construction that supported the housing market for most of the postwar period was gradually dissipated toward the end of the sixties.

A second development was the sharp increase in relative importance of multiple as compared to single detached new dwelling unit construction. Multiple dwellings rose from under 25 per cent of total housing starts in the early fifties to over 60 per cent of total starts in the late sixties. A third development was the increase in relative importance of non-family household formation, which refers primarily to young single persons who move out of their parents' home to live in separate accommodations, and middle-aged and elderly widows, widowers, bachelors, spinsters, and divorcees who live in separate accommodations from their families. During the 1951–6 period non-family household formation accounted for only 11.9 per cent of net household formation, while during the 1961–6 period it accounted for 30.1 per cent.[12] This shift in the nature of demand was one of the forces giving impetus to the shift toward multiple dwelling construction.

C. THE GENERAL STRUCTURE OF THE MORTGAGE MARKET

Mortgages are the primary debt form used to finance new residential construction, financing over 80 per cent of all housing starts; and residential mortgages are the primary form of mortgage debt, accounting for 82.2 per cent of all mortgage loans approved by lending institutions 1965–9.[13] The primary suppliers of mortgage credit for new construction in Canada are private financial intermediaries, the most important of which are life insurance companies, trust companies, mortgage loan companies, and the chartered banks, and Central Mortgage and Housing Corporation (CMHC), a crown corporation established to administer government housing programmes and make direct loans to the public when private financing is not available. Between 1965 and 1969 private financial intermediaries were the principal source of finance for 77 per cent of privately financed housing starts and 62 per cent of all housing starts; and CMHC was the principal source of finance for 20 per cent of all housing starts.[14]

Analogous to the housing market, the mortgage market is not a unified market like other security markets, but is a fragmented market characterized by "one of a kind" deals and local orientation. Mortgages, unlike bonds, are usually originated in small amounts for numerous unsophisticated borrowers and the rate and lending terms of the mortgage loans reflect not only generally prevailing capital market conditions, but local and regional conditions as well as the location, type, age, and quality of the security offered, and the creditworthiness of the borrower.[15] The individualistic nature of each mortgage loan results in little trade in outstanding mortgages and a very primitive secondary market.

Mortgage loans are usually made by advanced or forward commitments, a technique confined to the mortgage market (although direct bond placements are somewhat similar) whereby a builder, prior to obtaining interim financing and commencement of construction, seeks a commitment for permanent financing from an institutional investor. Terms and yield are arranged at the time of the commitment, which precedes the actual delivery of the mortgage and disbursement of funds by several months. This forward commitment procedure together with the localized and individualistic nature of mortgage transactions and the absence of a functioning secondary market tends to build a rigidity into the mortgage market and a stickiness into the response of mortgage yields to changing capital market conditions. As a result, mortgage yields tend to have a smaller amplitude than, and lag changes in, other capital market securities.[16]

The mortgage market in Canada subdivides into a number of categories, the major distinctions being between (i) private mortgage loans and government direct mortgage loans, (ii) mortgages made on the security of residential properties and mortgages made on the security of non-residential properties, (iii) mortgages made for new construction and mortgages made to refinance existing structures or real estate, and (iv) government insured mortgages made under the National Housing Act (NHA) and conventional mortgages. The relative importance of these categories may be seen from Table III.

Despite the differences that exist between these categories of mortgages the similarities are sufficient to allow a common treatment throughout most of this study. This aggregation, which greatly simplifies our exposition, is not without some costs since the general behaviour of the market participants may not be equally applicable for all categories. Whenever the distinctions between categories of mortgages become pertinent they will be discussed separately.

One distinction that should be made at the outset is that between government insured (NHA) and conventional mortgages. The basic differences between these mortgage forms are set out in Table IV and centre around the fact that NHA mortgages are government insured while conventional mortgages are not. Because the government reserves the right to determine which mortgages qualify for their insurance, NHA lending terms fall under government supervision. This contrasts with conventional mortgage terms which are virtually free of government regulation.[17]

Throughout most of the period under study the maximum yield that could be charged on a mortgage to qualify for government insurance was set by the government as follows: (a) between 1954[18] and November 22, 1966 by the governor in council on the basis of its assessment of current market conditions provided that the rate did not exceed the long term government bond yield by more than $2\frac{1}{4}$ per cent; (b) between November 1966 and June 1969 by a formula which tied the NHA ceiling to the average yield on long-term government bonds in the previous quarter, first being set at $1\frac{1}{2}$ per cent above this bond yield and then adjusted to $2\frac{1}{4}$ per cent above the bond yield. After June 1969 the rate that could be charged on NHA mortgages was set free to be determined in the market, thereby more

TABLE III
RELATIVE IMPORTANCE OF INSTITUTIONALLY INITIATED MORTGAGES, BY CATEGORIES, 1948-69

Year	Percentage of total institution initiations*			Percentage of new residential construction initiations†	
	New residential construction	Existing residential property	Non-residential property	Conventional	NHA
1948	48	28	24	48	52
1949	54	25	21	49	51
1950	59	22	19	27	73
1951	54	27	19	45	55
1952	60	24	16	36	64
1953	64	21	15	42	58
1954	71	16	13	41	59
1955	73	15	12	37	63
1956	68	18	14	46	54
1957	67	20	13	59	41
1958	68	17	15	49	51
1959	60	20	20	64	36
1960	53	22	25	66	34
1961	57	21	22	52	48
1962	56	24	20	62	38
1963	56	24	20	71	29
1964	50	28	22	77	23
1965	48	29	23	78	22
1966	47	29	24	79	21
1967	41	31	28	72	28
1968	66	21	13	58	42
1969	60	24	16	63	37

*In value terms. †In terms of dwelling units.
Source: Central Mortgage and Housing Corporation, *Canadian Housing Statistics*; and Central Mortgage and Housing Corporation, *Mortgage Lending in Canada*.

closely aligning the NHA and conventional markets. Because conventional mortgages have no special features to mitigate their inherent risk while NHA mortgages are virtually free from the risk of capital loss because of government insurance, conventional mortgages typically carry a higher interest rate and more stringent lending terms than do NHA mortgages.

In addition to government insured institutional mortgages, the National Housing Act also provides for CMHC to make mortgage loans directly to the borrower. Throughout this study these loans will be referred to as CMHC direct loans, and NHA loans, unless explicitly stated otherwise, will refer to government insured institutional mortgages.

D. OUTLINE AND SUMMARY OF FINDINGS

The main purpose of this study is to examine the organization of the postwar Canadian housing and residential mortgage markets with a view to analysing the role of and scope for government policy. The study is divided into three main sections, part B which examines the behaviour and structural relationships in the housing market, part C which does the same for the mortgage market, and part D which analyses the techniques and impacts of government intervention in these markets.

TABLE IV
COMPARISON OF NHA AND CONVENTIONAL MORTGAGE CHARACTERISTICS

Terms	NHA mortgages Prior to June, 1969	NHA mortgages After June, 1969	Conventional mortgages
1. Interest rate	Interest rate ceiling tied to the average yield on long-term government of Canada bonds in the previous quarter, after November 1966 Interest rate ceiling set by Governor in council, not to exceed by more than 2¼% long-term government of Canada bond yield, prior to November 1966	Free to be determined by the market	Free to be determined by the market
2. Term	Minimum of 25 years; maximum of 35 years	Minimum of 5 years; maximum of 40 years. Usually 20-30 years for new multiple construction, 5-10 years common for new single unit construction	No specified term; usually 5-25 years for new construction, 5-10 years for existing properties
3. Amortization period	Must be fully amortized over term	Up to maximum of 40 years; need not match term; usually 25-30 years	No specified requirement, usually 20-25 years
4. Loan to value ratio	Varies according to amount of mortgage but usually near 80%	Varies according to size of mortgage but usually between 80% and 90%	Usually between 66% and 75% Some financial institutions regulated to a maximum of 75% Over 75% if privately insured
5. Gross debt service to income ratio for owner occupied dwellings	Not to exceed 27% of borrower income	Not to exceed 27% of the income of the borrower, which may be augmented by 50% of income of spouse	No fixed amount, usually around 25%
6. Repayment privileges	Full repayment allowed for individual mortgagor after 3 years upon payment of additional 3 months interest	Full repayment allowed for individual mortgagor after 3 years upon payment of additional 3 months interest	Full repayment allowed for individual mortgagor after 5 years upon payment of additional 3 months interest
7. Insurance coverage	Federally insured for 100% of capital, interest up to 12 months, and maximum of $250 in legal fees	Federally insured for 100% of capital, interest up to 12 months, and maximum of $250 in legal fees	No government insurance; may be privately insured
8. Loan amounts	Maximum loan for single-family dwellings of $18,000 Maximum loan for multiple dwellings, $18,000 per unit	Maximum loan for single-family dwellings $25,000 Maximum loan for multiple dwellings, $18,000 per unit	No maximum except for some financial institutions limited to a percentage of paid-in capital
9. Coverage	New residential construction only (special provisions for home improvement loans also)	Residential properties only, both new construction and existing property; most loans for new construction	No restrictions, all real estate
10. Administrative aspects	Considerable delay and paper work pending approval	Considerable delay and paper work pending approval	Usually less paper work and delay than NHA loans
11. Secondary market	Secondary market developing, aided by CMHC	Some secondary market, aided by CMHC	Virtually no secondary market

Our study of the housing market begins in Chapter 2 with a discussion of the myriad of forces affecting this market, and attempts to systematize these influences and illustrate their interrelationships through an integrated stock-flow approach. This approach is used to describe the operation of a national housing market under the heroic assumption that there is a national market and that different forms of dwelling units are perfect substitutes for one another. This assumption is then removed, and the approach is used to describe the differences in behaviour between, and analyse separately, the single and multiple dwelling sectors of the housing market.

Within the framework of the approach developed in Chapter 2, the factors affecting the demand for and supply of housing are analysed in Chapter 3. The basic forces underlying the demand for housing accommodations are shown to be essentially the same as for other goods – demographic, income, price, the cost and availability of credit, and consumer preference. Demographic forces are not confined to population or family growth but include such variables as age composition, family size, child births, non-family household formation and number of doubled families. The importance of distinguishing between components is illustrated by the fact that family undoubling and net non-family household formation accounted for 30 per cent of the realized increase in housing demand between 1951 and 1966.

Variations in income are shown to have an impact on the demand for housing services both by influencing the quantity of housing dwellings desired and the quality of these dwellings. After surveying and attempting to reconcile various estimates of income elasticity (including our estimate derived in Chapter 4), it is concluded that the stock demand (including quality variations) elasticity with respect to permanent income probably lies between 0.6 and 1.0. Housing prices and rents are shown also to have an impact on the demand for housing services. However, the multi-dimensional nature of these prices, which not only reflect the nominal value of the dwelling but also the financing terms and conditions associated with the dwelling in the case of owner-occupancy dwellings, and parking, hydro, swimming pool and sauna use, free month's rent, etc., in the case of rental dwellings, makes reconciliation of various elasticity estimates impossible.

Credit variables are shown to exert a vital impact upon the demand for the ownership of single-family and rental dwellings. These variables affect the demand for the ownership of rental dwellings by affecting the expected profitability of new rental construction and single-dwelling construction, and affect the demand for home ownership by affecting the affordability of these homes. Because of the different mechanisms by which credit variables affect single and multiple dwelling construction, the influence of these variables (the cost of mortgage credit, the loan to value ratio, the amortization period, the term and repayment privileges) are examined separately for the single and multiple dwelling sectors.

The supply of new housing is shown to depend on both the production possibilities in the construction industry and on the supply of productive factors to the housing industry. Production possibilities refer to the substitutability of the different productive factors required for the development of the site, the construction of the dwelling, and the financing, administration and marketing of the dwelling. Our analysis indicates that the long-run supply curve for new housing is quite elastic since an ample supply of productive factors exists or can be developed and there is a high degree of potential factor substitutability. For example, labour and capital may be substituted for land via higher density land utilization; capital and unskilled labour may be substituted for skilled labour via increased prefabrication or systems building; labour and capital may be substituted for land location rent via land improvements and the provision of services and transportation facilities; and land and capital may be substituted for supervision and overhead via increased scale of operations. On the other hand, the short-run elasticity of supply is much lower since relatively less factor substitution is possible and there is a relatively inelastic supply of some factors of production.

The relationships described in the previous two chapters are quantified and analysed in Chapter 4 through the development of two econometric models of the housing market. The first model is more aggregative and ignores the distinction between the single and multiple dwelling sectors, while the second model is more disaggregative and concentrates upon this distinction. In addition to verifying the appropriateness of the approach of the previous two chapters, these models quantify a variety of economic relationships. One of the more important results of our econometric analysis is that the cost and availability of mortgage credit significantly affect residential construction activity, and that they exert different impacts upon single and multiple dwelling sectors, the cost of credit being more important in multiple construction and availability of credit more important in single dwelling construction. Other findings include the importance of the relationships between rent and construction costs or prices and construction costs in determining the volume of residential construction, the differential impact of rising land costs on single and multiple dwelling construction, and the positive impact that fluctuations in residential construction activity have on construction costs. Finally, the relationships indicated by our model were used to describe the long-run and cyclical variations in residential construction on a period-by-period basis.

Our study of the mortgage market begins in chapter 5 with a description and analysis of the mortgage instrument, institutional arrangements in the market and the investment characteristics of mortgages. The supply of mortgage credit comes from three main sources, private financial institutions, government agencies and corporations, and individual and non-institutional corporate lenders. Each of these sources are motivated by different forces in determining the volume of funds they wish to make available for mortgage lending. The volume of funds advanced by private financial institutions is primarily a function of the relative desirability of mortgages as a form of investment, and their inflow of funds; the volume of government lending is primarily a function of social priorities and general economic policy considerations; and the volume of individual lending is a function of a wide variety of economic and personal considerations. The factors affecting the mortgage lending behaviour of each of these lenders and their relative importance in the market during the postwar period are discussed.

Because private financial institutions (primarily consisting of life insurance companies, trust companies, mortgage loan companies, and the chartered banks) are the dominant participants in the mortgage market, accounting for 60 to 65 per cent of all new mortgage initiations, 70 to 75 per cent of all initiations for new residential construction, and 90 to 95 per cent of all non-government mortgage initiations for new residential construction, most of our discussion pertains to these institutions. Consequently, chapter 6 develops a portfolio selection model of financial institution investment behaviour and then applies this model to explain the mortgage lending activities of these institutions. An analysis of the role played by each of the major financial institutions in the capital markets in general and mortgage market in particular during the postwar period is also presented.

The model of financial intermediary investment behaviour described in chapter 6 is more formally derived and estimated for each major financial institution in the first section of chapter 7. Included are separate mortgage supply functions for each institution's total mortgage lending, total residential mortgage lending, conventional residential and NHA mortgage lending. These supply functions indicate the importance of relative yield considerations in the allocation of financial institution investment funds, as both the yield spread between mortgages and non-mortgage alternative security investments and between the conventional and NHA categories of mortgage investments significantly influence financial institution mortgage investment behaviour. The analysis indicates considerable variability in the interest sensitivity of these institutions' investment decisions, with the chartered banks and life insurance companies being most interest sensitive, trust companies next, and mortgage loan companies least senstive. The analysis also suggests considerable variation in the desired proportion of mortgages in each institution's investment portfolio. This proportion was 86 per cent for mortgage loan companies, 68 to 85 per cent for life insurance companies, and 71 per cent for trust companies after 1965; and 30 per cent for the chartered banks under the investment constraints in operation during the nineteen-fifties.

Because the asset size of financial institutions exerts a highly significant influence upon the volume of mortgage lending activity undertaken by financial institutions, a model was also developed and estimated to explain the net inflow of funds into these institutions. Because our purpose is to examine the interest sensitivity of institutional mortgage flows, this model focuses upon the interest sensitivity of inflows of funds and is not a complete model of the allocation of financial savings.

In order to obtain an indication of the over-all sensitivity of each institution's mortgage flows to changes in monetary conditions simulations were run combining the mortgage yield determination equation and the equations for mortgage approvals and net inflows of funds for each institution. These simulations indicated that monetary factors have a substantial influence upon the volume of Canadian financial institution mortgage approvals, influencing both the inflow of funds and portfolio investment decisions. When these influences are combined the chartered banks are most responsive to varying monetary conditions with the trust companies next, since both their inflows of funds and portfolio investment decisions are strongly influenced by monetary considerations. Life insurance companies, whose net inflows are least interest sensitive, and mortgage loan companies, whose portfolio decisions are least interest sensitive, follow behind the chartered banks and trust companies in over-all interest sensitivity, although their mortgage flows are also strongly influenced by monetary factors.

Our study of government policy begins in chapter 8 with a discussion of the anti-cyclical behaviour of residential construction activity and the extent to which monetary and fiscal policy may exacerbate or ameliorate this behaviour. Chapter 9 considers the impacts of the two major government selective housing programmes, the federal loan guarantee and insurance programme and the Central Mortgage and Housing Corporation direct lending programme, and concludes with a discussion of the policy dilemma posed by the conflict between policies designed to stabilize residential construction activity and policies designed to stabilize the level of general economic activity.

Although monetary policy is usually not designed specifically to influence the volume of residential construction activity, residential construction activity is profoundly influenced by it. In order to obtain an indication of the impact of monetary policy on residential construction the housing and mortgage market models developed in chapters 4 and 7 were simulated under different monetary assumptions. Under the most realistic assumptions, a policy of monetary restraint that would correspond to a 10 per cent increase in long-term bond yields after two quarters would generate an 8.1 per cent decline in housing starts in the first year, and a 13.0 per cent decline in the second year, which indicates that residential construction activity is highly sensitive to monetary policy. Moreover, although these estimates were derived during the period in which the NHA mortgage rate was administratively controlled, our analysis indicates that the elasticity is unlikely to differ significantly when the NHA mortgage rate is market determined.

Fiscal policy operates more indirectly upon residential construction, primarily by affecting the relationship between prices and rents and construction costs. A policy of fiscal ease which increases personal disposable incomes increases aggregate demand for housing and hence housing prices and rents. At the same time it increases general economic activity and hence construction costs. Because these influences are offsetting, and individually relatively small, the impact of fiscal policy is typically much smaller than that of monetary policy. If we can characterize the typical fiscal policy shift by a 5 per cent change in personal income tax rates, i.e., a 5 per cent surtax, and typical monetary policy shift by a 10 per cent change in long-term bond yields over two quarters, then our simulations indicate that a typical fiscal policy change has approximately one-tenth the impact upon housing starts that a typical monetary policy change has.

The federal loan insurance programme under the National Housing Act can influence residential construction activity by influencing the availability of funds for residential construction or by affecting the demand for this construction. Although this programme can be used for short-run stabilization purposes its major beneficial impact has been to increase the long-run supply of mortgage credit. From a short-run stabilization view its potential lies more in affecting the demand for new construction by varying the terms that qualify for NHA insurance than in affecting the supply of mortgage credit. Although it might seem that freeing the

NHA mortgage rate to be determined in the market is responsible for this, such is not the case since government scope for influencing the short-run supply of mortgage credit was relatively restricted even when this rate was administratively controlled. Government influence through this mechanism affected the mix of conventional and NHA housing starts and mortgage lending much more than the total volume of housing starts and mortgage lending.

Finally, our analysis indicates that the Central Mortgage and Housing Corporation direct lending programme has a very significant impact upon the volume of residential construction activity taking place in any period. However, all CMHC direct lending under section 40 is not "residual" in the sense of providing a net addition to the volume of residential construction, as is usually thought, since this lending generates reductions in the conventionally financed housing sector which offset approximately 20 to 25 per cent of the additional housing starts generated in the NHA financed sector.

B
The housing market

2
An Integrated Stock-Flow Model of the Housing Market

A. THE UNDERLYING FACTORS AND SIMPLIFYING ASSUMPTIONS

The housing market is a highly complex and diverse market complicated not only by its various components and their interrelationships but also by the large number of factors that affect it.[1] To begin with, transportation time and costs restrict the geographic substitutability of housing and in a loose way define local housing markets. Even within a market all housing units are not substitutable, since the size, location, age and sometimes financing restrictions of a dwelling impose market segmentation. Consequently, any discussion of national housing markets is at the outset forced to make the heroic simplifying assumption that the little overlap and substitutability that exists between regional and local submarkets is sufficient to cause these submarkets to respond similarly to basic economic variables.

Further complicating the housing market is the myriad of factors that affect it. A list of the most important of these factors would include the following.[2]
1. Demographic variables: (a) population size; (b) age-sex composition of the population; (c) number and size of family and non-family households; (d) internal migration and immigration.
2. Income and employment variables: (a) personal disposable income, past, present and expected; (b) income distribution; (c) employment and unemployment.
3. Consumer asset holdings, size and liquidity.
4. Price variables: (a) housing prices and rents; (b) alternative consumer good prices.
5. Development cost variables: (a) construction costs; (b) land costs; (c) interim or bridge financing costs.
6. Non-financial operating costs: (a) real estate taxes and operating expenses; (b) depreciation.
7. Financial variables: (a) mortgage rates; (b) non-price mortgage terms and mortgage availability – including loan to value ratios, amortization period, term to maturity, quality constraint; (c) imputed costs of equity funds; (d) availability of CMHC direct loans.
8. Consumer tastes and preferences.
9. Builder and developer organization, structure and expectations.
10. Government public housing involvement.
11. Housing stock variables: (a) size of housing stock; (b) location of housing

stock; (*c*) composition of stock (i) by age, (ii) by structural type, (iii) by quality; (*d*) intensity of occupancy; (*e*) vacancies; (*f*) exogeneous demolitions, conversions and housing removals.

12. Miscellaneous variables: (*a*) tax treatment of housing – i.e., no tax on imputed rents, depreciation allowance rates, etc.; (*b*) zoning regulations, transportation facilities, services, etc.

Other than for government public housing and the availability of CMHC direct loans, government housing programmes are not included since they are designed to influence other variables in the included list. Because government public housing expenditure has been relatively small, accounting for under 4 per cent of all housing starts 1946–69,[3] and depends on many factors not susceptible to economic analysis, this study confines most of its attention to the private sector and the determinants of private residential construction.

B. AN INTEGRATED STOCK-FLOW MODEL

The above list of variables includes factors affecting both the supply of new dwellings and the demand for new dwellings. These variables interact so as to determine the volume of new dwelling starts, and this interaction may best be described as occurring in a typical stock-flow manner.

Ignoring the distinctions between different sectors of the market and simplifying for descriptive purposes, at any given time a stock of dwelling units exists and this stock together with the demand for dwelling accommodations determines the price (or rent) for dwelling units and the number of units that will be vacant. The price (or rent) and vacancies, modified by what is set out below, are then compared with construction, land, and financing costs (and in the case of rental dwellings, operating costs) to determine the volume of residential construction that can profitably be undertaken. The level of construction activity is thus determined by its profitability subject to the availability of sufficient equity financing, construction or short-term bridge financing, and long-term mortgage debt financing.

This simplified model is shown in graphic form in Figure 1. Because of the high proportion of existing dwellings to new construction the stock of dwellings may be considered relatively inelastic in the short run and is represented by line SK – SK. The demand for housing is reasonably price sensitive (with an elasticity of approximately 1.0)[4] and is represented by line D – D. The intersection of SK – SK and D – D in Figure 1A determines a price P′ which exists for dwelling accommodations.[5] This price P′, determined by the demand and supply for dwelling stock, also becomes the obtainable price for new dwellings. Because new construction in any quarter augments the existing stock very little, this price in any quarter can be considered to be independent of the volume of new construction. Beyond some range the cost of new construction, represented by line C – C, can be considered to increase with the level of construction because of pressures exerted on the availability of funds, building materials, land, and labour.[6] In the absence of an effective availability of finance constraint the intersection of P′ – P′ and C – C in Figure 1B determines the volume of new construction at H′. The availability of

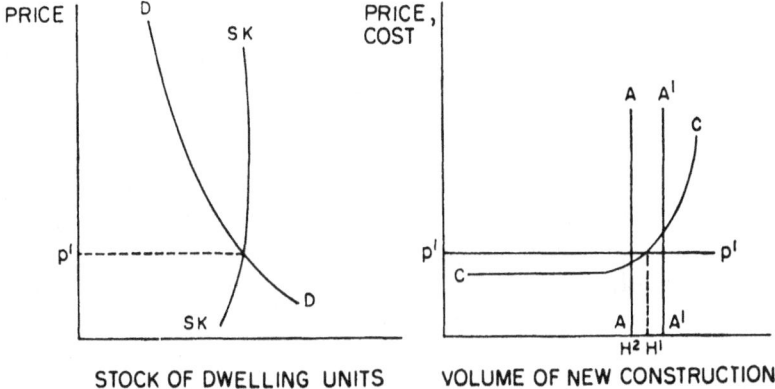

FIGURE 1 Graphic analysis of the stock-flow relationship in the housing market. A. Price determination. B. Volume of new construction determination.

funds constraint may be invariant with respect to price and cost, or have some very slight negative slope on the assumption that higher costs require more funds to finance a given volume of construction, and that the risk associated with a project increases with its price. Letting line A–A be an effective availability of finance constraint, the volume of new construction becomes H^2. If availability of finance is not an effective constraint, as in the case of line A'–A', the price-cost intersection determines the volume of construction.

The above representation assumes that the entire dwelling stock is utilized. However, this is not typically the case, since vacancies do arise. Vacancies can be built into our model by letting the stock of dwelling units and their demand jointly determine price and vacancy levels, and by inserting the capitalized expected cost of vacancies as an argument in the cost function C–C in Figure 1B.

If the housing market were a quickly adjusting market there would be some equilibrium level of vacancies, say 3 per cent – which would be a consequence of household mobility (that per cent that would enable people to change their accommodations without undue difficulty) – and whenever the vacancy factor deviated from this equilibrium prices would adjust: upward if vacancies were lower, downward if vacancies were higher, until this equilibrium were restored. However, the housing market is not perfect and consequently prices, rents, and vacancy levels can deviate from their equilibrium for considerable periods of time. These imperfections arise because of the adjustment lags on both the demand and supply side.

On the demand side, consumer reaction is slow because of the enormity of the housing decision (a house purchase being the largest expenditure most families ever make), fixed tenancies, transaction costs (in time, commissions, and possibly inappropriate furnishings), and inertia. On the supply side, the market is slow to adjust because of the time lags involved in altering or formulating construction plans (often subdivision or re-zoning is required before construction can even begin), and because new construction only adds 3.0 to 4.0 per cent annually to the housing stock. Consequently, decisions concerning the profitability of new construction are based not directly upon existing prices, rents, and vacancies, but rather upon projected equilibrium prices, rents, and vacancies, where current prices, rents, and vacancies serve to indicate future equilibrium levels.

The volume of construction that is undertaken in any period depends not only upon the volume that can profitably be undertaken, but also upon the availability of mortgage credit.[7] In a perfectly adjusting capital market this availability constraint would not arise because the interest rate would immediately adjust upward whenever the effective demand for funds exceeded the supply at a given rate. However, just as the housing market itself is not a perfect, fast adjusting market, neither is the mortgage market—the financial market which supplies most of the finance for new construction.[8] Because of the "one-of-a-kind" nature of mortgage transactions, the importance of customer goodwill, the prevalence of the forward commitment loan procedure, rigidities formerly imposed by an administered NHA mortgage rate, and the absence of a truly functioning secondary market, the mortgage rate has tended to adjust more slowly and have a smaller amplitude than other capital market rates, as Figure 2 indicates.[9] Consequently when capital markets tighten, bond yields tend to rise earlier, more rapidly and further than mortgage yields, increasing the relative attractiveness of bond investment vis-à-vis mortgage investment. Because bonds provide the main alternative investment opportunity to mortgages, an increase in the relative attractiveness of bond investment induces financial institutions to curtail their mortgage lending activity and ration mortgage credit (assuming the smaller and lagged mortgage rate adjustment response is insufficient to equilibrate the mortgage market) by altering the loan to value ratio,

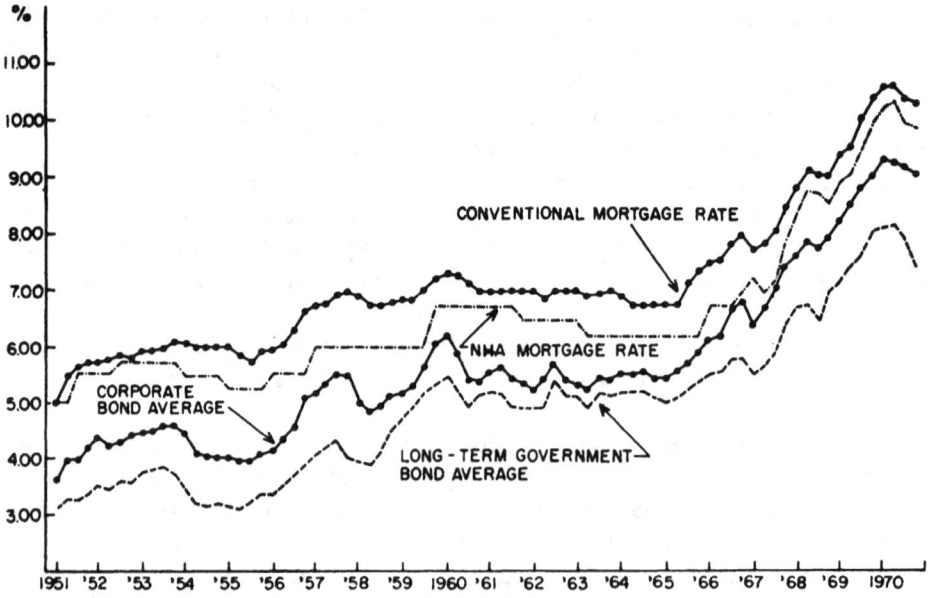

FIGURE 2 Selected interest rates, monthly series, 1951–70.

altering the amortization period, altering the term to maturity of the mortgage, arbitrarily refusing certain forms or qualities of loans, or, in the case of revenue producing properties, seeeking some or larger participation in the project. By such non-price credit rationing the market is equilibrated and the availability of funds exerts a constraining influence upon the residential construction market.

The relationship between the various demand and supply and the financial and real variables discussed above are shown in Figure 3. This flow chart shows that residential construction expenditure (IRC) is a function of current and lagged housing starts (HS). The volume of housing starts undertaken in any period depends upon a comparison of housing prices (PH), rent (R), and vacancy rates (SHV/SH) with construction and land costs (CLC), and financing costs (RM), and upon the availability of public Central Mortgage and Housing Corporation direct lending (CMHC) and private (MT) mortgage credit. Prices and vacancy rates are determined by each other, by the price of alternative goods and services (PGNE), permanent real disposable income (YD), demographic factors (DEM), and the cost and availability of mortgage credit. The current supply of housing dwellings (SH) depends upon the previous supply of housing dwellings and lagged housing starts. Construction costs depend upon the average hourly earnings of labour in the construction industry (WC), the cost of temporary or bridge financing (R03), and the current level of residential (IRC) and non-residential (INRC) construction relative to their respective industrial capacities. Land costs (L) are determined primarily by the demand for residential land. This demand is influenced by demographic variables, permanent real disposable income, the existing stock of housing units, and zoning, servicing, and transportation constraints (Z).

The availability of public mortgage credit, which arises via Central Mortgage and Housing Corporation (CMHC), is a policy variable, while the cost (RM) and other lending terms (MT) of private mortgage credit depend upon the demand for and supply of this credit. The demand for mortgage credit depends essentially upon

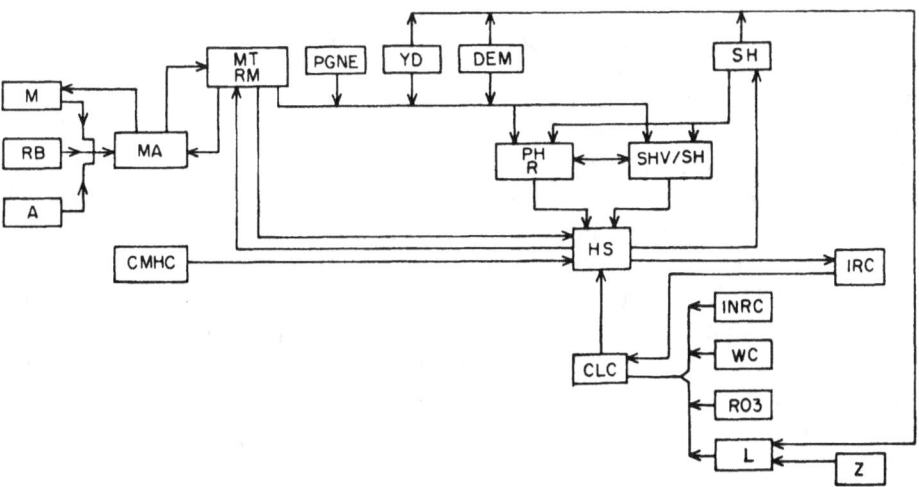

FIGURE 3 Flow chart of housing and mortgage markets.

the same factors as the demand for houses and the cost of alternative sources of funds; while the supply of mortgage credit, or institutional mortgage approvals (MA), depends upon the yield and other attributes of mortgage investments relative to those obtainable on alternative security investments (RB), the size of institutional investment portfolios (A), and the size of their existing mortgage holdings (M). The size of an institution's investment portfolio is taken to depend upon the yield paid on the institution's liabilities relative to the yield on alternative market securities, the public's wealth and the public's existing holdings of the institution's liabilities, although this relationship is not shown in the flow chart.

C. VARIATIONS BETWEEN THE SINGLE AND MULTIPLE DWELLING SECTORS

The major non-geographical distinction that exists within the national housing market is the distinction between single-family owner-occupied dwellings and multiple family rental dwellings.[10] The distinction indicates different motivation of the demanders of housing services in each class and of the builders or developers of new units in each class. Some market indication of these differences can be seen in Table v from the different cyclical and secular patterns in the prices and rents and volume of dwelling starts in each classification in the last two decades.

Table v indicates that multiple dwelling starts rose steadily and very significantly in both absolute and relative terms over the last two decades. In 1951 and 1952 multiple dwelling starts averaged only 18,600 units and were less than 25 per cent of total starts, while in the 1968–70 period they averaged 124,500 units and were 62.5 per cent of total starts. The vast majority of the growth in multiple starts was in apartment units which rose from an average of 13,000 units in 1951–2 to an average of over 102,000 units in 1968–70. In the last few years there has also been a very appreciable increase in the construction of row housing with construction of these units increasing from an annual average of approximately 2000 units in 1959–61 to 5100 units in 1965–6 and 13,800 units in 1969–70.

While multiple-dwelling construction was soaring, single-family construction showed considerable cyclical variation but little secular growth, and in 1949 single dwelling starts at 71,400 units were actually 676 units higher than in 1970. Single starts declined considerably in late 1950 and 1951 (to 53,000 in 1951) before beginning an upward movement that peaked in 1958 at 104,500 units and averaged 94,000 units annually 1955–9. Thereafter, single starts declined to approximately 75,000 units in 1961 and remained quite constant throughout the 1960s.

Differences between the rate of change of housing prices and rents also appear in the data in Table v. These data indicate that during the 1950s and 1960s housing prices and rents rose at an annual average of $4\frac{1}{2}$ per cent to $5\frac{1}{2}$ per cent (rents rose at 5.5 per cent, new NHA house prices at 4.5 per cent, the cost of new NHA homes adjusted for size at 3.7 per cent), and that housing rents rose more quickly than prices in the first half of the 1950s, and late 1950s and early 1960s, and more slowly in the mid-1950s and middle 1960s. The data also indicate distinctions between the new construction and existing home sectors, as prices on exist-

TABLE V
SINGLE AND MULTIPLE DWELLING STARTS,
AND PERCENTAGE CHANGE IN HOUSING PRICES AND RENTS, 1951-70

Year	Housing starts (in thousands)		Multiple starts as a percentage of total starts	Average Monthly rents	Percentage change in		
	Singles	Multiples			New NHA home cost, adjusted for size	New NHA house prices	Existing (MLS) house prices
1951	53.0	15.6	22.7	12.1	10.9	NA	NA
1952	60.7	21.5	26.2	8.7	4.3	7.1	NA
1953	70.8	51.6	42.2	7.2	1.0	3.1	NA
1954	78.6	34.9	30.7	9.9	4.3	6.8	NA
1955	99.0	39.3	28.4	3.0	2.7	7.1	NA
1956	90.6	36.7	28.8	6.1	5.3	10.7	3.5
1957	83.0	39.3	32.1	4.4	3.7	7.9	8.1
1958	104.5	60.1	36.5	7.1	2.9	−0.9	5.0
1959	92.9	48.4	34.3	0.9	1.7	1.7	3.3
1960	67.2	41.7	38.3	3.4	−1.9	−1.0	1.4
1961	76.4	49.2	39.2	2.1	0.5	0.7	−2.6
1962	74.4	55.5	42.7	3.7	0.3	2.2	3.3
1963	77.2	71.4	48.0	2.3	2.2	2.8	−3.1
1964	77.1	88.6	53.5	4.1	3.6	4.0	8.2
1965	75.4	91.2	54.7	5.2	4.4	4.5	8.5
1966	70.6	63.9	44.2	5.9	7.9	8.6	9.5
1967	72.5	91.6	55.8	7.7	4.0	8.1	9.9
1968	75.3	121.6	61.8	3.8	5.2	4.2	11.0
1969	78.4	132.0	62.7	9.0	7.9	2.7	9.3
1970	70.7	110.8	62.9	7.3	3.1	4.5	0.7

Sources: column 1, 2 and 5, and 6: Central Mortgage and Housing Corporation, *Canadian Housing Statistics* (1970), 10, 68, and 89; column 4, calculated from worksheets at Dominion Bureau of Statistics based on Labour Force Survey results; column 7, calculated from statistics published by Canadian Association of Real Estate Boards, *The Canadian Realtor* (Toronto), and the *Report* (Toronto).

ing homes (approximated by the average price of units sold through real estate board Multiple Listing Service (MLS)) rose more quickly than new home prices in the late 1950s and middle and late 1960s, and less quickly in the early 1960s.[11]

The different growth and cyclical behaviour in single and multiple dwelling starts and housing prices and rents indicate considerable differences in the variables and behaviour patterns of the participants in the single and multiple dwelling sectors of the housing market. A brief description of the dominant forces influencing the volume of new construction in each of these sectors is presented below.

(a) Multiple dwellings

Consistent with the stock-flow framework described in section B, the greater the final or user demand for rental dwellings relative to their supply, the higher will be the rents and the lower the vacancy rates for these dwellings and, consequently, the greater the likelihood that new construction projects will be profitable to undertake. Developers plan either to sell their buildings once they are completed and rented, or to retain them for long-term investments. The profitability of a project on a sale basis depends upon the relationship between its expected selling price and its total cost (including losses incurred during the initial renting period), and the profitability on an investment basis depends upon the developer's expected yield on invested capital. Both criteria are essentially the same because the price of real estate, just as other long-term investments, depends upon its yield, and hence the desirability of a project from either the "sale" or "investment" viewpoint ultimately depends upon the expected return on invested capital.

The return on the capital invested in a project depends upon a range of factors, the most important of which are: (i) the rent; (ii) the vacancy rate (both in equilibrium and during the initial rental period); (iii) the construction, development, land and interim financing costs; (iv) the operating costs, including realty taxes; (v) the mortgage costs; (vi) the non-price borrowing terms, such as the loan to value ratio, the amortization period, prepayment privileges and the appraisal value of the project[12]; (vii) the tax implications associated with the project – such as capital cost allowance.

In addition to the variables affecting return, the size of the mortgage loan plays an overriding role in determining whether construction can proceed or not because of the highly levered nature of residential construction. If, for example, mortgage lenders were to reduce the mortgage loan on a given project from 80 per cent of total cost to 70 per cent of cost (either by altering the loan to value ratio or appraisal value of the project) the equity required for the project would increase by 50 per cent, which could place the project beyond the financial capability of the developer.[13]

(b) Single dwellings

Single family dwellings are built both on a pre-sold custom basis (owner-builders are included in this category) and on a speculative basis by merchant builders (developers). The mechanism operating for the construction of custom-built homes is more direct than for speculatively-built homes so our discussion begins with this category.

(i) Custom homes
Some of the demand for single-family dwellings arises from people who desire a custom-built home, and consequently an increase in the demand for single-family dwellings usually leads to an increase in the construction of custom-built homes.[14]

The basic forces affecting the demand for custom homes (apart from tastes) are family incomes (permanent income appears more appropriate than current income in this connection), the cost of construction and land, and the cost and availability of mortgage credit. Cost of construction seems more appropriate than the price as a variable because price is usually determined on a cost plus basis and although the percentage mark-up varies over the cycle the prime determinant of the price of custom homes is their cost.

Mortgage credit influences the volume of single dwelling construction somewhat differently than it does the volume of multiple construction because the demanders of single dwellings usually own their homes rather than rent them. In the case of custom homes the owner arranges his own finance and hence his demand depends not only on his building costs but also upon the terms and conditions of his mortgage credit. The impact of mortgage terms will be discussed in more detail in the next chapter. For now, suffice it to say that higher borrowing costs and shorter amortization periods reduce effective demand by increasing monthly carrying costs, while a lower loan to value ratio or appraisal value does the same by increasing the required downpayment, thereby often putting the type of housing desired by a family beyond its financial capabilities.

(ii) Speculative homes
The market mechanism operating in the case of speculative-built homes is more analogous to multiple-dwelling construction than custom-built single-family homes, although it has some features similar to the custom-built market as well. When the demand for owner-occupied dwellings increases, the price of single-family dwellings increases relative to construction and land costs, and the speed at which homes are sold increases, increasing the profitability and hence the volume of this form of construction.

The cost and availability of mortgage credit are also very important in this sector and affect speculative building in a way similar to custom building since the purchaser of the home assumes responsibility of the mortgage. However, despite the fact that the mortgage terms affect the size of the downpayment and monthly carrying costs for the purchaser, they are also of major concern to the developer since the terms of the mortgage finance associated with his homes will have a pronounced effect upon his ability to sell them. Consequently, although mortgage conditions affect the final demand for single dwellings, much of the response to varying credit conditions in this market is a derived response based upon developer assessment of how these variations will influence the ultimate demand for dwellings.

From this discussion it is clear that the volume of residential construction is significantly influenced by the basic factors underlying the final demand for dwelling accommodations, and the cost and availability of mortgage credit. These factors are discussed in chapter 3.

3
Demand and Supply Factors in the Housing Market

A. INTRODUCTION

Most studies of the housing market concentrate upon the demand for housing services as the major force in determining housing prices and the volume of new construction. This is done under the assumptions that the stock of dwellings is essentially fixed in the short run and that in the long run the real resources for residential construction are potentially available in such volume that their supply will meet effective demand at current prices. Consequently, the availability of land, building materials, labour, entrepreneurs, and economic organization are taken for granted[1] and the supply of new construction is taken to be perfectly elastic. These are reasonable assumptions for long run periods of relatively normal economic conditions and consequently the emphasis in this chapter is on the demand side. However, supply considerations do exert considerable influence upon prices and construction activity in the short run and hence the nature of the supply constraints is also discussed.

B. FACTORS AFFECTING HOUSING DEMAND

The basic forces underlying the demand for housing accommodations are essentially the same as for other goods – population, income, prices, the cost and availability of credit, and consumer preferences – with the demographic and income variables being most important in the long run. In the short run, population growth may be accommodated in a relatively fixed housing inventory by varying the intensity of occupancy, but in the long run, especially under conditions of rising real incomes, demographic forces have been the strategic factors in determining the level of housing demand and residential construction.[2]

(a) Demographic forces
Demographic forces are not confined to population or family growth, but include such variables as age composition, family size, number of first and second child births, non-family household formation and the number of doubled families (families not living in separate dwellings of their own), which also play important roles in housing demand. The major forces are usually categorized as net family formation (the net sum of marriages, divorces, deaths of married persons, and net migra-

tion of families), net non-family household formation (net sum of individuals and groups of persons occupying separate dwellings), and net undoubling. Newly formed families whose head is young, new immigrants, and new non-family household formation (primarily young single persons who move out of their parents' home to live in separate dwellings, and middle-aged and elderly widows, widowers, and divorcees) tend to generate demand for rental accommodations, while families whose head is in the 25–35 age bracket and families experiencing first and second child births often shift their demand from rental to owner-occupancy accommodations.[3] Recently, completing the life cycle pattern, there has been a tendency for families to return to rental from owner-occupancy accommodations following the children's departure from the family home.

Some tentative quantitative support for the above profile comes from the characteristics of NHA new home borrowers, 70 to 75 per cent of whom shifted their type of tenure from tenant to owner. Of these borrowers in 1970, 54.9 per cent of the borrowers were between 25 and 34 years of age, and 71.7 per cent were between 25 and 39. Just under 9 per cent were younger than 25, and just under 10 per cent were between 40 and 44. 21.4 per cent had one child, 28.0 per cent had two children, 25.8 per cent had more than two children, and 24.8 per cent had no children in 1970. In 1966, 41.1 per cent had one child, 17.7 per cent had two children, and 20.7 per cent no children.[4]

In assessing the relative strengths of these various demographic forces for the future, it is interesting to note that between 1951 and 1966, the number of doubled families in Canada declined by approximately 140,000 families (from 9.8 per cent to 4.0 per cent of all families), while the number of non-family households (60 per cent of which consist of individuals over 55 years of age) rose by over 382,000. Since the number of family households in Canada rose by approximately 1,230,000 families between 1951 and 1966, undoubling and net non-family household formation accounted for 30 per cent of the realized increase in housing demand.[5] CMHC estimates that this percentage will increase in 1966–71 and then return to approximately 30 per cent between 1971 and 1981.[6] By traditional standards the net non-family formation component of net household formation after 1950 is exceptionally high.[7] This is likely to increase the responsiveness of housing demand to economic factors because the rate of family undoubling and of non-family household formation is likely to be more sensitive to income, unemployment, price, and rent variables than is the rate of net family household formation.

(b) Income
Variations in income have a substantial impact upon the demand for housing services by influencing the quality of housing accommodation desired, and the number of families or persons who feel they can afford their own dwelling. Rising real income stimulates the demand for new dwellings by enabling more families to afford the monthly carrying cost and downpayments required for home ownership, and by enabling more families and individuals to afford the monthly rental on rental accommodations. One effect of rising real income is therefore to increase

net household formation and hence the demand for new dwelling units. This increase normally occurs both in the single- and multiple-dwelling sectors. In the single-dwelling sector net demand increases because families shift their demand from rental to owner accommodations and occasionally some families are able to afford to undouble directly into single dwellings. In the multiple dwelling sector net demand increases because rising incomes stimulate net non-family household formation, earlier marriages, and net family undoubling,[8] and these increases outweigh reductions in demand arising from the shift of family demand from rental to owner accommodations. Because of the offset in the multiples sector it is not surprising that econometric studies indicate that the income elasticity for owner-occupied housing is probably higher than that for rental housing.[9]

A second effect of rising income is to increase the quality of accommodation desired within each class. This distinction between variations in the demand for physical units and for the quality of accommodations is highly arbitrary because the shift of a family's demand from rental to owner occupancy represents both a quality and structural shift. Nevertheless, the distinction is useful for reconciling various econometric results because some studies focus upon only the demand for dwelling units while others consider the demand for housing services, which includes both elements.

Considerable uncertainty exists at present as to the magnitude of the income elasticity of the demand for housing, with estimates ranging from 0.35 to 2.3 for Canadian and American studies. The uncertainty stems from a number of factors which include (i) different measures of income (permanent income yielding higher elasticities than current income): (ii) different dependent variables ranging from the number of dwelling units, to the value of dwelling units, to expenditures on housing services (both including and excluding imputed rents); (iii) different samples – from time series to cross-section, from renters to owners, to new home purchasers with Federal Housing Act mortgages; (iv) different models and consequently different included variables which may be multicollinear with the income variable.

The highest estimates of income elasticity come from cross-sectional analysis, where Reid[10] and Muth[11] obtained estimates in the 1.5 to 2.1 range. According to de Leeuw these estimates should be adjusted downward to the 1.35 to 1.45 range because the studies are based upon the market value of existing homes rather than upon per unit housing expenses and because they failed to account for imputed rent.[12] Furthermore, Reid ignored mortgage credit factors and used an averaging process which tends to wash out many relevant differences in housing components that should be explained by variables other than permanent income, and Muth failed to incorporate an adequate measure of interest cost and loan to value ratios in his work, both of which cause an upward bias in the income coefficient.[13]

The middle range of elasticity estimates come from de Leeuw (1.1)[14], Winger (1.05),[15] and Lee (0.89),[16] all using cross-sectional analysis, and Muth (0.88),[17] using time series data. These estimates are subject to adjustment also, with those of Lee, Winger, and Muth being adjusted downward slightly because of their use of market value rather than housing expenses and omission of imputed rent, and that of de Leeuw being adjusted downward for omitting mortgage credit factors. On the other hand, Winger's estimate should also be readjusted upward because of special features of his sample.[18] The net effect of these adjustments would be to increase the range from around 0.75 to 0.80 (for Lee and Muth) to 1.25 for Winger.

With the exception of a study by Uhler which uses a different estimation procedure,[19] the lowest elasticity estimates come from time series analysis. Included in this category are estimates of 0.7 to 0.8 by Lee,[20] and 0.5 by Oksanen[21] and Smith,[22] the latter both using Canadian data, and an estimate of 0.30 obtained from equation 7 in Chapter 4 of this study. The estimates by Lee should be adjusted downward a little for the same reasons as apply to his cross-sectional analysis. The estimates by Oksanen should also be adjusted downward slightly for the same reasons, but also readjusted upward because of his unusual specification of permanent income. If Friedman's definition of permanent income were used, the Oksanen model yields a permanent income elasticity of 0.70.[23] Netting out these various influences would leave a readjusted estimate around 0.60. Finally, the estimates by Smith (including that obtained in this study) require upward revision because the model is formulated in terms of the demand for physical dwelling units only and ignores quality shifts within structural classifications. The magnitude of the adjustment is difficult to estimate but would probably lead to an estimate of the elasticity for housing services in the 0.6 to 0.8 range.

The effect of these adjustments is to considerably narrow the range of the estimates of permanent income elasticity for housing services in Canadian and United States studies to between 0.6 and 1.4 with the majority of the estimates falling between 0.6 and 1.0. Consequently, the elasticity is likely to fall within the 0.6 to 1.0 range, being at the lower end for time series analysis and upper end for cross-section analysis.

(c) Prices and rents

Housing prices and rents affect the demand for housing in much the same manner as prices of other goods affect the demand for these goods. Ceteris paribus, and in the absence of destabilizing price expectations, an increase in the price of single-family dwellings reduces the demand for these dwellings in favour of rental dwellings and non-shelter commodities and services, and an increase in rents reduces the demand for rental dwellings in favour of single dwellings and non-shelter commodities and services. However, in the case of housing, the price-demand relationship is often clouded because of the multi-dimensional nature of housing prices.

The multi-dimensional nature of the price of multiple dwelling services (rents) is quite straightforward compared to that of the price of single dwellings. The true rent of multiple dwellings may differ from the nominal rent by extra charges for such items as hydro, parking, or be reduced by the granting of a "free" month's rent. It may also include some component for the use of saunas, swimming pool, and athletic facilities. These deviations are straightforward, relatively minor in value and easy to take account of, so that the nominal rent remains a relevant variable in the demand for rental accommodations. Conversely, in the case of single dwellings, it is usually not the nominal purchase price that is most relevant to purchasers, but the monthly carrying costs and cash required for a downpayment.[24] To the extent that variations in nominal price alter monthly carrying costs and immediate cash requirements these variations substantially alter the housing decision. However, they may be more than offset by varying financial arrangements, so that rising nominal housing prices and rising housing demand may co-exist, if financing terms are being liberalized. Consequently, the analysis of the relationship between single dwelling housing prices and demand depends critically upon the specification of credit variables. To further complicate matters prices of existing dwellings and of newly constructed homes may respond differently to variations in credit conditions. Because newly constructed homes carry mortgage financing at current rates while existing dwellings usually carry financing arranged in the past, rising interest rates shift the demand from new to existing dwellings. This reduces new home prices and raises existing home prices as the lower mortgage rate associated with existing dwellings is capitalized in the price. A similar capitalization in the price of newly constructed homes arises if interest rates increase appreciably during the construction period so that newly completed houses are being offered for sale with lower interest rate mortgages than homes currently under construction.

In view of the numerous dimensional problems in the price of single dwellings and variations in the response of different segments of the market to changes in financial variables, it is not surprising that no unanimity has been reached as to the magnitude of price elasticities.[25] Estimates range from zero (i.e., no significance) in an American cross-section study by Duesenberry and Kistin[26] and in a Canadian time series study by Oksanen,[27] to 0.35 in equation 7 in this study, to 1.0 or more in cross-section and time series studies by Reid,[28] Lee,[29] Muth,[30] de Leeuw,[31] and Chung.[32] Because these results are highly dependent upon the specification (or omission) of financial variables and the definition of price or rent, no attempt is made here to reconcile them. However, since equation 7 indicates a stock elasticity of 0.35 ignoring qualitative effects, and since qualitative effects are likely to be at least as strong or stronger, an over-all (quality and quantity) price elasticity for the demand for housing services of approximately 0.8 to 1.0 seems reasonable.

(d) Credit variables
The effect of credit variables on the user demand for housing occurs predominantly in the single-family sector since variations in credit terms only indirectly affect the demand for rental accommodation – by shifting demand from owner to rental accommodation when the credit terms for single-family homes are too onerous, and by reducing multiple-dwelling construction which ultimately leads to higher rents (thereby ameliorating with a lag the shift of demand into rental accommodations and reducing rental demand). However, credit variables do very strongly affect the profitability of new rental construction and the demand for the ownership of these dwellings, and thereby they exert a major influence upon the volume of new multiple dwelling construction.

(i) Impact on multiple dwelling construction

The demand for rental dwellings relative to their existing supply normally does not alter rapidly since variations in demographic, permanent income, and taste variables usually occur gradually, and new construction contributes only approximately 4 to 5 per cent annually to the multiple-dwelling stock. Consequently, if construction costs are relatively stable, a given expected rent-to-construction cost ratio can persist for a relatively long period[33] and the volume of new multiple-dwelling construction will depend upon the terms and availability of mortgage credit. The variables that are most important are the loan to value ratio, the amortization period and the mortgage rate.

Loan to value ratios.[34] Abstracting from risk considerations, an investment is worth undertaking when its expected return exceeds the expected opportunity costs associated with it. The opportunity cost associated with a multiple dwelling project is directly related to the nature of the financing and to the terms and availability of mortgage financing.

For example, let us assume that a corporation has the opportunity to construct an apartment building which will cost $1,000,000. The demand for rental dwellings relative to the available supply is such as to yield an expected net return of 7 per cent after all expenses except those that arise from the financing on a one-million-dollar capitalization.[35] This net return is expected to be constant for 25 years and the project is then expected to be worth $1,000,000. Financing is available by way of a 100 per cent of cost mortgage with an amortization term of 25 years, equal to the projected lifetime of the building. If the interest rate on this mortgage is less than 7 per cent – say 6 per cent – the investment is profitable for the company. In this case the company is able to completely finance the project out of borrowed funds, which have a real cost to the company of only 6 per cent since the funds which were obtained on the security of the apartment project could not have been used in any other manner, and the return received on these funds in every period exceeds their cost.

Assume now that the financing available still costs 6 per cent and has a term to maturity of 25 years, but that the loan to value ratio is reduced to 80 per cent of cost. In this case 20 per cent of the financing must originate from equity funds which could otherwise be utilized elsewhere. If the return on these equity funds would otherwise have exceeded 6 per cent it is no longer sufficient to say that the apartment project will be profitable if it returns over 6 per cent since the expected revenues will exceed the costs. Here, the cost on 20 per cent of the financing is no longer 6 per cent but rather the opportunity cost of the forgone alternative opportunities for this equity portion. If these equity funds would have yielded a return of 12 per cent in another venture, still neglecting variations in the certainty of the returns, the apartment project must yield over 7.2 per cent on its capitalization to be profitable. Under these circumstances, the project would not be undertaken.

If the apartment were expected to yield an 8 per cent return the project would still be undertaken since this represents a return of 16 per cent on the equity invested, which is in excess of the 12 per cent return obtainable on forgone alternatives. However, if the loan to value ratio was further reduced to 60 per cent, the required yield on capitalization for the project to be profitable would have to be 8.4 per cent and the project once again would be unprofitable.[36]

Therefore, it can easily be seen that variations in the mortgage loan to value ratio greatly affect the desirability of investment in rental real estate, and the sensitivity of investment to changes in this ratio increases as the yield obtainable on alternative investment opportunities increases. Finally, the impacts of short term alterations in loan to value ratios are not symmetrical. These ratios are usually lowered in periods of expanding economic activity and rising interest rates when yields on alternative investment opportunities are typically greatest, while the ratios are raised when credit conditions are easing and alternative investment opportunities are less profitable. This causes alterations in the loan to value requirement to exert a stronger restraining impact in periods of tightening conditions than a stimulating impact in periods of credit ease.

Amortization period. A variation in the amortization term of mortgage financing alters the desirability of a prospective project by affecting the time path of the flows of funds associated with an undertaking. Returning to our previous example, let us assume that a company is considering the construction of a $1,000,000 apartment building which is expected to generate a net rental income of $72,460 for 50 years and zero net income thereafter. Financing is available by way of a 100 per cent loan to value ratio mortgage bearing an interest rate of 6 per cent, but with an amortization term of only ten years. In order to fully amortize the mortgage loan in ten years the yearly payments required would be $135,868 or $63,408 a year in excess of net rental revenue, and this excess must come out of equity funds. As shown in Figure 4, the company would have a net cash outflow of $63,408 a year for the first ten years and a net cash inflow of $72,460 for the next 40 years from this investment. If the yield the company would have to forgo on these equity funds exceeds $9\frac{3}{4}$ per cent the opportunity cost of undertaking this investment would exceed its return and the investment should not be undertaken,[37] again abstracting from risk differences associated with alternative investments.

Suppose, instead, the mortgage had a 20-year amortization period. In this case yearly amortization payments would be $87,185 and the company would have a net outflow of $14,750 a year for the first 20 years and a net inflow of $72,460 for the next 30 years. It would now require a yield on alternative uses of equity funds of over 12 per cent to make such an investment unattractive. If a 30-year amortization period were available, the company would have payments of $72,650 a year, resulting in a net outflow of $190 a year for 30 years and net inflow of $72,460 for the last 20 years, so that virtually no equity funds would ever be required. If the amortization period exceeded 30 years, a positive net cash flow would result throughout the lifetime of the investment.[38]

Since the shorter the amortization period the greater the likelihood of a negative flow of funds, which would involve the company in equity financing and thereby raise the opportunity cost of the investment, the longer the amortization period the more desirable the undertaking. This is true even when the company faces a positive net flow over the entire lifetime of the investment, since a longer amortiza-

34   RESIDENTIAL MORTGAGE MARKETS

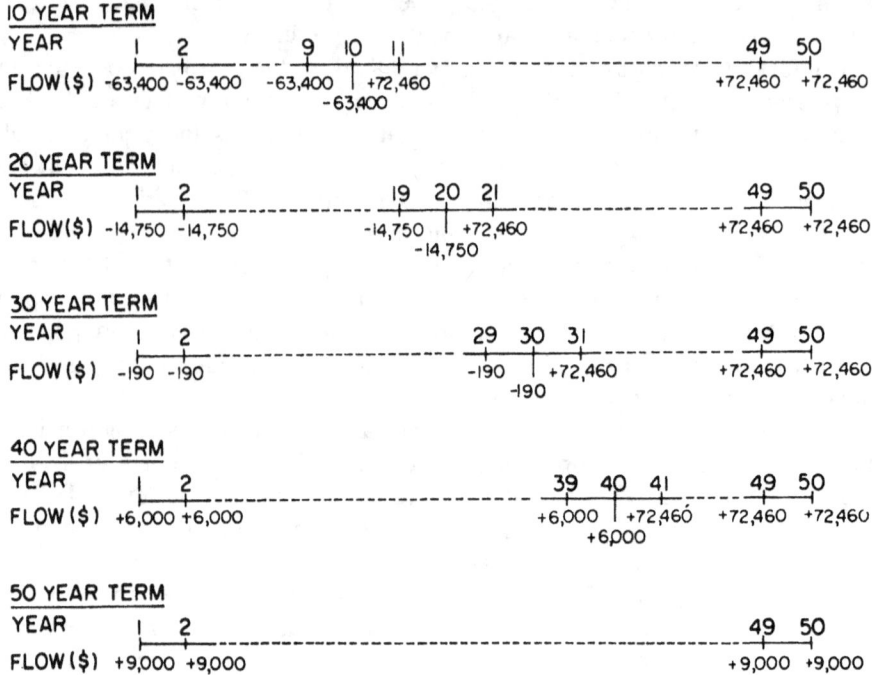

FIGURE 4   Time flows of funds according to various mortgage amortization terms associated with a hypothetical investment – 100 per cent loan to value ratio

tion period results in larger inflows in the earlier years of the investment which, together with the very high rate of time preference that most companies have, results in the future income stream having a higher present value for the company than that arising from an income stream equivalent at the market discount rate but with a larger proportion of its net inflow of funds in the latter years – i.e., at a company's high rate of time preference, the present value of the income stream associated with the 50-year mortgage amortization term exceeds that associated with the 40-year term.

A similar analysis is true for any loan to value ratio, except that the longer the amortization period the more favourable the early year cash flow and the more quickly the company's equity is returned (where net cash flows are positive in all but year one), or the smaller the net outflow required from equity funds to retire the mortgage (where net cash flows are negative during the term of the mortgage). Therefore, changes in the amortization period associated with a mortgage affect the desirability of a prospective investment and, thereby, the volume of residential rental construction.

Interest rate and repayment privileges. The higher the interest charges associated with a mortgage the less desirable is an investment principally financed by way of mortgage funds. Another consideration affecting the desirability of an undertaking is the possibility of early repayment – which would enable refinancing if any of the above costs or terms were expected to improve. In the absence of such provisions companies might delay committing themselves to a project until the expected improvement in terms occurs, rather than undertaking rather onerous terms for a long period. On the other hand the easier the repayment provisions the more readily projects will be undertaken, since all that is necessary is for the project to yield sufficient returns in the period prior to improvement of terms to cover the expense of refinancing for the project to be profitably undertaken immediately rather than waiting. Hence, the interest rate and repayment privileges associated with a mortgage also affect the volume of construction.

(ii) Impact on single dwelling construction
The volume of single dwelling construction is directly related to the demand for owner-occupied dwellings since variations in demand are reflected in the price and hence profitability of speculative building and directly in the volume of custom building. The demand for owner-occupancy housing is greatly affected by the terms and availability of housing credit because most families are quite sensitive to the downpayment and monthly payment requirements for a home purchase.[39]

The extent to which housing credit enters into the housing decision depends upon the liquid position of the purchasing family. Families with sufficient funds to completely finance their purchase without mortgage credit are naturally less constrained by financial variables, and their housing decision may be separated into a purchasing decision, where relative prices are important, and a financing decision, where the relationship between the cost of mortgage credit and expected yield on alternative investments is important. Families with insufficient funds to completely finance their purchase are more constrained and forced into a joint financing and purchasing decision, where the most relevant variables are no longer price and interest costs but the size of the required monthly payment and downpayment.

The relative importance of these groups may be estimated from Table VI which shows that approximately 28 per cent of households with mortgage debt have mortgage debt exceeding their net worth, and about 61 per cent have mortgage debt equal to 50 per cent or more of their net worth. In the extreme case, where a family would have been willing to hold all its net worth in a house, it could have obtained a home without resorting to mortgage financing when its net worth was equal to or greater than the value of the house. Since the usual loan to value ratio for new residential financing at the time the survey upon which Table VI is based ranged from 66 per cent for conventional to 80 per cent for NHA mortgages, a family's net worth would have to have been at least 125–150 per cent of the amount of the mortgage at the time of purchase. Table VI, however, refers not to a family's net worth at the time of the mortgage origination but at the time of the survey, so that the majority of families would have had time to increase their net worth to mortgage debt ratio. This would automatically occur as a family met its mortgage payments if it did not incur further debt, since each payment involves a return of capital and, therefore, results in both an increase in net worth and reduction in debt, and hence, it is likely

TABLE VI
FREQUENCY AND SIZE OF TOTAL MORTGAGE DEBT OF FAMILIES BY NET WORTH GROUPS, 1962

Net worth groups	Average mortgage debt of debtors only	Distribution of debtors
Negative to zero	$ 8,600	0.6%
$1-999	11,070	0.9
1000-4499	9,380	7.2
4500-7499	8,370	19.1
7500-9999	6,880	10.9
10,000-14,999	7,080	22.3
15,000-24,999	7,970	21.2
25,009-49,999	9,820	9.7
50,000 and over	15,010	8.1

Source: Royal Commission on Banking and Finance, "Consumer Survey" in the *Appendix Volume* (Ottawa 1964), Table 69

that many families who at the time of the survey had highly favourable net worth to mortgage debt ratios were unable at the time of purchase to finance their home out of equity funds. It is likely that, on the average, a minimum ratio of net worth to mortgage debt of 2 to 1 would be required at the time of the survey for a family to have been able to obtain its home without mortgage financing if it so desired, and a less conservative guess may be a ratio of 3 to 1, since net worth probably has increased more than a 2 to 1 ratio implies, especially since it was calculated on estimated market value of assets which, for a typical household, has appreciated since the time of purchase. If the 2 to 1 ratio is accepted, 61 per cent of mortgage debtors could not have purchased their homes without mortgage financing, 18 per cent could have, and 21 per cent fall into a net worth category that is unclear. If the 3 to 1 ratio is appropriate, 82 per cent could not have financed their homes without mortgages, 8 per cent could have, and 10 per cent fall into an ambiguous range. Therefore, it would appear that 70 to 80 per cent of mortgagors required their mortgages to finance the purchase of their homes (although they may have been able to purchase less expensive homes without mortgage financing), which makes the availability of mortgage financing on terms that are easily affordable a vital factor in determining the level of demand for owner-occupancy residential construction. Factors affecting this affordability are discussed below.

Downpayment. Larger downpayment requirements increase the minimum liquid savings that families require to enter the housing market and reduce the housing expenditure that a given downpayment will support, thereby significantly reducing housing demand. During the 1960s the average downpayment required on new NHA single and semi-detached homes ranged from 39 per cent of the mean family income of NHA borrowers in 1961 to 49 per cent in 1967, with the average being around 42 per cent,[40] and average personal net saving as a percentage of disposable income ranged from 5.5 per cent to 9.7 per cent and averaged 7.6 per cent. These figures mean that approximately $5\frac{1}{2}$ years were required for a family to accumulate sufficient savings for the downpayment on an average priced NHA home. Since downpayment requirements are usually higher for conventionally financed homes, a longer period would be required to accumulate the necessary equity. Therefore, the downpayment requirement is clearly an effective constraint upon housing demand, and the above figures suggest that a 10 per cent increase in the required downpayment on an NHA home would force the average family to postpone its home purchase by over 6 months in order to accumulate the additional equity. This conclusion is further substantiated by the Royal Commission on Banking and Finance Consumer Survey which found that 15 per cent of the families who purchased homes with mortgage credit during the 1957–62 period would either have purchased no home (9 per cent) or a cheaper home (6 per cent) if downpayment requirements had been 10 per cent higher.[41]

Changes in downpayment requirements (which arise from changes in the price of the home, the relationship between appraisal value and price, and the loan to value ratio) may have a very great effect upon the demand for homes since more families are brought into the market and those already present are able to increase their expenditures when personal liquid savings requirements are reduced. This is especially true as the loan to value ratio approaches 100 per cent of the price, since the purchasing power of a given downpayment is doubled every time the downpayment requirement is halved, i.e., if the loan to value ratio increases from 50 to 75 per cent, 60 to 80 per cent, 80 to 90 per cent, or 90 to 95 per cent, then the purchasing power of a given downpayment doubles, and the impact of a 5 per cent increase in the loan to value ratio on purchasing power and size of mortgage obtainable increases. However, while equal successive reductions have a larger impact on purchasing power of a given downpayment, they may have a smaller impact on increasing demand for residential houses, since downpayment requirements lose much of their effectiveness as a limitation upon the price which a purchaser can offer or as a barrier to entry into the housing market as the loan to value ratio increases, especially when it exceeds 80 to 90 per cent.

Monthly payments. The size of the monthly mortgage payment (principal and interest) required for a home purchase has a very significant affect upon the demand for owner-occupied dwellings by limiting the number of households able to carry the payment out of current income. The Royal Commission on Banking and Finance "Consumer Survey" found that if monthly payments had been 10 per cent higher 32–40 per cent of families purchasing a home with mortgage credit 1957–62 would not have purchased a home (20–25 per cent) or would have purchased a cheaper home (12–15 per cent).[42]

The size of the monthly payment required for a home depends upon the price of the home, the loan to value ratio, the mortgage interest rate, and the amortization period (the number of years required for the mortgage to be fully repaid out of monthly payments). Apart from reducing monthly payments by reducing the price or loan to value ratio (the latter on balance, curtailing demand by raising the required downpayment), the monthly mortgage payments may be reduced by lowering the interest rate and thereby the interest portion of each payment, or by lengthening the repayment term which spreads the capital repayments over longer periods, and thereby reduces the principal portion of each payment.

An intuitive feel of the impact of monthly mortgage payments on housing demand may be gained from the following exercise. Consider a typical new NHA financed home in Canada in 1970. According to Central Mortgage and Housing Corporation, *Canadian Housing Statistics 1970*, Table 103, such a house cost $21,895, had a $4206 downpayment, and had monthly payments of $189.05, and monthly tax payments of $46.97. Adjusting these figures and the mortgage rate somewhat for exposition purposes, assume the typical home cost $22,000, had a $17,800 NHA mortgage at 8.5 per cent with a 25-year amortization period. In this case monthly mortgage payments would be $141.50, and an approximate breakdown of expenses would be as follows: mortgage payments, $141.50; taxes, $47.00; heat, $27.00; insurance, $3.00; utilities, $12.00; maintenance, $12.00; total, $242.50. Assuming a maximum of 25 per cent of before tax income should be spent on housing, and ignoring the opportunity cost of the downpayment, the gross annual income required to support this home would be $11,640. Assume now that the interest rate were to rise by 1 per cent to 9.5 per cent, then monthly mortgage payments would increase to $153.26 and the gross annual income required to support this home would increase over $560 to $12,204. In areas where housing prices are higher (say Toronto where the average home sold by multiple listing service was approximately $31,500 in the first half of 1969) the change in income necessitated by such an increase in the interest rate would, of course, be larger.[43] On the other hand, if the amortization term of the mortgage were also increased, so the mortgage became a 9½ per cent mortgage amortized over 40 years, monthly mortgage payments would decline slightly to $140.98, total carrying costs would decline to $241.98 and the required annual income would decline to $11,615.

The relative importance of changes in the interest rate and amortization term upon the monthly payment may be seen from Table VII. This table indicates that rising interest rates can be substantially offset by an increase in the amortization term, for example a 5-year increase in the amortization period of a 7.5 per cent 25-year mortgage more than offsets a 0.5 per cent increase in the interest rate, but that as the interest rate and amortization period increase, the extent to which an increase in the amortization period can be used to offset rising interest costs

TABLE VII
MONTHLY LEVEL PAYMENTS REQUIRED TO AMORTIZE $1000 AT VARIOUS INTEREST RATES AND AMORTIZATION PERIODS

Interest rate[1]	Amortization period in years						
	10	15	20	25	30	35	40
9.5%	$12.84	$10.33	$9.20	$8.61	$8.28	$8.04	$7.92
9.0	12.58	10.05	8.89	8.28	7.93	7.69	7.56
8.5	12.32	9.76	8.59	7.95	7.59	7.35	7.21
8.0	12.06	9.48	8.28	7.63	7.25	7.01	6.86
7.5	11.81	9.21	7.99	7.32	6.91	6.66	6.50
7.0	11.56	8.93	7.69	7.00	6.59	6.32	6.14
6.5	11.31	8.66	7.41	6.70	6.26	5.98	5.79
6.0	11.07	8.40	7.12	6.40	5.95	5.65	5.45
5.5	10.82	8.14	6.84	6.10	5.64	5.33	5.12
5.0	10.58	7.88	6.57	5.82	5.34	5.02	4.80

[1]Compounded semi-annually.
Source: *Monthly Amortization Mortgage Payments* (Boston 1965).

declines. An important implication of this relationship is that housing demand may be stimulated by financial variables even during periods of rising mortgage rates, but that the capacity to do this is reduced as the amortization period lengthens.

Econometric estimates of the impact of variations in mortgage lending terms upon housing demand and new construction are difficult to untangle because of the ingenious way in which they have often been specified. For example, Break[44] created a composite credit variable consisting of the mortgage rate (RM) divided by the product of the mortgage maturity term (MT) and loan to value ratio (LV), i.e., RM/(MT x LV). He found housing start elasticities with respect to this composite credit variable of between −0.1 and −1.4 with the majority between −0.3 and −0.5, but since the influence of variations in RM, MT and LV are all likely to be different, the implications of a change in one variable are far from clear. Lee[45] used two separate variables, the loan to value ratio and a composite variable, the product of the mortgage rate and amortization term (RM x MT) and obtained stock demand elasticities of −0.27 for the mortgage cost burden and 0.90 for the loan to value ratio. Other studies have used interest rates for various proxies, and our simulations in chapter 8 indicate an average housing start elasticity over two years of −1.06 with respect to the bond rate assuming mortgage rates also adjust, an average elasticity over two years of −0.36 with respect to the NHA mortgage rate, and an average elasticity over two years of −0.76 with respect to the mortgage rate average (RM). Of primary importance, however, is the fact that regardless of how they are specified in almost all cases mortgage credit variables are very significant.

(e) Other variables
A number of other variables affect the demand for housing and influence the volume of residential construction including inflationary expectations, real estate taxes, special tax treatment of housing, the age composition of existing housing stock and consumer tastes and preferences.

Inflationary expectations influence housing demand by shifting future demand into the present. If people anticipate rising prices with increased downpayment requirements they may opt for housing purchases today rather than delay the purchase with the possibility that downpayment requirements will increase faster than their savings, or that their income will not support higher mortgage payments. Similarly if developers of multiple dwelling projects anticipate rising construction costs they may accelerate building plans, rationalizing that the carrying costs arising from higher vacancies (the result of building in advance of the demand) and higher mortgage rates will more than be offset by savings in construction costs. This is especially likely if high interest rates are anticipated to continue into the fututre so that future competitors will not be able to obtain more favourable financing before rising construction costs will have eroded any advantage that falling financing costs might give.

Higher realty taxes and other operating expenses reduce the demand for housing by increasing the carrying costs associated with housing. On the other hand the fact that imputed rent accruing to residents of owner-occupied dwellings is not considered in taxable income is a tax advantage that increases the demand for owner-occupied dwellings and housing in general.[46] And, of course, anything that affects consumer preferences for housing relative to other consumer goods affects the volume of new construction.

C. FACTORS AFFECTING HOUSING SUPPLY

In most empirical work supply constraints are given relatively little attention and we do not depart from this practice. However, the major reason why only a summary of supply factors is presented here is that relatively little is known in a macroeconomic context, although considerable information is available on a technical basis.

The supply of new housing depends upon both production possibilities and the supply of productive factors to the housing industry.[47] Production possibilities refer to the substitutability of the different productive factors required for the development of the housing site, the construction of the dwelling, and the financing, administration, and marketing of the dwelling. Some idea about production possibilities may be obtained by looking at relative factor shares and the elasticity of substitution of one factor for others in production.

Information about relative factor shares in new construction can be deduced from the Report of the National Commission on Urban Problems in the United States[48] and cost data in *Canadian Housing Statistics*. Assuming that the northeast and midwest United States have cost structures similar to Canada, and integrating the US and Canadian data, we get a breakdown of the components of single-family housing costs as shown in Table VIII. This indicates that site costs, acquisition, and improvements account for approximately 20 per cent of total costs and that construction costs account for 77 per cent. Within the construction category, labour accounts for 26 per cent, materials for 31 per cent and supervision and administration (including profits) 17 per cent. Representative figures for multiple dwelling construction are more difficult to obtain because of the enormous variability that arises depending upon the size of the project and whether it is high or low rise. However, median figures presented by the report of the National Commission on Urban Problems indicate that the figures presented in Table VIII are reasonably appropriate for multiple construction as well, although the proportionate cost for the site should be reduced to approximately 15 per cent, and construction costs increased to over 80 per cent, and the material-labour mix shifted more heavily in favour of materials.

Table VIII suggests that a number of substitutions are possible in the development process. These substitutions include the substitution of labour and capital costs for land location rent via land improvement and the provision of services, and transportation; the substitution of capital and unskilled labour for skilled labour in construction via increased prefabrication or systems building; the substitution of materials and labour for land via higher density land utilization; and the substitution of land and structure for supervision and overhead via increased scale of operations. The actual substitutability that is possible depends not only on technological feasibility but also on a myriad of institutional and political constraints.

TABLE VIII
COMPONENTS OF SINGLE FAMILY HOUSING COSTS, IN PER CENT, 1968 approx.

		Per cent
Site costs		20
acquisition	9	
improvements	11	
Construction costs:		77
labour	26	
materials	31	
finance	3	
supervision and administration	17	
Marketing		4
Total		101

Source: derived from *Building the American City*, reprint of the National Commission on Urban Problems, 91st congress, 1st session, House Document, no. 91-34 (Washington, 1968), 418-25; Central Mortgage and Housing Corporation, *Canadian Housing Statistics* (1970), 70, 88, 89; Central Mortgage and Housing Corporation, *Manpower and Material Components of the Residential Building Programme*, Economic Research Bulletin, no. 68 (Ottawa, 1957).

(a) Land cost versus construction cost
Between 1951 and 1970 land costs rose from 9.6 per cent to 19.7 per cent of the total cost of construction of new single detached NHA homes in Canada, as a result of a 74 per cent increase in construction costs and 308 per cent increase in land costs.[49] Substituting these values into an equation derived by Muth gives an elasticity of substitution of construction cost for land of 0.68 in the construction of single detached dwellings.[50] The elasticity is probably higher for the construction of all dwellings because rising land costs lead to higher density land utilization and a shift in favour of multiple- from single-dwelling construction.

The implication of this substitution of density for land is that to the extent that zoning regulations, building codes and technology permit, economization of land will occur through an increase of the value of construction per unit of land. Consequently, even though land physically is in fixed supply, the effective supply of urban land may be thought to be somewhat elastic via this mechanism. Furthermore, to the extent zoning regulations, building codes or technology change so as to allow a higher density utilization the elasticity is increased, so that in the long run the supply of land is reasonably elastic even within the confines of a fixed urban area.[51] In the short run, however, this elasticity is substantially reduced, and should be considered to be quite low.

(b) Location rent versus land improvements and social services
The relationship between land prices and public investment decisions is becoming

increasingly recognized. New roads, rapid transit systems, sewers, and water lines yield sizable benefits to adjacent properties and greatly enhance their value.[52] At the same time, rising land values in urban centres increase the pressure for new roads, transportation systems, sewers and water to bring more land into effective use. Since the provision of transport facilities and services generate alternatives to more centrally located land, the materials and labour embodied in this construction are substitutes for land location rent. Moreover, since land values generally decline with distance from the core or central business district even when serviced and possessing similar transportation facilities because of the real costs imposed by additional travelling time, in a sense the long-run supply curve of residential land is quite elastic. That is, since rising land prices in the urban core induce the provision of public services which increases the supply of lower priced residential land, the long-run supply curve is elastic.[53] The time lags in this process are so great that for all practical purposes the supply of land through increased accessibility should be considered relatively inelastic.

A second mechanism by which the supply of land may be increased is via increased spending to upgrade inferior lands already adequately provided with public services. Although the scope for land improvement is limited such substitutability exists, which increases somewhat the elasticity of supply.

(c) Labour versus material inputs

Between 1951 and 1970 wage rates of all construction workers in Canada rose 214 per cent, residential building material costs rose 41 per cent, and the composite building material and wage rate index rose 151 per cent, while the cost of construction per square foot of NHA single detached dwellings rose only 71 per cent.[54] The considerably lower rate of increase of cost of construction per square foot compared to the composite index indicates that technological adjustments occurred in the building industry to increase the relative importance of building materials (the more slowly rising cost component) from the time the weights for the composite index were determined[55] and to economize on factor inputs.

This adjustment is the logical response to relatively faster rates of wage increases than material cost increases and was made possibly by larger scale mass production and increased prefabrication. Mass production economizes on labour by allowing a more continuous, highly specialized construction process and enabling improved scheduling and material distribution. Increased prefabrication reduces labour costs per unit as production is shifted from high-cost on-site labour to generally lower-cost off-site labour, and from labour in general to power driven machinery. Prefabrication also reduces labour costs by eliminating interruptions in the production process.[56]

These adjustments would suggest that the supply curve for new houses is reasonably elastic because relatively faster cost increases of one factor of production generate technological changes to reduce their importance. Although this is true for the long run, it is not particularly valid in the short run since short run obstacles to this process include buyer acceptance, building code compliance, and labour union obstacles, all of which limit the innovation possible within a short time span. Moreover, since factor substitution is limited in the short run, the supply elasticity depends upon the availability of individual factor inputs. In a non-controlled free market economy the usual assumption is that an increase in the price offered by an industry for a factor of production will increase the supply of that factor for the industry, and availability problems should not arise. However, in periods of rapidly expanding demand, or if non-market barriers to entry exist, availability of factor inputs may become an effective constraint.

Between 1946 and 1953 Central Mortgage and Housing Corporation *Annual Reports* contained such comments as "shortages of building materials and, in some instances, building labour, has been the limitation upon the volume of residential construction" (1946, 9); "the main reasons for this (lower construction) have been shortages of material and a dilution in the skilled working force" (1947, 18); "decline in starts can be attributed in part to difficulties ... to obtain materials" (1950, 4); and "it appeared unlikely that material and labour supplies ... would be sufficient to maintain the 1950 rate of housebuilding" (1951, 3). By 1954 these references to material and labour shortages had disappeared but the immediate postwar experience clearly illustrated that in a rapidly expanding economy the aggregate demand for scarce supplies can exceed their availability, and sectors such as housing can have difficulty attracting the necessary inputs in the face of rising competing industrial and defence demands. Prior to 1954 a major constraint upon the volume of new construction was shortages of materials such as bathtubs, furnaces, and nails, and skilled labour,[57] and the short-run supply of new housing was relatively inelastic.

In the more recent postwar period restrictive practices on the part of the building trade unions have also reduced the elasticity of supply. By maintaining extremely strict apprenticeship regulations and limiting the supply of "licensed" skilled craftsmen while simultaneously increasing the proportion of union projects, the trade unions have increased the effective supply price of additional skilled craftsmen.[58] Although the long-run effect of this constraint has been to spur the industry into increased fabrication and use of less skilled off-site labour, the short-run effect is reduced elasticity.

(d) Industrial structure

Unlike the building trade unions, entry into the industry at the entrepreneurial level has traditionally been open and the industry has been characterized by a number of small participants, although the scale of operations has been increasing and the industry is now becoming more concentrated. An idea of this concentration can be gained from statistics on NHA building. In 1961, 42 per cent of all NHA dwellings were constructed by builders producing less than 26 NHA units each, and only 24 per cent were constructed by the 2 per cent of the builders producing more than 100 units. In 1970, only 24 per cent of the NHA dwellings were constructed by builders producing less than 26 units and 48 per cent were constructed by the 4 per cent of the builders producing more than 100 NHA units each.[59] The high proportion of small builders means that entrepreneurial inputs have been relatively high and the potential for economization exists. Because large-scale operations also reduce scheduling, distribution and production delays, it is not clear that increased operating size will reduce the proportion of entrepreneurial inputs relative to labour, but it should reduce both labour and entrepreneurial input relative to materials and land. Because of ease of entry and potential economies of scale the industrial structure is compatible with a high supply elasticity.

(e) Conclusion
We can conclude from the foregoing discussion that the usual assumption that the long-run supply curve for new housing is very elastic is reasonable since there is a high degree of potential factor substitution and that an ample supply of productive factors exists or can be developed. The short-run elasticity of supply, on the other hand, is probably much lower since relatively less factor substitution is possible, and time lags, barriers to entry in the building trade unions and shortages of accessible, serviced land constrain development.

4
Econometric and Empirical Analysis of the Canadian Housing Market

In the previous two chapters we developed a model to explain the housing market and volume of new residential construction, and we examined the various forces affecting the demand and supply of dwelling units. The purpose of this chapter is to subject our model to the rigour of econometric estimation, and then use it to describe the recent behaviour of the market.

A. ECONOMETRIC ANALYSIS[1]

(a) The aggregate model
The model described in chapter 2 and graphically illustrated in Figure 3 is summarized in functional form and estimated in equations 1 to 14. Underlying this model is the usual heroic assumption, removed in section (*b*), that the behaviour of the participants in the single- and multiple-dwelling sectors of the market are similar and that prices, rents, vacancy rates and construction costs in these sectors vary proportionately. This enables us to develop an aggregative model and ignore the distinction between the single and multiple sectors.

(i) Housing prices and vacancy rates
A key variable in determining the volume of housing activity is the price and vacancy rate of the existing housing stock. This is determined by the interaction of the demand for dwellings and the existing stock. Because we are interested in the volume of new construction the model focuses upon the number of physical dwelling units rather than on quality or housing service variables.

The family demand for housing units (DSH/FAM) is a function of permanent real family disposable income (YD/FAM), the price of dwelling units (PH), the price of alternative goods and services (PGNE) and the cost (RM) and availability (AV) of mortgage credit. The demand for housing is expressed on a family basis because families occupy approximately 83 per cent of Canadian dwelling units,[2] and accurate data on non-family households are not available. Furthermore, although demographic variables are strategic in determining housing demand in the long run, in the short run demographic variations may be absorbed by varying the intensity of occupancy, and their short-run influence tends to be collinear with the other arguments of the demand function.[3]

(1) DSH/FAM = d(YD/FAM, PH, PGNE, RM, AV).

The per family stock of dwellings (SH/FAM) consists of units that are occupied (SHOC/FAM) and those that are vacant (SHV/FAM). Ignoring the FAM deflator, the stock of dwelling units existing in any period is identically equal to the stock of the previous period plus completions (C) and conversions (CON) less removals and demolitions (RD). If conversions, removals and demolitions are considered to be a function of past stock, and completions a function of lagged starts, the supply of housing units is a function of the previous stock and lagged starts, i.e.,

$$\text{CON} = b \text{SH}_{t-1}, \quad \text{RD} = b_1 \text{SH}_{t-1}, \text{ and } \text{C} = \sum_{i=0}^{n} c_i \text{HS}_{t-i}, \text{ then}$$

$$\Delta \text{SH} = (b-b_1) \text{SH}_{t-} + \sum_{i=0}^{n} c_i \text{HS}_{t-i}, \text{ and}$$

$$\text{SH} = (1+b-b_1) \text{SH}_{t-1} + \sum_{i=0}^{n} c_i \text{HS}_{t-i}. \text{ Hence,}$$

(2) $\quad (\text{SH}/\text{FAM}) \equiv (\text{SHOC}/\text{FAM}) + (\text{SHV}/\text{FAM}) = s[(\text{SH}/\text{FAM})_{t-1},$

$$\sum_{i=0}^{n} \beta_i (\text{HS}/\text{FAM})_{t-i}].$$

Housing prices and vacancies can now be determined by the interaction of the demand for and supply of housing units.

(3) $\quad$ PH $= p(\text{YD}/\text{FAM}, \text{PGNE}, \text{RM}, \text{AV}, \text{SHOC}/\text{FAM}, \text{SHV}/\text{FAM}).$
(4) $\quad$ SHV/FAM $= v(\text{YD}/\text{FAM}, \text{PGNE}, \text{RM}, \text{AV}, \text{SHOC}/\text{FAM}, \text{PH}).$

Before these equations can be estimated some slight modifications are required in their specification because of data limitations. First, because reliable vacancy data are not available for most of the estimation period the vacancy equation (equation 4) cannot be estimated, the vacancy variable (SHV/FAM) must be deleted from the model for estimation purposes, and the separate (SHV/FAM) and (SHOC/FAM) variables must be replaced by a total housing stock variable (SH/FAM). These modifications, although unfortunate, do not cause serious bias as long as prices are a good indicator of market conditions.[4] Second, because the availability of credit is not a directly observable variable and because satisfactory loan to value ratio and amortization-term variables which are often used to represent credit rationing are not available in Canada, a proxy credit rationing variable, the differential between mortgage and bond yields (RM−RB), was used to represent private credit rationing or availability effects in this study. In addition, another variable, the volume of Central Mortgage and Housing Corporation direct lending (CMHC) was introduced to represent the availability of public mortgage credit. The justification for these variables is developed more fully in chapters 5 to 7.

The validity of the specified equations was tested by fitting ordinary least squares regressions to seasonally unadjusted quarterly observations over the 1954 to 1967 period. Because some statistical series are not available as early as 1954 some regressions in this chapter are estimated over a shorter period, with each regression beginning in the first quarter that data permit after 1954. The estimation period, t ratios (bracketed), R^2, standard error of estimate (SEE), and Durbin-Watson statistic (DW) are reported for all regressions. In addition, an R^2 adjusted for seasonality ($\overline{\overline{R^2}}$) is presented when appropriate.[5] Q1, Q2 and Q3 are first, second, and third quarter seasonal dummy variables, respectively. The precise definition and source of the variables included in this study are presented in Appendix A.

Estimates of the housing stock and price equations are presented in equations 5 and 6,[6] and indicate the general appropriateness of our specification. The coefficients on the lagged housing start variable in equation 5 were estimated by the Almon technique using second and third degree Almon variables.[7]

(5) $\quad$ SH $= 1.000$ SH$_{t-1}$ $+ 0.213$ HS $+ 0.339$ HS$_{t-1}$ $+ 0.248$ HS$_{t-2}$ $+ 0.086$ HS$_{t-3}$
$\qquad$ (776.94) $\quad$ (3.01) $\quad$ (5.19) $\quad\quad$ (4.74) $\quad\quad$ (4.46)

2Q'54 $-$ 4Q'67, SEE $= 6.44$, $R^2 = 0.999$, DW $= 2.03$.

(6) $\quad$ PH $= 128.72 + 1.39$ Q1 $+ 2.75$ Q2 $+ 1.41$ Q3 $+ 61.83$ (YD/FAM)$_{t-1}$
$\qquad$ (4.72) $\quad$ (1.69) $\quad\quad$ (3.32) $\quad$ (1.74) $\quad\quad$ (4.55)

$\qquad - 288.27$ (SH/FAM) $+ 1.99$ PGNE$_{t-1}$
$\qquad$ (8.85) $\quad\quad\quad\quad\quad$ (10.14)

1Q'57 $-$ 4Q'67, SEE $= 1.88$, $R^2 = 0.98$, $\overline{\overline{R^2}} = 0.97$, DW $= 1.33$.

Equation 5 indicates that the existing housing stock is determined by the past stock of houses and current housing completions, where housing completions are represented by past housing starts. The lagged housing stock coefficient of 1.0 suggests that demolitions and removals equal conversions (i.e., that $/b/ = /b_1/$) since these variables were assumed to be a function of the lagged stock. The coefficients on the lagged housing start variables indicate an average construction period of just over one-and-one-half quarters assuming housing starts are uniformly distributed within each quarter.[8]

The housing price regression indicates that housing prices vary directly with permanent real disposable income per family and the price of alternative goods and services, and inversely with the per family size of the existing housing stock. Unfortunately our cost-of-credit and credit-rationing variables failed to perform as anticipated and were omitted. The credit-rationing variable had the wrong sign and the cost-of-credit variable was insignificant. One explanation for these failures is the fact that credit variables have a stronger influence on the quality of housing demanded than on the unit or stock demand; and that those stock-demand influences that exist fall primarily on the allocation of housing demand between owner and rental units rather than on the total demand for housing. A second explanation arises from the capitalization of existing mortgage credit. Traditionally, rising interest rates are expected to reduce housing demand and hence housing prices by increasing monthly carrying costs, and this is likely if the mortgage cost associated with a home purchase is responsive to current market conditions. However, in many cases the mortgage associated with a home was arranged in the past at the rate prevailing at that time, so that an increase in current rates improves the previously arranged financing with the result that this low interest mortgage is capitalized in the form of higher house prices. This sequence is possible also on newly constructed homes, if rates rise rapidly. This occurs because the mortgage, which is assumed by the purchaser, is usually arranged by the builder prior to the commencement of construction, thus allowing a considerable time lag between the arrangement of the mortgage and the sale of the house. Consequently, an increase in the current mortgage rate decreases the demand for and price of housing requiring new financing (including vendor mortgages) and increases the price of housing with existing financing. Furthermore the total demand for housing may not decline if expectations are that higher financing costs will persist because demand may be shifted from the future to the present to take advantage of homes available with "bargain" financing. The net impact of rising financing costs on housing prices is therefore ambiguous, and the insignificance of credit variables in the housing price regression reflects this ambiguity.

A third possibility is that the specification of the price and interest rate variables in this study are inappropriate to reflect the interest rate effect on prices. The housing price variable is an average of an index of housing prices compiled by Multiple Listing Service sales (co-operative sales by members of Canadian real estate boards) which roughly approximates an index of prices of existing houses, and an index of new NHA home prices, which approximates an index of prices of newly constructed homes. Because of the diverse forces which can operate on these two segments of the house market it is possible that our price variable, which is a composite of two house prices, is not sensitive enough to reflect variations arising from interest rate changes. Moreover, it is possible that the mortgage rate variable, which is an average of the prime conventional mortgage rate of six life insurance companies and the actual NHA mortgage rate, is inappropriate to reflect rate variations in the house resale market where vendors of existing homes often "take back" a mortgage to facilitate the sale of their home, since terms on secondary mortgage finance only loosely vary with primary financing terms.

In interpreting these results extreme caution must be exercised as a consequence of the presence of serially correlated residuals in the price regression, indicated by the low Durbin/Watson statistic,[9] and the inclusion of a lagged dependent variable in the housing-stock equation. This variable biases the Durbin/Watson statistic toward 2.0 and inhibits the detection of serial correlation.[10] In an effort to eliminate these problems autoregressive transformations using the procedure suggested by Hildreth and Lu were performed.[11] This procedure assumes that the residuals (μ) in the regressions are generated by a first-order and autoregressive scheme

$$\mu = \rho \mu_{t-1} + \epsilon$$

and attempts to select the ρ that minimizes the residual variance of the specified equation. In the work that follows, whenever serial correlation is indicated by the Durbin/Watson statistic or is undetectable because of the inclusion of a lagged dependent variable an autoregressive transformation is conducted. The transformed regression and value of the autoregressive parameter are presented in an appendix to the appropriate chapter or immediately below the ordinary least squares estimate whenever the autoregressive parameter ρ lies outside the range −0.1 to 0.1 (i.e., whenever $|\rho|>0.1$).

The results of the autoregressive transformation in the housing stock regression indicate that serial correlation is not a problem since the ρ which minimizes the residual variance of equation 5 is −0.032. However, the price regression presents a problem because the search procedure indicates that a ρ greater than 1 minimizes the residual variance of equation 6. This is unsatisfactory because it implies an explosive process and suggests that a first-order autoregressive transformation may not be appropriate. Nevertheless, because the price equation has no lagged dependent variable a Theil-Nagar transformation was performed and the results are presented in the appendix to this chapter.[12] The results of this transformation indicate some substantial coefficient changes, but do not affect the significance of the included variables.

Finally, expressing equation 1 in linear form and substituting from equations 5 and 6 gives equation 7.

(7) $\quad$ DH/FAM $=0.45+0.0049$ Q1 $+0.0096$ Q2 $+0.0049$ Q3 $+0.22$ (YD/FAM)$_{t-1}$
$\quad\quad -0.0035$ PH $+0.0070$ PGNE$_{t-1}$.

(ii) Housing starts

Housing starts (HS) have been described as a function of the price of houses (PH), vacancy rate (SHV/SH), construction and land costs (CLC), and the cost (RM) and availability of private (MT) and public (CMHC) mortgage credit. Deleting the vacancy variable and replacing the availability of private mortgage credit variable with a proxy variable, the yield differential between mortgages and bonds (RM−RB), because of data limitations; specifying the house price−construction cost variables in relative terms; and introducing a dummy variable (WW) (taking the value 1 in the last quarters of 1963 to 1965 and zero elsewhere) to represent the impact of the government winter housebuilding incentive programme that provided a $500 per dwelling subsidy for 1 to 4 unit dwellings substantially constructed between December 1 and March 31, gives equation 8.

(8) $\quad$ HS $=h$ (PH/CLC, RM, RM−RB, CMHC, WW).

Estimates of the housing start equation are presented in equation 9

(9) $\quad$ HS $= -14.85 - 21.65$ Q1 $+7.22$ Q2 $+6.39$ Q3 $+8.88$ WW $+104.58$ (PH/CLC)
$\quad\quad$ (0.79) $\quad$ (11.92) $\quad\,$ (4.17) $\quad\,$ (3.69) $\quad$ (2 77) $\quad\quad\quad\quad$ (4.28)

$\quad\quad -10.70$ RM$_{t-1}+6.07$ (RM−RB)$_{t-1}+1.87$ (CMHC/PH) $+6.07$ (CMHC/PH)$_{t-1}$
$\quad\quad\,$ (4.16) $\quad\quad\quad$ (2.58) $\quad\quad\quad\quad$ (1.31) $\quad\quad\quad\quad\quad$ (4.88)

1Q'57−4'Q67, SEE $=3.57$, $R^2=0.94$, $\bar{R}^2=0.73$, DW $=1.76$.

The regression results tend to confirm the appropriateness of the housing start specification since the volume of housing starts is significantly influenced by the ratio of housing prices to construction and land costs, the availability of private mortgage credit (represented by the RM−RB variable), the availability of public mortgage credit (expressed as the constant dollar value of CMHC direct lending) and the cost (RM) of mortgage credit. The sum of the coefficients on the CMHC variables indicates that an additional million dollars in CMHC direct lending in constant 1957 dollars would generate an additional 80 housing starts.[13] Finally, the coefficient on the winter housebuilding incentive dummy variable (WW) indicates that this programme was quite successful in breaking the usual fourth quarter decline in housing starts.

(iii) Construction and land costs

To complete the housing sector, consideration must be given to the factors affecting construction costs and land costs. The measure of construction costs in this section is an index of the average cost of construction (including land costs) per square foot on new government-insured single detached dwellings. Variations in this index were assumed to be influenced by changes in average hourly earnings in construction (WC), changes in temporary or bridge financing costs (R03),[14] changes in land costs (L), changes in the cost of building materials, and the delays and bottlenecks that arise as current residential construction (IRC) and non-residential construction (INRC) press against their respective industrial capacities. Since changes in the cost of building materials are highly correlated with changes between residential and non-residential construction and their respective industrial capacities, the building material variable was deleted from the model and its impact was assumed to be reflected in the coefficients on the capacity variables and a sales tax dummy variable (DVST). DVST, which has the value 1 from 3Q'63 to 4Q'65 and zero elsewhere, was included to reflect the influence of the imposition in stages of a sales tax on building materials between June 1963 and December 1965.[15] The degree of capacity utilization in residential and non-residential construction was assumed to be represented by the deviations of residential and non-residential construction expenditure from their seasonally adjusted logarithmic trends. The equation is specified in natural logarithms (ln) in terms of annual changes in quarterly form in equation 10 because of the inclusion of the wage variable and the amount of random noise inherent in the measure of construction costs. Although this procedure does not introduce bias into the estimates it does impair the efficiency of the least squares estimates by building serial correlation into the model and reducing the number of truly independent observations.[16]

(10) $\ln \text{CLC} - \ln \text{CLC}_{t-4} = c[(\ln \widehat{\text{INRC}} - \ln \widehat{\text{INRC}}), (\ln \widehat{\text{IRC}} - \ln \widehat{\text{IRC}}),$
$(\ln \text{WC} - \ln \text{WC}_{t-4}), (\ln \text{L} - \ln \text{L}_{t-4}), (\ln \text{R03} - \ln \text{R03}_{t-4}), (\text{DVST})]$.

The estimated construction and land cost regressions and the estimated linear trend regressions for $\ln \widehat{\text{INRC}}$ and $\ln \widehat{\text{IRC}}$ are presented in equations 11 to 13, where T is a time trend beginning in 1Q'52.[17]

(11) $\ln \text{CLC} - \ln \text{CLC}_{t-4} = -0.006 + 0.037 \, (\ln \text{INRC} - \ln \widehat{\text{INRC}})_{t-1} + 0.070$
(1.20) (1.67) (2.73)

$(\ln \text{IRC} - \ln \widehat{\text{IRC}})_{t-1} + 0.36 \, (\ln \text{WC} - \ln \text{WC}_{t-4}) + 0.07 \, (\ln \text{L} - \ln \text{L}_{t-4})$
(5.24) (1.59)

$+ 0.020 \, (\ln \text{R03} - \ln \text{R03}_{t-4}) + 0.017 \, \text{DVST}$
(2.07) (2.72)

3Q'55–4Q'67, SEE = 0.017, $R^2 = 0.73$, DW = 1.16.

(12) $\ln \widehat{\text{INRC}} = 6.25 - 0.370 \, \text{Q1} - 0.086 \, \text{Q2} - 0.105 \, \text{Q3} + 0.0085 \, \text{T}$
(118.65) (7.16) (1.67) (2.03) (8.09)

1Q'53–4Q'67, SEE = 0.14, $R^2 = 0.75$, DW = 0.33.

(13) $\ln \widehat{\text{IRC}} = 5.93 - 0.349 \, \text{Q1} - 0.092 \, \text{Q2} - 0.008 \, \text{Q3} + 0.0027 \, \text{T}$
(141.89) (8.51) (2.24) (0.20) (3.19)

1Q'53–4Q'67, SEE = 0.11, $R^2 = 0.66$, DW = 0.70.

Land costs, measured as an index of the cost of land used in the construction of new NHA single detached dwellings, are assumed to be determined by the demand for residential land.[18] The cost of land (L), therefore, is thought to vary directly with population (POP), permanent real disposable income, and expectations as to future land prices (where expectations are extrapolative and represented by past changes in land prices), and inversely with the size of the existing housing stock.

(14) $\text{L} = -84.1 + 0.022 \, \text{POP} + 0.028 \, \text{YD} - 0.081 \, \text{SH} + 0.65 \, \triangle \text{L}$
(4.16) (4.38) (4.93) (3.29) (5.43)

2Q'54–4Q'67, SEE = 4.70, $R^2 = 0.96$, DW = 0.98.

(iv) The mortgage market

The importance of the mortgage market to the housing sector is apparent from the above discussion, since the terms and availability of mortgage credit have a direct bearing both on the user demand for housing and on the willingness and ability of builders and developers to undertake new construction. Because the determination of mortgage rates and terms depends both on the supply of and demand for this credit and because the factors affecting the supply of mortgages are discussed in chapters 5 and 6, the estimation of a mortgage rate equation is postponed until chapter 7.

(b) The dis-aggregate model

In this section the assumption that the behaviour of the participants in the single- and multiple-dwelling sectors of the housing market are similar and that prices, rents, vacancy rates and construction costs in these sectors vary proportionately, is removed, and separate single and multiple sector housing market models are estimated.

(i) Housing prices, rents, and vacancy rates

A number of modifications are required in our specification to reflect the differences that exist between the single and multiple dwelling sectors. A key variable in determining the volume of housing activity undertaken in each sector is the relationship between the value of new completed dwellings and their construction cost. In the case of multiple dwelling construction the completed value of a project largely depends upon current rents and vacancy rates on existing multiple dwellings, while in the case of single dwelling construction the value largely depends upon current prices and vacancy rates on newly completed single dwellings.

Rents (R) and vacancy rate in multiple dwellings (SHVM/SHM) are determined by the demand for rental accommodation and their existing supply, and prices and vacancy rate in single dwellings (SHVS/SHS) are determined by the demand for single-family accommodations and their supply.[19] These sectors are strongly interwoven because the demand for rental dwellings depends not only on the price (rent) of these dwellings but also on the price of competing owner-occupancy accommodations, while the demand for owner-occupancy accommodation depends both on the price of this accommodation and the rent on multiple-dwelling units. A second inter-relationship exists in the response of housing demand in each sector to credit variables. If we ignore qualitative effects, a major impact of credit variables on housing demand occurs in the allocation of final housing demand between rental and owner accommodation. When credit terms become more stringent, the demand for owner occupancy housing declines. However, much of this demand for housing is not eliminated but shifted to a demand for rental accommodation as families postpone their shift from rental to owner-occupancy dwellings and undouble into rental rather than owner-occupancy accommodations. Because tighter credit conditions do not affect rents from the supply side except with a considerable lag, this shift in demand causes a net increase in the demand for rental accommodation. Consequently, more stringent credit terms are likely to affect housing prices and rents in opposite ways, increasing rents via a net increase in the demand for rental dwellings and reducing house prices via a net reduction in the demand for owner occupancy dwellings.

In our model the demand for single dwellings (DSHS) is expressed on a per family basis (FAM) because family units are the main occupiers of single dwellings and the demand for multiple dwelling units (DSHM) is expressed on a per capita basis (POP) because the occupancy of these dwellings is not confined to families. Although this is not a very sophisticated way of introducing demographic variables, these variables are very elusive in quarterly models and this specification proved most satisfactory. The demand functions for single and multiple dwellings are presented in equations 15 and 16.

(15) $\text{DSHS}/\text{FAM} = ds\,(\text{YD}/\text{FAM}, \text{PH}, \text{R}, \text{PGNE}, \text{RM}, \text{AV})$.

(16) $\text{DSHM}/\text{POP} = dm\,(\text{YD}/\text{POP}, \text{PH}, \text{R}, \text{PGNE}, \text{RM}, \text{AV})$.

For scaling purposes the stock of single dwellings (SHS) is expressed on a per family basis and the stock of multiple dwellings (SHM) is expressed on a per capita basis in equations 17 and 18.

(17) $\text{SHS/FAM} \equiv (\text{SHSOC/FAM}) + (\text{SHSV/FAM}) = ss\,[(\text{SHS/FAM})_{t-1},$

$\sum_{i=0}^{m} \beta_i\,(\text{HSS/FAM})_{t-i}]$

(18) $\text{SHM/POP} \equiv (\text{SHMOC/POP}) + (\text{SHMV/POP}) = sm\,[(\text{SHM/POP})_{t-1},$

$\sum_{j=0}^{n} \beta_j\,(\text{HSM/POP})_{t-j}].$

Housing prices, rents and single and multiple dwelling vacancies can now be determined by the interaction of the respective demand and supply functions.

(19) $\text{PH} = q\,(\text{YD/FAM, R, PGNE, RM, AV, SHSOC/FAM, SHSV/FAM}),$

(20) $\text{R} = r\,(\text{YD/POP, PH, PGNE, RM, AV, SHMOC/POP, SHMV/POP}),$

(21) $\text{SHSV/FAM} = sv\,(\text{YD/FAM, R, PH, PGNE, RM, AV, SHSOC/FAM}),$

(22) $\text{SHMV/POP} = mv\,(\text{YD/POP, PH, R, PGNE, RM, AV, SHMOC/POP}).$

Because satisfactory vacancy data do not exist and because housing stock statistics are compiled on a rental and owner-occupied basis, rather than a multiple and single dwelling basis in Canada, some modifications are required before estimation. These modifications consist of deleting the vacancy equations from the model, combining the occupied and vacant housing stock variables into a single housing stock variable, and replacing the stock of multiple (SHM) and stock of single (SHS) dwelling variables with the stock of rental (SHR) and stock of owner-occupied (SHO) dwelling variables in equations 17 to 20. The housing stock equations 23 and 24 are estimated in undeflated form to avoid the introduction of heteroscedasticity.[20] The coefficients on the lagged housing start variables in these housing stock equations were estimated by the Almon technique using second and third degree Almon variables.[21]

The estimated housing stock and price and rent regressions are presented in equations 23 to 28. Two sets of estimates of the price and rent regressions are presented, one set (equations 25 and 26) with the mortgage rate variable included and one set (equations 27 and 28) with it excluded.

(23) $\text{SHO} = 0.9989\,\text{SHO}_{t-1} + 0.281\,\text{HSS} + 0.400\,\text{HSS}_{t-1} + 0.285\,\text{HSS}_{t-2}$
   (1172.57)   (4.63)   (8.27)   (6.88)

   $+ 0.098\,\text{HSS}_{t-3}$
   (6.21)

2Q′54–4Q′67, SEE = 4.16, $R^2 = 0.999$, DW = 2.23.

(24) $\text{SHR} = 0.9998\,\text{SHR}_{t-1} + 0.090\,\text{HSM} + 0.277\,\text{HSM}_{t-1} + 0.279\,\text{HSM}_{t-2}$
   (809.56)   (1.18)   (7.18)   (5.82)

   $+ 0.179\,\text{HSM}_{t-3} + 0.058\,\text{HSM}_{t-4}$
   (5.10)   (4.75)

2Q′54–4Q′67, SEE = 3.14, $R^2 = 0.999$, DW = 1.38.

(25) $PH = 181.11 + 0.84\, Q1 + 1.98\, Q2 + 0.88\, Q3 + 16.72\, (YD/FAM)_{t-1}$
    (4.07) (1.02)   (2.35)   (1.13)   (1.10)

  $- 402.90\, (SHO/FAM) + 1.60\, PGNE_{t-1} + 0.28\, R_{t-1} - 1.28\, RM_{t-1}$
    (8.50)   (4.30)   (1.26)   (.68)

1Q'57 – 4Q'67, SEE = 1.81, $R^2 = 0.98$, $\bar{R}^2 = 0.98$, DW = 1.30.

(26) $R = -42.05 + 0.82\, Q1 + 1.38\, Q2 + 1.61\, Q3 + 270.07\, (YD/POP)_{t-1}$
    (1.92) (1.37)   (2.20)   (2.76)   (4.79)

  $-1345.42\, (SHR/POP)_{t-1} + 1.39\, PGNE_{t-1} + 0.13\, PH_{t-1} + 2.12\, RM_{t-1}$
    (3.44)   (5.81)   (1.21)   (1.79)

1Q'57 – 4Q'67, SEE = 1.34, $R^2 = 0.99$, $\bar{R}^2 = 0.99$, DW = 1.16.

(27) $PH = 168.74 + 0.84\, Q1 + 1.91\, Q2 + 0.90\, Q3 + 23.74\, (YD/FAM)_{t-1}$
    (4.19) (1.02)   (2.30)   (1.17)   (2.16)

  $-392.32\, (SHO/FAM) + 1.56\, PGNE_{t-1} + 0.21\, R_{t-1}$
    (8.83)   (4.28)   (1.07)

1Q'57 – 4Q'67, SEE = 1.80, $R^2 = 0.98$, $\bar{R}^2 = 0.98$, DW = 1.25.

(28) $R = -40.32 + 0.87\, Q1 + 1.56\, Q2 + 1.53\, Q3 + 226.44\, (YD/POP)_{t-1}$
    (1.79) (1.42)   (2.45)   (2.55)   (4.32)

  $-1294.72\, (SHR/POP)_{t-1} + 1.56\, PGNE_{t-1} + 0.18\, PH_{t-1}$
    (3.23)   (6.85)   (1.62)

1Q'57 – 4Q'67, SEE = 1.38, $R^2 = 0.99$, $\bar{R}^2 = 0.98$, DW = 1.20.

The housing stock regressions indicate that the housing stock in each sector is determined by the stock in the previous period and current housing completions, where current completions are represented by past housing starts. The lagged housing stock coefficients of less than 1.0 (0.9989 in equation 23 and 0.9998 in equation 24) suggest that housing demolitions and removals in both sectors exceed conversions since these variables were assumed to a function of lagged stock. Coefficients on the lagged housing start variables indicate an average construction period of approximately two-and-one-third quarters for multiple dwelling projects and one-and-two-thirds quarters for single housing units.[22] The fact that the sum of the coefficients of the multiple housing start variables is considerably below 1 and that the sum of the coefficients of the single housing start variables is above 1 arises from classification inconsistencies inherent in the use of SHR and SHO as approximations for SHM and SHS, respectively. These results indicate that not all multiple dwellings, which include duplexes and row housing, are used for rental purposes. Finally, the Hildreth-Lu transformations confirm the absence of serial correlation, yielding ρs of –0.112 and –0.026 in the SHO and SHR regressions, respectively, and transformed coefficients virtually identical to those in the untransformed regressions.

The price and rent regressions are quite consistent with the theory developed earlier. Housing prices and rents vary directly with permanent real disposable income, the price of competing housing, and the price of alternative goods and services; and inversely with the respective stocks of housing. Housing prices seem to vary inversely with the cost of mortgage credit, and rents seem to vary directly with this cost, which is consistent with the notion that rising financing costs shift demand from owner to rental housing. However, the deletion of the mortgage cost variable in equations 27 and 28 seems to have little or no effect on the explanatory power of the regressions. The R^2s remain the same and the SEE rises slightly in one case, while the deletion of the mortgage cost variable allows the income variable to become much more significant in the housing price regression. Therefore, although the mortgage rate variable performs as anticipated it does not appear to play a leading role in price and rent determination. On the other hand, it must be remembered that our price, rent, and mortgage cost variables are all inexact representations of true market conditions and consequently the likelihood of a strong correlation is diminished.

Since the Hildreth-Lu search procedure yielded autoregressive parameters greater than 1 in the housing price and rent regressions, a Theil-Nagar autoregressive transformation was used in an attempt to eliminate serial correlation. The transformed regressions presented in the appendix do not indicate any startling changes although they generally increase the significance of the price of competing dwelling accommodation variables and reduce the significance of the alternative goods and services variable (PGNE). These regressions also tend generally to increase the importance of the effects of income on housing prices.

Finally, equations 23 to 26 can be used to determine the parameters of equations 15 and 16 specified in linear form, and the calculated equations are presented in equations 29 and 30.

(29) $\text{DSHS/FAM} = 0.45 + 0.0021\, Q1 + 0.0050\, Q2 + 0.0022\, Q3 + 0.042\, (\text{YD/FAM})_{t-1}$
$- 0.0025\, (\text{SHO/FAM}) + 0.0042\, \text{PGNE}_{t-1} + 0.0007\, R_{t-1} - 0.0032\, \text{RM}_{t-1}.$

(30) $\text{DSHM/POP} = 0.031 + 0.00061\, Q1 + 0.0010\, Q2 + 0.0012\, Q3 + 0.20\, (\text{YD/POP})_{t-1}$
$- 0.00074\, (\text{SHR/POP}) + 0.0010\, \text{PGNE}_{t-1} + 0.000096\, \text{PH}_{t-1} + 0.00\,6\, \text{RM}_{t-1}.$

(ii) Housing starts

The major differences to be incorporated in a two-sector housing market model compared to a single sector model arise from the substitutability of one form of construction for another. Developers have the option of building multiple or single dwelling units (although usually not on the same site) and the extent to which they undertake construction in one sector depends upon its expected profitability. This substitutability is introduced into our specification in a number of ways. First, single housing starts (HSS) are specified as a function of housing prices while multiple dwelling starts (HSM) are specified as a function of rents. Consequently, in a period in which rents increase relative to housing prices, ceteris paribus, multiple dwelling construction will increase relative to single dwelling construction. Second, if developers think that higher borrowing costs can be passed on to purchasers of single-family dwellings more easily than to tenants in multiple dwellings, rising mortgage rates will cause multiple-dwelling construction to fall more sharply than single dwelling construction. Third, land costs play an important role in determining the form of construction to be undertaken since rising land costs encourage higher density land utilization. This should lead to an increase in the volume of multiple dwelling construction relative to single-dwelling construction. Although increasing land costs will also tend to discourage both forms of construction by reducing their profitability the net impact of rising land costs is likely to be an increase in multiple dwelling starts and a reduction in single dwelling starts.[23] Finally, government preferences affect the volume of construction in each sector through the availability of CMHC direct loans for single dwelling construction (CMHCS) and CMHC direct loans for multiple dwelling construction (CMHCM).

Summarizing this discussion in functional form after introducing the winter housebuilding incentive dummy variable (WW) gives equations 31 and 32.

(31) HSS = hs (PH, CC, L, RM, MT, CMHCS, WW, SHVS/SHS),

(32) HSM = hm (R, CC, L, RM, MT, CMHCM, WW, SHVM/SHM),

where CC is an index of construction costs per square foot of new NHA single detached dwellings excluding land costs and MT is a measure of the stringency of non-price mortgage lending terms or the availability of private mortgage credit.

The estimated equations for single and multiple housing starts are presented in equations 31 and 32 after deleting the vacancy variable, substituting a proxy credit rationing variable (RM − RB) for the availability of private mortgage credit and expressing the house price–construction cost, and rent–construction cost variables in relative terms.

(33) HSS = 18.82 − 12.70 Q1 + 5.06 Q2 + 4.20 Q3 + 4.87 WW + 18.43 $(PH/CC)_{t-1}$
       (1.12) (8.60)   (3.29)   (3.02)   (2.03)   (0.86)

  − 2.35 RM_{t-1} + 5.65 $(RM-RB)_{t-1}$ − 0.12 L + 2.30 (CMHCS/PH)
   (1.24)   (2.94)   (1.97)   (2.03)

  + 4.94 $(CMHCS/PH)_{t-1}$
   (4.68)

1Q'57 − 4Q'67, SEE = 2.89, R^2 = 0.89, $\bar{R}^2$ = 0.62, DW = 2.00.

(34) HSM = 6.77 − 8.17 Q1 + 2.46 Q2 + 2.55 Q3 + 2.58 WW + 34.97 $(R/CC)_{t-1}$
       (0.52) (5.45)   (1.46)   (1.70)   (1.05)   (3.02)

  − 6.28 RM_{t-1} + 0.18 $(RM-RB)_{t-1}$ + 0.072 L + 11.29 (CMHCM/PH)
   (3.29)   (0.09)   (1.06)   (2.21)

  + 7.30 $(CMHCM/PH)_{t-1}$
   (1.66)

1Q'57 − 4Q'67, SEE = 3.02, R^2 = 0.85, $\bar{R}^2$ = 0.78, DW = 1.51.

These regressions confirm the appropriateness of the model and accentuate some distinctions between the single and multiple dwelling sectors. The private credit rationing variable is very significant in the single dwelling sector but insignificant (although with the correct sign) in the multiple sector. On the other hand, the demand restraining effects of rising mortgage costs exert a much stronger impact upon multiple starts than single starts. Although this result is more pronounced than we had anticipated, it is consistent with the preceding discussion since developers of multiple projects are likely to be very sensitive to interest costs, which substantially affect the profitability and cash flow of their projects, and require little non-price credit rationing. On the other hand, builders of single unit dwellings are building for home purchasers who, constrained by an over-all budget constraint but not a profitability test for each purchase, have the latitude to allocate more of their household budget to housing. Also, these purchasers are concerned primarily with monthly and downpayment requirements, which are quite sensitive to variations in non-price lending terms as well as to interest costs, rather than with interest costs alone. Consequently, on the demand side, builders of single-unit dwellings are likely to be less responsive to interest cost variations than builders of multiple-unit dwellings, as the interest elasticity measured at the means of -0.80 for single compared to -2.19 for multiple housing starts indicates, and they require non-price rationing to equilibrate their sector of the market.

The likelihood of greater non-price rationing in the single dwelling sector is reinforced on the supply side by the tendency of financial institutions to favour large corporate borrowers who dominate multiple dwelling construction rather than smaller builders who are prevalent in the construction of single-unit dwellings. This preference arises both because institutions wish to maintain the goodwill of prime borrowers with whom they deal on a continuing basis and because individual, as opposed to corporate, borrowers have the statutory right to discharge their mortgages after three to five years upon payment of a bonus of three months' interest. This means that if interest rates are high and expected to decline only corporate borrowers can be "locked-in" to the higher interest rate for the full term of their loan while individual borrowers cannot. The significance of the government direct lending variable (CMHC) in the multiple equation is not inconsistent with the lack of private rationing in this sector since Central Mortgage and Housing Corporation lending occurs at a lower rate than is charged for conventional mortgage finance.

The larger sum of the coefficients on the multiple than on the single government direct lending variable indicates that a given increment in government mortgage lending in constant 1957 dollars for multiple dwellings will generate considerably more dwelling starts than if this lending were for single dwelling construction. Land costs are shown to play an important role in the mix of single and multiple dwelling starts as rising land costs increase the proportion of multiple to single dwelling construction. Although the rent to construction cost ratio is quite significant in the multiple sector the ratio of housing prices to construction cost is not really significant in the single sector, although the sign is correct, probably because of the inclusion of custom built homes and the very great difficulties in properly measuring housing prices.

(iii) Construction costs

Because land costs enter the disaggregated housing start equations separately, the construction cost variable was redefined in this section to exclude land cost.

The measure of construction cost (CC) used in this section is an index of the average cost of construction (excluding land cost) per square foot on new government-insured single detached dwellings. Variations in this index were assumed to be influenced by the same variables as in the previous section with the exception of land costs. This estimated construction cost regression is presented in equation 35, and essentially reconfirms the earlier result obtained in equation 11.

$$(35) \quad \ln \text{CC} - \ln \text{CC}_{t-4} = -0.0090 + 0.015 \, (\ln \widehat{\text{INRC}} - \ln \text{INRC})_{t-1}$$
$$(2.13) \quad (0.76)$$

$$+ 0.104 \, (\ln \widehat{\text{IRC}} - \ln \text{IRC})_{t-1} + 0.425 \, (\ln \text{WC} - \ln \text{WC}_{t-4})$$
$$(4.22)) \quad (6.36)$$

$$+ 0.013 \, (\ln \text{R03} - \ln \text{R03}_{t-4}) + 0.021 \, \text{DVST}$$
$$(1.39) \quad (3.38)$$

3Q'55–4Q'67, SEE = 0.016, R^2 = 0.76, DW = 0.83.

B. EMPIRICAL ANALYSIS

(a) Long-run trends

The foregoing econometric analysis clearly indicates the validity of our housing model and substantiates its specification and applicability for the postwar period. The purpose of this section is to describe and analyse the basic behaviour of the residential construction market during this period within the framework of our model.

Canada entered the postwar period with a very severe shortage of housing accommodation as a consequence of a sharply reduced building programme during the depression and the war. Between 1931 and 1945, Canada averaged fewer than 39,000 dwelling completions annually, compared with an annual average of over 55,000 completions for the five years preceding this period, and of over 77,000 completions for the five years immediately following this period.

In 1951, although the housing situation had improved substantially, 9.8 per cent of all Canadian families and 13.0 per cent of Canadian families in metropolitan areas did not have separate dwelling accommodations of their own. Moreover, substantial numbers of families required improved accommodations since the 1951 Census indicated that 13.4 per cent of all dwellings and 9.7 per cent of urban dwellings were in need of major repair. The 1951 Census also indicated that 31.7 per cent of all dwellings were without the exclusive or shared use of flush toilets, 39.2 per cent were without the exclusive or shared use of an installed bath or shower, and 43.1 per cent were without hot and 26 per cent were without either hot or cold running water.[24] Consequently 30 to 35 per cent would be a very conservative estimate of the proportion of Canadian families in physical need of new housing accommodation in 1951, and this backlog of pent-up demand was the dominant feature of the housing market in the 1950s and early 1960s.

Some indication of the persistence and severity of the housing backlog can be seen from Table IX. Despite the rapid improvement in housing standards in the

TABLE IX
MEASURES OF HOUSING CONDITIONS, 1951-70

	Percentage of Canadian families not maintaining their own households		Percentage of Canadian dwellings without the use of essential facilities		
	All areas	Metropolitan areas	Flush or chemical toilets	Piped hot and cold water	Installed bath or shower
1951	9.8%	13.0%	20.3%	43.1%	39.2%
1956	7.7	10.0	20.4*	28.9*	28.5*
1961	5.7	6.8	12.8	19.8	19.1
1966	4.0	4.5	8.4	12.6	12.8
1970	NA	NA	4.2	5.5	8.1

NA Figures not available.
*Figures are for 1957.
Source: Central Mortgage and Housing Corporation, *Canadian Housing Statistics* (1968), 64, and (1970), 96.

fifties, the 1961 Census found that 5.7 per cent of Canadian families were still without separate dwelling accommodations of their own, 5.6 per cent of the housing stock was in need of major repair (and an additional 20 per cent in need of minor repair), 14.1 per cent of all dwellings were without the use of flush toilets, 19.1 per cent were without the use of an installed bath or shower, and 19.8 per cent were without hot running water.[25] These latter deficiencies did not fall below 10 per cent of all dwellings until the mid-1960s so that although the backlog of housing need had been sharply reduced it was far from eliminated even through most of the sixties.

Compounding the initial backlog problem was a very high rate of net family formation in the first two-thirds of the 1950s when net family formation occurred at a level that was not matched again until the second half of the sixties. This high level was spearheaded by both high marriage rates and high levels of immigration.

Apart from the political pressure that the inadequately housed can exert on the government to initiate subsidized housing, a backlog of unsatisfied housing need can only generate an increased volume of residential construction if it can be translated into effective demand, i.e., when the people desiring new dwelling accommodations are able to pay for them. As discussed previously, the affordability of residential accommodations increases with rising per family and per capita disposable income, lower rents and housing prices, and more liberal price and non-price financing terms. Although housing prices and rents rose throughout the postwar period, and rose at a faster rate than the general price level, the affordability of housing generally increased throughout the 1950s and 1960s.

Table x presents selected price and income average annual rates of increase from 1957 (the first year for which all our series exist) to 1970. These figures indicate that the annual average increase in the cost of NHA homes was 3.2 per cent, in the average price obtained through real estate board Multiple Listing Service sales (approximating price changes for existing homes) was 4.8 per cent, in the labour force survey of average monthly rents was 4.7 per cent (all of the foregoing series being unadjusted for quality and size variations), in the Dominion Bureau of Statistics rental index was 1.6 per cent, and shelter index was 3.3 per

TABLE X
SELECTED PRICE AND INCOME AVERAGE ANNUAL RATES OF INCREASE, 1957-70

	Per cent
Housing prices and rents	
Cost of NHA homes per square foot	2.8
Cost of NHA homes	3.2
Average MLS selling price	4.8
Home ownership index – DBS	4.7
Average monthly rents – labour force survey	4.7
Rental index – DBS	1.6
Shelter cost index – DBS	3.3
Down payment and monthly payments on NHA homes	
*Average down payment requirements	0.8
†Average monthly gross debt service	6.3
General price indices:	
Consumer price index	2.5
GNE implicit price deflator	2.7
Incomes	
Personal disposable income per family	4.9
Personal disposable income per person over 19	4.9
Personal disposable income per person	5.0

*These requirements fell substantially in 1958. Between 1958-70, the annual rate of increase was 2.7 per cent.
†Average increase for 1958-1970 period.
Sources: Bank of Canada, *Review* (Dec. 1972); Central Mortgage and Housing Corporation, *Canadian Housing Statistics* (1965) and (1971); and Dominion Bureau of Statistics, Labour Force Survey.

cent. Perhaps a more meaningful measure of the affordability of new homes than the nominal purchase price is a combination of downpayment requirements and monthly gross debt service payments, consisting of monthly mortgage payments and tax payments. Although this information is available only for new NHA homes it indicates that the average annual increase in downpayment requirements was 2.7 per cent and in monthly gross debt service was 6.3 per cent between 1958 and 1970.[26] In comparison to these shelter cost increases, personal disposable income per family rose at an average annual rate of 4.9 per cent, personal disposable income per capita rose at an average annual rate of 5.0 per cent, and personal disposable income per person over 19 years of age rose at an average annual rate of 4.9 per cent. Therefore, although shelter costs rose more quickly than other commodities (the consumer price index rose at an average annual rate of 2.5 per cent and the GNE implicit price deflator rose at an average annual rate of 2.7 per cent) housing accommodations became slightly more affordable during the 1950s and 1960s.[27]

(b) Cyclical variation

Although the general trend was toward increased affordability of housing, improved housing standards and increased residential construction activity, Figure 5 indicates that this progress was not without cyclical variations as new residential construction is one of the most volatile components of gross national product. Using housing starts as a crude short-run indicator of the trend in housing standards, improvement occurred rapidly from the end of the war to 1958, with only the

FIGURE 5   Quarterly housing starts seasonally adjusted at annual rates, 1948–70

1951–2 and late 1956 to early 1957 periods experiencing a lower level of starts than the previous postwar peak. A substantial slowdown in housing starts began in 1959 and despite a steady improvement beginning in 1961, it was not until 1964 that housing starts returned to their 1958 peak. This expansion was reversed briefly in 1966, but then continued vigorously in the last part of the 1960s. With an average annual level of housing starts of 199,000 for 1968–70 Canada almost tripled its 1946–8 average of 72,700 starts, although population and the rate of net family formation were less than double the 1946–8 levels.

(i) 1946 to 1950: Canadians entered the postwar period with a high degree of liquidity, liquid assets had tripled while GNP had only doubled since 1939, and a large backlog of pent-up demand in all sectors.[28] Monetary policy was geared to maintaining a bond price support programme which held long-term government bond yields at 2.50 per cent,[29] and although fiscal policy was deflationary most of the surplus was used to redeem government of Canada securities which increased the liquidity of the private sector and offset much of the fiscal restraint. With housing need so great, liquidity so strong, and no monetary restraint as financial institutions stood ready to meet any demand for mortgage financing that passed credit analysis and offered a rate of return containing a minimum risk premium over government bonds, residential construction activity expanded steadily and rapidly, constrained only by the availability of building materials and labour and the lack of qualified and well organized builders.[30]

(ii) 1951 to mid-1952: in October 1950, with inflation threatening as a result of the outbreak of the Korean war and resultant pressures placed on the economy, the Bank of Canada rediscount rate was raised, signalling the end of the bond price support programme and the freeing of interest rates.[31] Interest rates, gradually at first and then more vigorously, moved upwards under pressure exerted in the corporate sector where business and industry were experiencing unusually heavy demands for funds. By early 1951 government bond yields broke the 3 per cent barrier for the first time in the postwar period, despite continuing net redemptions by the government and net purchases by the Bank of Canada. Although credit conditions tightened, mortgage financing was still readily available from most lenders but demand for this financing slackened in the face of soaring construction costs in the latter part of 1950 and early 1951 and the application of selective credit controls against housing for the first time in February 1951.

For some unexplained reason, despite the existence of a high and rising volume of residential construction, a large scale physical need for housing, an ample availability of mortgage financing, and high levels of personal savings and personal disposable incomes, there had been fear in 1949 and early 1950 that the demand for housing "would not be sufficiently strong to sustain the current volume of housing."[32] The government, therefore, cut NHA downpayment requirements in half and further stimulated an already strong effective demand for housing. This demand, which coincided with wartime and industrial claims on the economy, exerted such pressure on material and labour supplies that it became obvious that these supplies were insufficient to maintain the previous rate of construction[33] and in February 1951 the government restored NHA downpayment requirements to their previous level. Despite this measure residential construction costs rose over 15 per cent in 1951, and the consumer price index over 10 per cent, which, together with increased personal sales and excise taxes and expectations that NHA downpayment requirements would again be reduced, resulted in a temporary slackening in demand and a sharp contraction in residential construction activity.

(iii) Mid-1952 to 1955: by 1952 inflationary pressures had eased, materials, supplies and labour had become freer, the postwar pent-up demand for new housing had been reinforced by the curtailment of residential construction in the previous year, by large scale immigration, large net family formation and child births, increasing incomes and favourable expectations, and residential construction regained its vigour. This strength in demand was sufficiently strong to drive the conventional mortgage rate up 1.1 per cent, from 5.0 per cent to 6.1 per cent, between 1951 and 1953, while the long-term government bond yield rose only 0.6 per cent, from 3.1 per cent to 3.7 per cent.

In early 1953 bond market activity increased as the government became a net issuer of long-term debt, the Bank of Canada became a net seller of government securities and the chartered banks reduced their bond holdings to protect their reserve positions. The resultant increase in bond yields caused a pause between mid-1953 and mid-1954 in the upward trend in housing starts, and as Figure 6 indicates, a new decade was ushered in in which the availability of mortgage financing was to be a crucial determinant of the timing of fluctuations in residential construction expenditures.[34] Prior to this, the volume of residential construction depended upon the availability of building materials and labour and the capacity of the building industry.[35]

In an attempt to ameliorate deficiencies in the availability of mortgage credit, the National Housing Act was revised in 1954 to empower the chartered banks to enter the mortgage market. At approximately the same time, but quite unrelated, the tightness in the capital markets eased toward the end of 1953 as net new issues of corporate securities declined, demand for bank loans eased and government net bond redemptions increased, and bond yields slipped toward their 1951

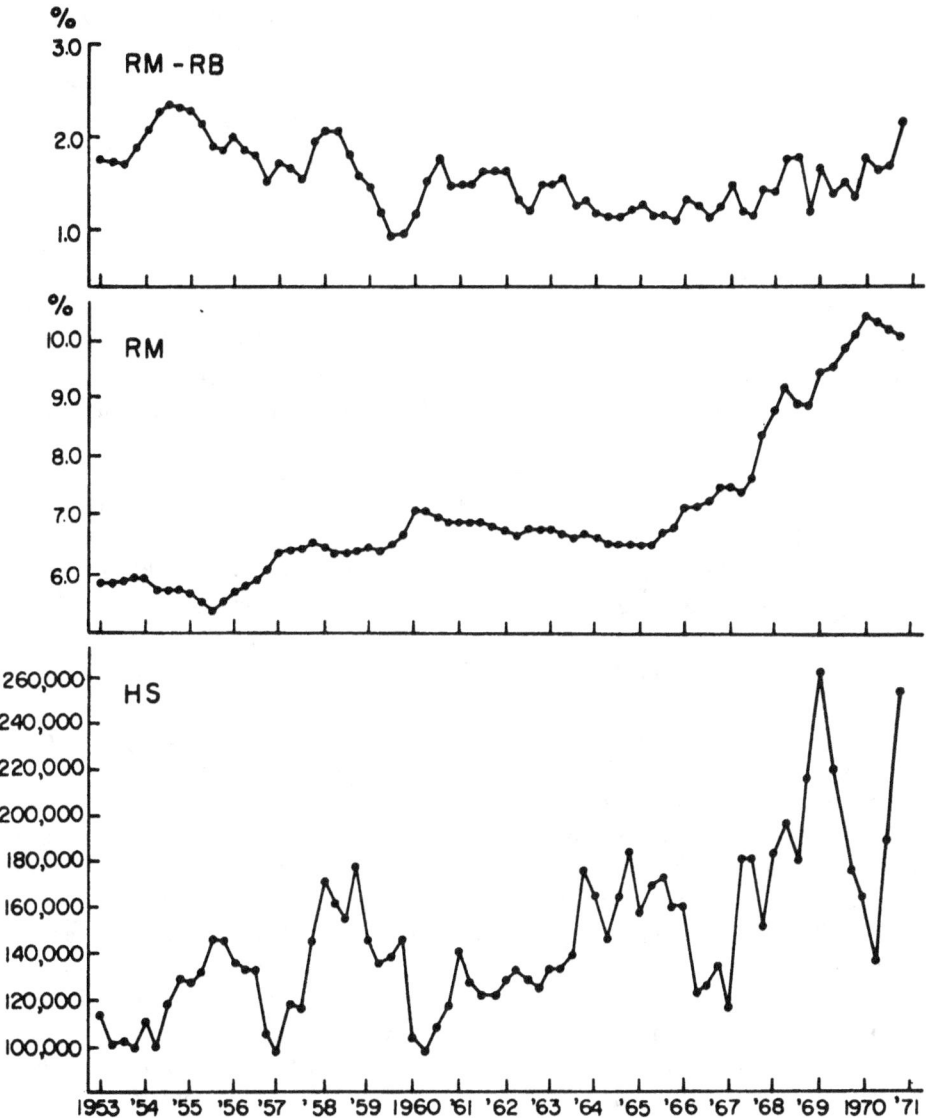

FIGURE 6 Housing starts, mortgage yields and mortgage–bond yield differential, 1953–70

levels.[36] These events substantially increased the availability of funds for mortgage investment (the conventional mortgage rate remaining strong near 6 per cent in the face of continuing high demand) and housing starts increased sharply from mid-1954 to the end of 1955.

(iv) 1956 to mid-1957: buoyed up by an investment boom which was triggered by world-wide fears of a raw material shortage, the Canadian economy entered another period of expansion in the latter part of 1954 and early 1955. Capital investment took place at a tremendous pace, with expansion in industrial and commercial plant construction, and power, communication, and public services. Unusually heavy demands were placed upon the capital market and, led by corporates, provincials and municipals, bond yields rose rapidly,[37] severely limiting the availability of funds for residential construction[38] and causing a sharp decline in new housing starts and residential construction expenditure. The NHA mortgage yield maximum was increaaed to try and alleviate pressures but had little effect upon the availability of mortgage credit.

(v) Mid-1957 to 1958: the economic expansion of the previous period began to falter in April 1957 and by mid-1957 had passed its peak as domestic spending became less vigorous. Monetary conditions eased throughout 1957 as net new corporate bond issues and demand for bank loans fell off sharply, and the government continued its net redemptions of long-term bonds. The declining yields on bonds resulted in an increase in the attractiveness of mortgage investment, and private housing starts rose rapidly. During this period Central Mortgage and Housing Corporation, still concerned with the deficiencies in the availability of mortgage financing, began using its direct lending powers with a vengeance and, together with attempts to further stimulate demand by reducing downpayment requirements and increasing maximum loan amounts, pushed housing starts to an all time high that was not to be reached again until 1965. This period also saw multiple dwelling starts increase in importance to approximately one third of all starts.

(vi) Mid-1958 to 1960: the economic decline of 1957 was quite brief, and gave way to expansion in April 1958. Unfortunately, mindful that they were too timid and too late in restraining the previous boom, and influenced by fears of inflation, the monetary authorities virtually froze the money supply in 1958[39] and, together with extremely large net government borrowings of over $1140 million in 1958, tightened the capital markets despite the fact that the recovery was only in its initial stages. This tightness was further increased by the ill-timed conversion loan of 1958, which "ushered in not only a period of much higher interest rates but one of widespread and continuing instability in the financial markets."[40] Altogether the latter half of 1958 (from May 1 on) witnessed the conversion of $5800 million of fairly short-term government bonds and net new issues of $838 million of long term government bonds. This substantially lowered the public's holdings of more liquid assets and was responsible for a sharp rise in interest rates during the last quarter of 1958 to the first quarter of 1960. During this period, despite a 7 per cent level of unemployment, the long-term government bond yield rose from 4.18 per cent to 5.43 per cent.[41]

Coincident with this period of rising bond yields, housing starts plummetted during 1959 and the first half of 1960. With the decline of CMHC direct lending in 1960, which buoyed up housing starts for 1958 and 1959, second quarter 1960 housing starts at 98,000 declined to only 55 per cent of fourth quarter 1958 starts, on a seasonally adjusted basis at annual rates.

(vii) 1961 to mid-1965: by early 1961 the general contraction of the economy had stopped and an economic expansion hesitatingly began. Bond yields, which had been artificially high because of the market disruptions and suspicions emanating from the conversion loan, began a long period of gradual decline in mid-1960, which was interrupted only temporarily by the foreign exchange crisis and resultant monetary restraint of mid-1962.[42] Toward the end of 1962 this crisis had ended and monetary conditions returned to their previous levels. From the fourth quarter of 1962 until the middle of 1965 bond yields remained extremely stable fluctuating within a very narrow band. (The long-term government bond average oscillated between 4.94 per cent and 5.28 per cent for almost three years.)

During this period, unfettered for the most part by monetary restraint, and stimulated by rising incomes and employment, favourable expectations and a diminished but still significant backlog of unsatisfied demand, housing starts increased steadily (except for a brief pause in 1962) to a new postwar peak in 1965. This expansion was led by multiple dwelling starts which rose from approximately 38 per cent of total starts to over 53 per cent in 1964 and 1965. This sharp rise in multiple dwelling construction coincided with sharply rising land costs which stimulated higher density land utilization and a sharp increase in non-family household formation (partly made possible by the recovery in the economy) which generates a demand for multiple-dwelling accommodation.

During this period the role played by Central Mortgage and Housing Corporation also increased significantly as housing starts financed directly by Central Housing and Mortgage Corporation increased continuously from 15,618 starts in 1960 to over 30,000 units in 1964 and 1965.

(viii) Mid-1965 to 1966: the economic expansion of the early sixties accelerated around mid-1965 and credit conditions which previously had been relatively relaxed began to tighten under the strain. This tightening, sometimes reinforced, sometimes ameliorated by monetary policy, continued at varying rates from mid-1965 until the end of 1969 when long-term government bond yields peaked at over 8.3 per cent.[43] The initial tightening in mid-1965 was reinforced toward the end of the year and in early 1966 by a policy of monetary restraint. Despite an increase in CMHC financed housing starts of over 8000 units in 1966, this restraint exerted the usual confining impact on residential construction and housing starts once again declined sharply.

(ix) 1967 to 1970: despite the continuation of a very strong aggregate demand the Bank of Canada moved to ease credit conditions in mid-1966.[44] This policy was reflected in somewhat lower bond yields in the first half of 1967 and a sharp revival in housing starts in mid-1967.

However, the high rate of increase in the money supply in late 1966 and 1967 (using the narrow definition of the money supply, the money supply rose at an average annual rate of 10 per cent during the last half of 1966 and 16 per cent during 1967)[45] was in no small way responsible for a sharp increase in the rate of inflation and even more important in the expectation that this higher rate of inflation would persist. Because inflationary expectations soon become incorporated in higher nominal interest rates[46] it was not surprising that interest rates moved up rapidly after the middle of 1967, with the long-term government bond yield reaching 6.54 per cent at the end of 1967, 7.30 per cent at the end of 1968 and 8.33 per cent at the end of 1969. Much more surprising was the increase and high level of housing starts maintained throughout 1968 and early 1969.

Despite the high cost of mortgage money, the high yield on competing securities and a decline in CMHC financed housing starts to approximately 27,000 units annually, residential construction soared from 164,123 housing starts in 1967 to the new heights of 196,878 and 210,415 starts in 1968 and 1969 respectively. Most of this increase occurred in multiple dwelling starts which jumped again to account for over 60 per cent of all housing starts. This sharp increase and high level of housing activity is extremely difficult to explain in the face of high interest rates. However, a number of institutional factors combined in this period to produce a high volume of residential construction.

First, inflationary expectations were very strong in the economy as a whole,[47] and especially in the residential construction sector where wage rates and land cost were each increasing at almost 10 per cent a year. Under these circumstances developers were induced to undertake new projects, and especially multiple projects, even in the face of high interest costs because delay was expected to mean considerably higher land and construction costs. Consequently, any possible saving in financing costs that might be anticipated by a delay in construction was expected to be more than offset by increases in other costs. Second, this inflationary psychology on the part of the public caused many potential home purchasers to move forward their purchase plans before rising house prices outpaced their financial capacity, with the result that housing demand was temporarily maintained by families stretching their budgets to purchase a home "while they could afford it." Third, although nominal interest rates had risen considerably and were extremely high, real costs of capital were not.[48] Variations in the real cost of capital differed from variations in nominal costs for many developers both because the increase in nominal rates primarily reflected inflationary expectations and because some components in the real cost of capital were falling for a number of major developers because of their evolution to major corporation status. This coming of age of a large number of Canadian construction companies occurred almost simultaneously in this period and enabled these companies to obtain large quantities of funds by way of debentures as opposed to mortgages. This large transfer of funds to the construction industry somewhat mitigated both the effects of rising nominal interest rates and generally reduced availability of funds, and postponed the contraction in building activity.

The contraction in private housing starts which normally would have been expected to occur in the second half of 1968 failed to materialize until late 1969 and 1970, and then was substantially blunted by CMHC financed housing starts, primarily in the form of starts for low income groups. In 1970, CMHC financed housing starts rose to over 59,000 units from 26,416 units in 1969, and accounted for over 30 per cent of all starts. Nevertheless, both total housing starts and privately financed housing starts declined sharply throughout most of 1969 and 1970.

(c) Summary

During the postwar period the volume of housing starts rose at an average annual rate of increase of approximately 5 per cent. This long-run growth was facilitated by a strong underlying demand for housing accommodation, an initial severe housing shortage, generally favourable demographic factors and rising real incomes. On the other hand this growth was not without substantial cyclical variation. Prior to 1953 the volume of residential construction activity depended essentially upon the availability of building materials and labour and the capacity of the building industry. Thereafter, fluctuations in the cost and availability of mortgage financing and the volume of direct lending activity provided by Central Mortgage and Housing Corporation became the crucial determinants of the timing of fluctuations in residential construction. Toward the end of the sixties fluctuations in housing starts were characterized by inflationary expectations and then government attempts to activate demand via aids for low income housing. By 1970 the government was firmly implanted as a major participant in the housing market, directly financing over 30 per cent of all housing starts (80 per cent of which were for low income housing), and multiple dwelling construction had become the dominant form of construction, accounting for over 60 per cent of all housing starts.

APPENDIX: TREATMENT OF SERIAL CORRELATION

In an attempt to remedy the serial correlation in the residuals of those equations where serial correlation was indicated by a low Durbin-Watson statistic (equations 6, 9, 11, 25–8, 31–3) or was not detectable because of the use of a lagged dependent variable[1] (equations 5, 14, 23, and 24) autoregressive transformations using the procedure suggested by Hildreth and Lu[2] were attempted. This procedure assumes that the residuals (μ) in our regressions are generated by a first-order autoregressive scheme

(A1) $\quad \mu_t = \rho \mu_{t-1} + \epsilon_t$

and attempts to select that p which minimizes the residual variance of the specified equation. The transformed regressions and autoregressive parameter are presented in equations A2 to A10.

Aggregate model

(A2) $\quad$ SH^3 = 1.000 SH$_{t-1}$ + 0.212 HS + 0.339 HS$_{t-1}$ + 0.248 HS$_{t-2}$ + 0.086 HS$_{t-3}$
$\qquad\quad$ (784.50) $\quad$ (3.01) $\quad\quad$ (5.23) $\quad\quad$ (4.77) $\quad\quad$ (4 49)

$\quad$ SEE = 6.44, $\rho = -0.015$, DW = 2 00.

(A3) $\quad$ HS = −13.46 − 21.48 Q1 + 7.04 Q2 + 6.28 Q3 + 8.76 WW + 102.33 (PH/CLC)
$\qquad\quad$ (0.67) (12.35) $\quad$ (4.07) $\quad$ (3.77) $\quad\quad$ (2.76) $\quad\quad$ (3.89)
$\qquad\quad$ − 10.45 RM$_{t-1}$ + 5.84 (RM − RB)$_{t-1}$ + 1.77 (CMHC/PH) + 5.76 (CMHC/PH)$_{t-1}$
$\qquad\qquad$ (3.84) $\qquad\quad$ (2.34) $\qquad\qquad$ (1.23) $\qquad\qquad$ (4.65)

$\quad$ SEE = 3.56, $\rho = 0.094$, DW = 1.89.

(A4) $\ln \text{CLC} - \ln \text{CLC}_{t-4} = -0.004 + 0.015\ (\ln \text{INRC} - \ln \widehat{\text{INRC}})_{t-1}$
       $\qquad\qquad\qquad\quad (0.49)\ \ (0.53)$
       $\qquad + 0.024\ (\ln \text{IRC} - \ln \widehat{\text{IRC}})_{t-1} + 0.33\ (\ln \text{WC} - \ln \text{WC}_{t-4})$
       $\qquad\quad (0.92) \qquad\qquad\qquad\qquad (3.55)$
       $\qquad + 0.10\ (\ln \text{L} - \ln \text{L}_{t-4}) + 0.021\ (\ln \text{R03} - \ln \text{R03}_{t-4}) + 0.014\ \text{DVST}$
       $\qquad\quad (1.82) \qquad\qquad\qquad (1.92) \qquad\qquad\qquad\qquad (1.52)$
       $\text{SEE} = 0.015,\ \rho = 0.606,\ \text{DW} = 1.89.$

(A5) $\text{L} = -4.20 + 0.009\ \text{POP} + 0.020\ \text{YD} - 0.026\ \text{SH} + 0.45\Delta\text{L}$
       $\qquad\ (1.43)\ \ \ (1.74) \qquad (2.93) \qquad (1.06) \qquad (6.21)$
       $\text{SEE} = 3.92,\ \rho = 0.441,\ \text{DW} = 1.31$

Dis-aggregate model

(A6) $\text{SHO}^4 = 0.9989\ \text{SHO}_{t-1} + 0.280\ \text{HSS} + 0.401\ \text{HSS}_{t-1} + 0.287\ \text{HSS}_{t-2}$
       $\qquad\quad (1297.99) \qquad\quad (4.77) \qquad\quad (9.11) \qquad\quad (7.38)$
       $\qquad + 0.099\ \text{HSS}_{t-3}$
       $\qquad\quad (6.59)$
       $\text{SEE} = 4.13,\ \rho = -0.123,\ \text{DW} = 2.05.$

(A7) $\text{SHR}^5 = 0.9997\ \text{SHR}_{t-1} + 0.154\ \text{HSM} + 0.277\ \text{HSM}_{t-1} + 0.257\ \text{HSM}_{t-2}$
       $\qquad\quad (587.45) \qquad\quad (2.08) \qquad\quad (5.29) \qquad\quad (4.53)$
       $\qquad + 0.159\ \text{HSM}_{t-3} + 0.051\ \text{HSM}_{t-4}$
       $\qquad\quad (4.07) \qquad\qquad (3.82)$
       $\text{SEE} = 2.96,\ \rho = 0.350,\ \text{DW} = 2.02.$

(A8) $\text{HSS} = 18.72 - 12.70\ \text{Q1} + 5.06\ \text{Q2} + 4.20\ \text{Q3} + 4.87\ \text{WW} + 18.58(\text{PH/CC})_{t-1}$
       $\qquad\ (1.11) \quad (8.61) \qquad (3.29) \quad (3.02) \quad (2.03) \quad\ (0.87)$
       $\qquad - 2.35\ \text{RM}_{t-1} + 5.65\ (\text{RM} - \text{RB})_{t-1} - 0.12\ \text{L} + 2.29\ (\text{CMHCS/PH})$
       $\qquad\ (1.23) \qquad\ (2.93) \qquad\qquad\quad (1.97) \quad (2.03).$
       $\qquad + 4.93\ (\text{CMHCS/PH})_{t-1}$
       $\qquad\ (4.67)$
       $\text{SEE} = 2.89,\ \rho = 0.004,\ \text{DW} = 2.00.$

(A9) $\text{HSM} = 3.34 - 8.33\ \text{Q1} + 1.51\ \text{Q2} + 2.09\ \text{Q3} + 2.58\ \text{WW} + 28.16\ (\text{R/CC})_{t-1}$
       $\qquad\ (0.19)\ (6.70) \quad (0.94) \quad (1.63) \quad (1.21) \quad (1.98)$
       $\qquad - 5.15\ \text{RM}_{t-1} + 0.60\ (\text{RM} - \text{RB})_{t-1} + 0.11\ \text{L} + 6.55\ (\text{CMHCM/PH})$
       $\qquad\ (2.08) \qquad\ (0.24) \qquad\qquad\quad (1.38) \quad (1.39)$
       $\qquad + 4.57\ (\text{CMHCM/PH})_{t-1}$
       $\qquad\ (1.06)$
       $\text{SEE} = 2.91,\ \rho = 0.348,\ \text{DW} = 1.81.$

(A10) $\ln \text{CC} - \ln \text{CC}_{t-4} = 0.0096 - 0.013\ (\ln \text{INRC} - \ln \widehat{\text{INRC}})^*_{t-1}$
       $\qquad\qquad\qquad\quad (0.53)\ \ (0.55)$
       $\qquad + 0.041\ (\ln \text{IRC} - \ln \widehat{\text{IRC}})_{t-1} + 0.235\ (\ln \text{WC} - \ln \text{WC}_{t-4})$
       $\qquad\quad (2.09) \qquad\qquad\qquad\qquad (2.86)$
       $\qquad + 0.017\ (\ln \text{R03} - \ln \text{R03}_{t-4}) + 0.021\ \text{DVST}$
       $\qquad\quad (1.98) \qquad\qquad\qquad\qquad (2.29)$
       $\text{SEE} = 0.012,\ \rho = 0.900,\ \text{DW} = 2.02.$

(*This variable has the wrong sign and is insignificant.*)

Unfortunately, our search procedure indicates that a ρ greater than one minimizes the residual variance of equations 6 and 25–8 and this is unsatifactory since it implies a first-order autoregressive transformation may not be appropriate. Nevertheless, since these equations have no lagged dependent variables a Theil-Nagar transformation was attempted.[6] These results are presented in equations A11 to A15.

Aggregate model

(A11) $\text{PH} = 125.43 + 1.18\,\text{Q1} + 2.53\,\text{Q2} + 1.34\,\text{Q3} + 68.06\,(\text{YD}/\text{FAM})_{t-1}$
          (3.57) (1.78)   (3.40)   (2.08)   (4.15)

          $- 275.22\,(\text{SH}/\text{FAM}) + 1.80\,\text{PGNE}_{t-1}$
             (6.45)   (7.79)

SEE $= 1.75$, $\rho = 0.335$, DW $= 1.79$.

Disaggregate model

(A12) $\text{PH} = 182.41 + 0.59\,\text{Q1} + 1.65\,\text{Q2} + 0.83\,\text{Q3} + 28.55\,(\text{YD}/\text{FAM})_{t-1}$
          (3.69) (0.90)   (2.20)   (1.35)   (1.57)

          $- 392.68\,(\text{SHO}/\text{FAM}) + 1.27\,\text{PGNE}_{t-1} + 0.30\,R_{t-1} - 0.040\,\text{RM}_{t-1}$
             (6.60)   (3.61)   (1.26)   (0.02)

SEE $= 1.67$, $\rho = 0.350$, DW $= 1.75$.

(A13) $\text{PH} = 181.88 + 0.58\,\text{Q1} + 1.63\,\text{Q2} + 0.83\,\text{Q3} + 29.29\,(\text{YD}/\text{FAM})_{t-1}$
          (4.15) (0.90)   (2.26)   (1.38)   (1.97)

          $- 390.88\,(\text{SHO}/\text{FAM}) + 1.25\,\text{PGNE}_{t-1} + 0.30\,R_{t-1}$
             (6.91)   (3.73)   (1.48)

SEE $= 1.64$, $\rho = 0.375$, DW $= 1.79$.

(A14) $R = -17.61 + 0.49\,\text{Q1} + 1.05\,\text{Q2} + 1.57\,\text{Q3} + 346.17\,(\text{YD}/\text{POP})_{t-1}$
          (0.73) (1.11)   (1.95)   (3.50)   (5.36)

          $- 1617.66\,(\text{SHR}/\text{POP})_{t-1} + 0.99\,\text{PGNE}_{t-1} + 0.24\,\text{PH}_{t-1} + 2.57\,\text{RM}_{t-1}$
             (3.30)   (4.49)   (2.09)   (1.71)

SEE $= 1.18$, $\rho = 0.420$, DW $= 1.58$.

(A15) $R = -18.26 + 0.49\,\text{Q1} + 1.14\,\text{Q2} + 1.43\,\text{Q3} + 298.39\,(\text{YD}/\text{POP})_{t-1}$
          (0.74) (1.08)   (2.05)   (3.13)   (4.99)

          $- 1427.82\,\text{SHR}/\text{POP})_{t-1} + 1.12\,\text{PGNE}_{t-1} + 0.29\,\text{PH}_{t-1}$
             (2.95)   (5.09)   (2.50)

SEE $= 1.21$, $\rho = 0.400$, DW $= 1.51$

C
The mortgage market

5
The Structure and Basic Trends in the Postwar Residential Mortgage Market

The importance of the mortgage market to the Canadian economy is apparent from the previous chapters since the terms and availability of mortgage finance exert a significant impact upon the volume of residential construction activity, and since variations in these variables are one of the main routes by which monetary influences are transmitted to the real sectors of the economy. Because the demand for residential mortgage credit can be derived from the demand for housing and because supply considerations have dominated the market for most of the postwar period, the focus of this and much of the subsequent two chapters is on the supply of mortgage credit. This approach leads to the specification of financial institution mortgage supply functions and a mortgage rate determination model in chapter 7.

A. THE MORTGAGE INSTRUMENT

Before discussing the sources of mortgage finance it is useful to consider the investment properties of mortgages since the nature of the mortgage instrument does much to determine the private supply of mortgage credit. Unlike other security markets the mortgage market is really a series of overlapping submarkets characterized by "one of a kind" deals, special considerations and local orientation. Mortgages range from small single-family residential mortgages which in many ways approximate consumer loans to large multiple dwelling mortgages which in many ways approximate corporate direct placement bonds or debentures. This diversity in characteristics causes the rate and lending terms of mortgage loans to reflect not only generally prevailing capital market conditions, but also local and regional considerations and the location, type, age, and quality of the security offered, and the creditworthiness and sophistication of the borrower.[1] This diversity also results in little trade in outstanding mortgages and in a very primitive, virtually non-existent secondary market in Canada.

(a) Mortgage yields and terms

(i) The identity problem
Analysis of the mortgage market in Canada is considerably complicated by the existence of not one but many mortgage rates, and by the fact that the nominal

mortgage rate is only one of numerous price and non-price variables that adjust over the cycle. At any point in time a heirarchy of nominal rates exist on different categories of mortgage loans, with rates typically being lowest for NHA CMHC direct mortgage loans, and successively rising for each of the following categories: (*a*) NHA CMHC direct mortgage loans, (*b*) NHA approved lender loans, (*c*) conventional single-dwelling loans, (*d*) conventional pre-leased commercial and indusial loans, (*e*) conventional apartment, townhouse, and multiple tenancy commercial and industrial loans, (*f*) conventional hotel and motel loans, and (*g*) conventional second mortgages.[2] This variation within the mortgage classification means that there is likely to be considerable variation in rates within the mortgage market itself, and not all of these variations will be reflected in movements of a representative rate. This problem is compounded in Canada since consistent monthly data exist for only three of the above categories, NHA CMHC direct loans, NHA approved lender loans and the prime conventional mortgage loans. Because data exist for both NHA loan categories[3] the major problems occur with the conventional mortgage rate.

First, the only conventional mortgage rate series available is the prime conventional mortgage rate charged by six life insurance companies and, while probably representative of all life insurance companies, it may not be completely representative of the rates charged by other lending institutions. Second, it is the prime rate on all classifications of properties so that the series is affected by changes in the mix of life insurance company mortgage lending, for example, between residential and non-residential and between single-family and multiple dwelling residential. Third, it is the prime rate charged and not an average rate so that it fails to reflect variations in life insurance company willingness to give borrowers the prime rate when market conditions vary, i.e., it does not reflect increased stringency that would occur if the proportion of loans made at the prime rate changed.

Apart from these complications particular to the prime conventional rate, any nominal mortgage rate provides an incomplete portrayal of mortgage market conditions because it is only one of many dimensions to the mortgage loan contract. In addition to the nominal rate, the mortgage contract specifies non-price variables such as the size of the loan, the amortization period, the maturity term, and repayment privileges; and price variables that affect the effective rate such as the compounding period, legal and finders fees, and, in the case of revenue-producing properties, possible equity participation. The non-price variables are discussed in more detail below and are mentioned here only as a reminder that the true desirability of mortgages to investors and true cost to borrowers vary with non-price as well as price variables.

More pertinent, the effective mortgage rate may vary considerably from the nominal rate by other conditions of the mortgage contract. First, a nominal 6 per cent mortgage rate on an annual compounding period becomes 6.09 per cent if compounded semi-annually, and 6.167 per cent if compounded monthly. Second, if the borrower is required to pay legal, finders, and/or other initiation fees, the effective rate may increase considerably. For example, during periods of monetary stringency, as in 1968 and 1969, lenders commonly charge legal and finders fees in the vicinity of 5 per cent on new mortgage loans, which adds 1.08 per cent to the effective rate on a 5-year mortgage and 0.55 per cent to the effective rate on a ten-year mortgage. In periods of monetary ease these fees often decline to the vicinity of 2 per cent or less. Third, after the mid-1960s a new phenomenon of equity participation in revenue-producing real estate began as part of the mortgage arrangement for some institutions. In its simplest form, in consideration of its mortgage loan, the lending institution would receive in addition to the nominal interest rate and fees, x per cent of the gross revenue generated by the financed project. A common factor on these arrangements was 2 per cent, which would add approximately 25 to 40 basis points to the nominal rate in the first year, and more over the contract term, if gross revenues increase. More complicated variants involve the lender purchasing the land and leasing it back to the borrower at some rental, so that the borrower pays both ground rent and mortgage payments to the lender. The simultaneous determination of land price, land rental, and the nominal mortgage rate make it impossible to unscramble the effective mortgage rate (i.e., the rate that would apply if the other transactions were at "arm's length"). This unscrambling is also impossible in a simpler procedure whereby the lender; in consideration of making a mortgage loan at some nominal rate, obtains the opportunity to buy an equity interest in the project.[4]

Although it is clear that the nominal mortgage rate data available in Canada provide an inadequate portrayal of market conditions, the lack of alternatives forces us to utilize what we have. Fortunately, a recent American study by Guttentag, for the 1951 to 1966 period,[5] suggests that variations in fees and non-price lending terms for this period may not be as important as previously thought,[6] and it is variations in these variables rather than their levels which would impede our analysis. Also, significant equity participation as part of the mortgage lending process did not arise until the latter half of the 1960s, and even then was confined to a relatively small segment of the market. Consequently, it is reasonable to assume that, despite numerous deficiencies, our mortgage rate series are a reasonable representation of general market conditions for most of the postwar period.

(ii) Cyclical amplitude and responsiveness of mortgage yields
During the postwar period the nominal conventional mortgage interest rate lagged behind and had a narrower cyclical amplitude than other security yields, as Figure 2 indicated. The typical market adjustment process would begin with short-term high grade securities such as treasury bills, and short-term government securities. Movements in the yields on these securities would shortly thereafter be reflected in long-term government bond yields, and then in provincial, municipal and corporate bond yields. Finally, after a lag of one to twelve months, the length of lag varying with the rapidity of the movement in other security yields, changing market conditions would be reflected in changing nominal mortgage yields. This lagged adjustment process and the relative narrowness of mortgage rate fluctuations are attributable to a number of factors peculiar to the mortgage market.

Forward commitment procedure and direct negotiations. A significant feature of the mortgage lending process is the forward commitment procedure whereby a builder, prior to commencing construction, seeks a commitment for permanent financing from an institutional investor.[7] A typical sequence begins with an application by the borrower for a mortgage commitment. This application is reviewed by the loan committee and after some lag, the length depending upon capital market conditions, the nature of the project, the borrower, and the customer relationship between the borrower and the institution, a commitment is given or the loan refused. If a commitment is given a time-table for the disbursement of funds is established. This may call for an almost immediate disbursement of funds or disbursement in stages over a considerable period of time as construction proceeds. In any event the interest rate and other terms are negotiated and determined at the commitment stage, which precedes the disbursement of funds by some period.

The forward commitment procedure not only causes a problem of timing between the commitment and disbursement of funds but also introduces the problem of attrition – mortgage commitments that are not exercised. Attritions arise when construction is postponed or forgone, when projects are altered to reduce their value, and when funds may be obtained elsewhere on more favourable borrowing terms. The latter situation is likely to occur only in periods of easing monetary conditions since the lapsing of a commitment usually entails the loss of a deposit or commitment fee.

The forward commitment procedure combined with the direct negotiation procedure in the market provide one explanation for the stickiness in the response of mortgage yields.[8] First, because frequent changes in mortgage rates can cause loss of goodwill for a lender in a market where his reputation in the eyes of the borrower has considerable significance, mortgage lenders try to avoid fine gradations in interest rates and to delay rate adjustments until market trends are clearly defined. Since a pervasive market movement cannot be immediately distinguished from a temporary one, mortgage yields lag bond yield adjustments.[9]

Second, when current mortgage yields decline requests arise for reductions in the yield on outstanding commitments and, since the borrower can go elsewhere for funds, some adjustment toward the more favourable current rate is often granted. Even when some disbursements have already been made, especially in the case of unsold single dwellings, there is some incentive to reduce the mortgage rate to allow the builder to remain competitive and maintain goodwill.[10]

Pressures are therefore placed upon lenders to reduce the rate on outstanding commitments and loans on unsold homes when current mortgage rates fall. However, when current rates rise, commitments remain binding on the lender. This creates strong incentives for lenders to resist downward pressure on yields for as long as possible, since equivalent gains could not be realized from a subsequent rise in yields. Similarly, incentives to raise rates are not as strong as might normally be anticipated unless these new levels are expected to be maintained for a reasonable length of time. This means, once again, that alterations in mortgage yields are delayed until market trends are well established.

Absence of secondary market. The localized nature of the mortgage market and prevalence of "individual" arrangements has inhibited the development of a secondary market, and consequently the mortgage rates quoted are for initiations. Because of the negotiated nature of transactions and lender desires to maintain good borrower-lender relationships, primary rate adjustments usually lag adjustments on outstanding issues.[11] Since other security yields are taken from yields on outstanding issues, mortgage yields will tend to lag adjustments in other security yields. Furthermore, the lack of a secondary market prohibits effective interest arbitrage because the discount desired by dealers to purchase outstanding mortgages often makes the transactions cost exceed the expected gain.[12]

Fees, quality variations, and adjustments in non-price terms. A third explanation for the relatively slow adjustment in mortgage yields focuses upon the other contractual terms of the mortgage contract. First, since the nominal mortgage yield is only one, albeit the major one, of the price components, adjustments may take place in the other components such as fees and other charges by the lender. Since fees and other charges vary cyclically, the true price variation exceeds the yield variations and, if this is the fast adjusting price component, may explain some of the lag in the rate adjustment.[13] Second, non-price terms such as the loan to value ratio, amortization period, and contract term, could vary more quickly than the mortgage rate, affecting the quality of the loan and consequently the interest yield net of risk premium. In such a situation some of the burden of the market adjustment is removed from the market rate to non-price considerations which enables mortgage yields to fluctuate more narrowly and respond more slowly than yields in more highly standardized security markets where price is the prime point of negotiation and other terms show little variability.[14] Finally, it could be argued that in periods of economic expansion inflation improves the quality of conventional mortgages more than it does the quality of high grade bonds, so that mortgage rates need adjust relatively less.[15]

While all the factors discussed above no doubt contribute to the stickiness of the mortgage rate, they all presume that pressures originate in the bond market, either because of increasing economic activity and private demands for funds, or because of government policy. However, if market pressures originate in the mortgage market because of a sharp increase in the demand for mortgage credit the mortgage rate may lag insignificantly behind other security yields, or even lead them. Consequently, although external shocks will take longer to be reflected in mortgage yields than other security yields for the reasons discussed above, if a market shock originates in the housing sector, mortgage yield adjustments need not lag and may lead adjustments in other security yields.

(b) Investment properties of mortgages

(i) Marketability and liquidity
Since mortgages are long-term investments with a usual term to maturity of 5 to 30 years, and since there are virtually no secondary market transactions in mortgages except at very large discounts, mortgages are traditionally considered to be a very illiquid form of investment. However, there is a substantial difference

between the liquidity or marketability of an individual mortgage and the liquidity of a large mortgage portfolio. Most mortgages are fully amortized, which results in a substantial monthly inflow of funds and provides institutions with capital that may be used to satisy other needs. For example, between 1954 and 1967 trust companies received annual mortgage repayments equivalent to 17.6 per cent of their total mortgage portfolios, mortgage loan companies received annual repayments equivalent to 12.8 per cent of their total mortgage portfolios, and life insurance companies received annual mortgage repayments equivalent to 8.4 per cent of their total mortgage portfolios.[16] The life insurance company proportions are much lower than the trust and loan company proportions because they desire longer maturity terms in their investments to better match the maturity structure of their life contingency obligations.[17] Therefore, if liquidity is defined as "the attribute which makes a sufficient portion of a portfolio convertible into cash within a reasonable time by regular payments or self liquidation, prompt sale without substantial loss or by use as collateral for loan purposes to meet institutions' maximum requirements for cash,"[18] then large mortgage portfolios must be considered quite liquid even if individual mortgages are not.

(ii) Foreclosure and ultimate capital risk

Residential mortgage loans are normally so large in relation to a borrower's income and net worth, in the case of single-unit owner-occupancy residential mortgages, and in relation to projected cash flows, in the case of multiple unit rental dwellings, that the lender must look primarily to the property itself as the ultimate security for his capital, although loans customarily carry the borrower's personal covenant.[19] The probability that the borrower will be able to meet his payments remains a vital consideration in mortgage lending since institutions desire not only to avoid capital losses – which occur when the unamortized portion of the mortgage exceeds the capital recovered on the sale of a foreclosed property – but also to avoid foreclosures, which are costly in time, goodwill, and legal fees. While the probabilities of capital loss and foreclosure are difficult to estimate they decrease as lending terms become more stringent and, therefore, the degree of the risk associated with mortgage lending varies inversely, and the desirability of mortgages as investments directly, with the restrictiveness of the lending terms.[20]

Loan to value ratio and downpayment size. The loan-to-value ratio determines the loan amount and downpayment requirement, given the value of the real property, and is a measure of the "property risk" associated with a mortgage. The property risk is the probability that the value of the underlying security will sometime in its life fall below the outstanding loan balance, encouraging default and saddling the lender with a loss, if it occurs, since mortgage contracts do not provide for an increase in the amount of the security or a quick calling of the loan. The loan to value ratio provides the margin of protection against declining property values, and also sets the amount of equity the borrower stands to lose in case of default. Hence, the lower the loan-to-value ratio, the greater the lender's hedge against declining property values and the greater the borrower's incentive to satisfactorily discharge his obligation under the mortgage.

Amortization term. The amortization term of a mortgage affects its risk in two ways. First, the shorter the amortization period, the smaller is the property risk, since the more quickly the existing loan to value ratio is decreased and borrower's equity in the loan is increased, and the smaller the uncertainty and difficulty in estimating security values over the lifetime of the mortgage. On the other hand, the shorter the amortization term, ceteris paribus, the larger is the monthly payment required to discharge the mortgage and hence the greater the default risk arising from insufficient income to meet monthly payments. However, the net effect is such that lender risk is usually considered to increase with the length of the amortization period.

Debt service to income ratio. In the case of single-family dwelling mortgage loans, the proportion of income that a family must devote to house maintenance, taxes and mortgage amortization payments has a large bearing on the probability that the family will be able to meet its mortgage payments and weather temporary adversity. The lower the gross debt service to income ratio, the smaller the likelihood of mortgage default. As a general rule of thumb a ratio exceeding 23 to 25 per cent is considered precarious[21] (although the maximum ratio for an NHA mortgage is 27 per cent), while a ratio below 20 per cent is considered quite satisfactory.

Maturity term. The maturity term of a mortgage affects its investment desirability in two ways. First, the shorter the maturity term the more liquid a mortgage is, and hence the more desirable the investment for investors with a strong liquidity preference, such as chartered banks, trust companies and mortgage loan companies. Second, the maturity term affects the matching of asset and liability term structures so as to hedge maturity risk. For most investors, obligations are generally short term and hence the shorter the maturity term the more desirable the investment. However, some investors, like life insurance companies and pension funds, have very long-term obligations and consequently for them the longer the maturity term the more desirable the investment from the hedging maturity risk viewpoint.

Repayment provisions. Provisions made for the repayment of the mortgage loan also have a large influence upon the risk associated with the loan. Mortgages carrying full amortization provisions bear much less ultimate capital risk than mortgages that are not fully amortized and require a large balloon payment at maturity since, at any point of time during the loan, the actual loan to value ratio is smaller and capital outstanding less than under other repayment schemes. Moreover, since larger monthly payments are required to fully amortize a mortgage, repayment difficulties become evident earlier, which reduces the risk of capital loss if foreclosure becomes necessary.

(iii) Predictability of investment flows

The predictability of the flows associated with an investment refers to the likelihood that repayment flows will take place normally over the full contract term of the mortgage rather than in some unexpected manner such as by early repayment of the loan. This abstracts from the possibility that the loan might not be repaid and refers only to the timing of the repayment of the loan. In Canada any individual, as opposed to corporate, borrower has the legal right to repay an NHA mortgage three years and a conventional mortgage five years after commencement, on any subsequent anniversary date of the mortgage, on payment of three months' interest. As a result, mortgagees are subjected to the possibility of large-scale prepayments in periods of rapidly falling interest rates, which would necessitate the reinvestment of funds at an inauspicious time. However, since this privilege applies only to individual borrowers, who on the whole are not sophisticated in financial dealings, large-scale early repayments have not been as common as might be expected. Nevertheless they do occur, especially in the conventional sector and by corporations who have negotiated repayment clauses. Somewhat offsetting the desirability of early repayment are the large transactions costs in the form of legal and other fees associated with new mortgage loans. On the other hand, the refinancing pressure is reinforced by the fact that the borrower can further reduce his monthly payments since the mortgage base is reduced by his previous principal repayments. Early repayment of NHA mortgages for refinancing purposes has been rare because until recently it meant that refinancing must be by way of conventional mortgages (NHA mortgages until 1967 were virtually confined to new construction) with their higher interest rate, lower loan to value ratio and generally shorter amortization period. Nevertheless, the possibility of early repayment is sufficiently strong to have a significant negative impact upon the desirability of mortgage investments for some institutions.[22]

In summary, mortgages are long-term investments with fairly low risk of capital loss. This is especially true for NHA mortgages which are virtually 100 per cent insured as to capital and interest. Capital risk on conventional mortgages and foreclosure risk on conventional and NHA mortgages vary with the loan to value ratio, amortization term, debt service to income ratio, and nature of repayment terms of the mortgage, as well as with the appraisal skills of the lender. Mortgages are relatively non-marketable securities, although there is a small secondary market in NHA mortgages, but because of the substantial monthly capital inflows that arise in large mortgage portfolios, large mortgage holdings are not as illiquid a form of investment as is often supposed. On the other hand, the asymmetry introduced by the possibility of early repayments without corresponding call provisions reduces the attractiveness of mortgage investment.

B. SOURCES OF MORTGAGE FINANCE

The supply of mortgage credit comes from three main sources, private financial institutions, government agencies and corporations, and individual and non-institutional corporate lenders. Each of these financing sources are motivated by different forces in determining the volume of funds they wish to make available for mortgage lending, and each responds differently to changes in the general level of economic activity and employment, and changes in the capital markets. The volume of funds advanced by private financial institutions is primarily a function of the relative desirability of mortgages as a form of investment and their inflow of funds; the volume of government lending is primarily a function of social priorities and general economic policy considerations; and the volume of individual lending is a function of a wide variety of economic and personal considerations, with loans made in conjunction with the sale of their home being most important.

To understand the functioning of the mortgage market, each of the sources of funds must be examined separately. Because government direct lending is really a government policy variable and individual and non-institutional corporate lending is primarily residual, most of our discussion is devoted to the lending behaviour of private financial institutions.

(a) Private financial institutions

Private financial institutions, referring primarily to life insurance companies, trust companies, mortgage loan companies, and the chartered banks (but including "other institutions" such as Quebec savings banks, mutual benefit, and fraternal societies), are the dominant participants in the mortgage market. This may be seen from the fact that they account for 60–65 per cent of all new mortgage initiations, 70–75 per cent of all mortgage initiations for new residential construction and 90–95 per cent of all non-government mortgage initiations for new residential construction. Between 1965 and 1970 they were the principal source of finance for 76 per cent of privately financed housing starts and 59 per cent of all housing starts. By comparison, Central Mortgage and Housing Corporation was the principal source of finance for 20 per cent of all housing starts, and equity funds and other sources were the principal source for the remaining 21 per cent of all housing starts.[23]

Financial institutions are financial intermediaries with pools of funds gathered by the sale of their obligations to the public in their role as collector of private savings and drained by their purchases of other market obligations.[24] Each institution's share of the public's savings is governed by the public's preferences as to how they wish to hold their savings, each institution's ability to meet these preferences through their debt obligations, and the relative yield offered on their obligations.

Because a large factor in determining the public's preference for the obligations of the various institutions is the rate of interest the obligations yield, institutions compete for desirable investments that will earn a satisfactory return and enable them to offer competitive rates for funds. The proportion of funds that institutions make available for mortgage lending, therefore, depends upon the relative desirability of mortgages as an investment. This desirability depends upon both the yields obtainable on mortgages relative to other investments. and upon the properties of mortgages in relation to the various specific investment requirements of each institution. These requirements vary between institutions depending upon the local versus national orientation of the institution, the nature of the institution's debt instrument, its emphasis on long-term as opposed to short-term lending, the size of the institution, the extent of the institution's branch operations and the legal constraints under which the institution operates. These differences result in each institution having a different utility function, a different optimum asset mix, and a different perspective from which to view asset characteristics. Consequently, mortgages satisfy different investment needs for each of the different institutions, which results in each institution playing a different role in the mortgage market according to the relationship between its specific investment needs and the ability of mortgages to satisfy these needs. A model of financial intermediary investment behaviour and of their inflow of funds is presented separately for each of the major institutions in the next two chapters.

(b) Individual, non-institutional corporate and other lenders

Individual and non-institutional corporate lenders comprise a very wide heterogeneous group of mortgagees ranging from individuals who acquire a mortgage on the sale of their home or through intra-family transactions to professional operators seeking high-yielding mortgage investments through brokers or their own connections, from private non-profit institutions like hospitals and universities to institutionally administered estate, trust, and agency funds, to incorporated business firms. These lenders initiate approximately 20 per cent of all new mortgage loans and they held an estimated 30 per cent of all outstanding mortgages in 1969, this proportion having declined from 44 per cent in 1950. However, these lenders have a much smaller impact upon the market, especially the new construction market, than these figures indicate since, with the exception of the institutionally administered portion, most individual lending is of a residual nature on properties that lending institutions will not finance because of location, condition, or type. Moreover, a large portion of the funds made available for mortgage lending by private non-institutional sources is done partially in response to non-market considerations which results in a segment of the mortgage market being relatively insensitive to changing yield considerations. This tends to build rigidities into the volume of their mortgage lending and makes this segment of the market less interesting when our main concern is with variations in the volume of residential mortgage lending and residential construction. As a result, most of our study pertaining to the private sector of the market will be devoted to the institutional segment of the market, which accounts for most of the variation in the volume of mortgage financing forthcoming from private sources.

(i) Individuals

Individuals held approximately 35 per cent of non-institutional (private and public) mortgages outstanding and approximately 10 per cent of the total mortgages outstanding in Canada in 1969.[25] Their investment is limited to fewer individuals than stocks or bonds since the Royal Commission on Banking and Finance "Consumer Survey" indicated that 5.8 per cent held mortgages compared to 29.1 per cent for bonds and 12.3 per cent for stocks. The survey indicated that mortgages accounted for approximately 6 per cent of individuals' total assets and 15 per cent of their non-stock financial assets.[26] Although the percentage of individuals holding mortgage investments increases as incomes increase, [27] investment in mortgages is more highly correlated with occupation than income, with lawyers, notaries, and construction contractors showing the advantages of low information costs, and having the highest proportion of mortgage interest to total investment income of any occupation class.[28]

Individual mortgage lending is primarily of a residual nature as individuals usually advance funds on the security of second mortgages which institutions are generally precluded from accepting, on the security of properties that are regarded by institutions as providing insufficient security because of location, quality or type, and in conjunction with the sale of their homes.[29] In the latter case the mortgage loan is ancillary to the house sale transaction since acceptance of a mortgage as partial payment may be the only way to effect a sale. Although there is a relationship between primary and secondary market conditions, the connection between nominal rates on these securities can be quite loose because of lack of arbitrage and competition, and because there are additional variables, such as the nominal purchase price of the house upon which a mortgage is "given back," which affect the nominal rate charged on these residual loans. On the other hand, secondary lenders initiating new loans are often just as professional as any institution in the selection of their portfolio, consciously seeking out high-yielding, fairly safe, first or second mortgages, and they are highly sensitive to market conditions.

(ii) Non-institutional corporations

Non-institutional corporations, which include small loan companies, holding companies, and other corporations, and institutions whose mortgage lending operations are ancillary to their principal function, in 1969 held about 23 per cent of the mortgages in this section. These corporations have little national impact but are often very important locally, especially in areas poorly serviced by institutional lenders. Their loans are made for investment purposes and respond to the usual market influences. Since they are predominantly active in outlying areas, and have an oligopolistic position, their mortgage yields are somewhat higher than in urban areas. Because of the larger yield spread between mortgages and other securities received by these corporations, their investment decisions are less sensitive to marginal variations in alternative security yields than are financial institution decisions.

(iii) Estate, trust, and agency (ET&A) funds

Mortgages held in estate, trust, and agency funds (including institutionally administered pension funds), in 1969 accounted for approximately 29 per cent of the mortgages in this category. These mortgages are included here even though they are administered by trust companies because the beneficial ownership belongs to private individuals. Since these funds are administered by institutions their investment is quite sensitive to changing relative yields, but less so than actual institutional funds, since the investment of these funds must be in accordance with the terms laid down in the trust agreement. For example, the investment of pension funds, which are the fastest-growing segment of these ET&A funds and account for 60 per cent of total funds, are often constrained by the wishes of the originator of the fund. This often results in a high proportion of funds being invested in issues of the employer. In 1968, municipal and provincial employees' funds, which accounted for 18 per cent of total trusteed pension plan assets, held 3.8

per cent of their portfolios in mortgages, 5.2 per cent in stocks, 52.3 per cent in provincial and 20.7 per cent in municipal securities; industrial pension plans accounted for 57 per cent of total pension plan assets and approximately 77 per cent of both corporate bonds and stocks held by pension plans; federal crown corporations and government agencies held 11.5 per cent of pension plan assets and over 35 per cent of government of Canada securities held by pension plans.[30] All of this indicates that factors other than risk, yield, and liquidity considerations influence portfolio investment decisions for pension plans. Various other rigidities are built into segments of ET&A funds so that these funds, while influenced by relative yield considerations, are less sensitive to yield factors than are financial institution funds.

(iv) Caisses populaires and credit unions
Caisses populaires and credit unions held approximately 14 per cent of the mortgages included in this category in 1969. These societies or unions are co-operative or self-help societies which supply loans to fellow members at more favourable rates than they could obtain elsewhere. They consider lending to their members their main function and, therefore, devote about 30 per cent of their assets to short-term, small residential mortgage loans and 37 per cent to other types of member loans. As a result of the obligation these societies feel toward meeting the needs of their members, and the fact that they obtain very high returns on their loans, especially their home mortgage loans, the investment pattern of these institutions is little affected by changing yields on alternative investments. In addition to this the yields paid on their shares and deposits have not influenced their inflow of funds as much as their co-operative nature, location of offices, hours of business, and more favourable lending rates for funds which they make available to members who may be considered less credit worthy by other institutions lacking the personal knowledge of their character.[31] This means that the inflow of funds into, and the investment pattern of, these co-operative societies are much less sensitive to changing relative interest yields than financial institutions.

(c) *Government agencies and corporations*
The government agency most closely associated with the mortgage market is Central Mortgage and Housing Corporation (CMHC), a crown corporation which administers the government housing and mortgage activities.[32] In this role it makes funds available to the private sector in its capacity as lender of last resort and finances special programmes usually designed to provide housing for low income groups. At the end of 1969 CMHC held approximately 21 per cent of all outstanding mortgage debt (including debt held by individuals), and typically accounted for approximately 18 per cent of all private and public institution mortgage initiations and approximately 25 per cent of institutional mortgage initiations for new residential construction. However, in unusual circumstances such as 1969 and 1970 when private financial institutions sharply curtailed their lending activity, CMHC has provided almost 40 per cent of the mortgage finance for new residential construction.

The government first became a supplier of mortgage funds in 1935 when it undertook to make loans for new residential construction jointly with authorized financial institutions by contributing 25 per cent of the amount of the loan, while the institution provided the other 75 per cent.[33] The institution selected and administered these loans subject only to certain general constraints placed by the government on the lending terms, so that in reality the government became a silent partner advancing 25 per cent of the amount of mortgage loans when their general specifications were met and when requested to participate by the lending institution. This enlarged the pool of funds available for mortgage lending but did not alter the nature of the mortgage lending decision in that mortgage loans were still initiated by lending institutions according to their relative desirability as an investment, although this desirability was affected by the participation of government in the market, especially after 1938 when this participation carried with it a partial guarantee against loss for the institution's capital.[34]

This lending partnership between financial institutions and the government lasted until 1954, when the joint loan programme was terminated, and government participation in the market shifted to direct lending under the authority previously given to CMHC to use public funds to make residential construction loans when private funds were not forthcoming. CMHC seldom used this authority prior to 1957, but thereafter CMHC became a large-scale mortgage lender in its capacity as a lender of last resort. In 1967 CMHC began to accelerate its role as financier of government programmes for low income housing and by 1968 the majority of its lending was for this purpose.

Since CMHC is a public institution the volume of its mortgage lending is regulated not by the relative desirability of mortgage investments compared to alternative investments, but according to social priorities and general economic policy considerations. Consequently, CMHC direct lending is treated as a policy variable throughout this study.

C. HISTORICAL PROFILE OF THE RELATIVE ROLE OF MORTGAGE MARKET PARTICIPANTS

During the postwar period the relative role of the various participants in the mortgage market shifted radically. These shifts occurred both in the relative importance of the major categories of lenders, and in the relative importance of participants within the institutional sector.

Table XI, which shows the proportion of outstanding mortgage debt held by the major sources of mortgage funds, indicates three major shifts. First, and most dramatic, the relative role of the personal sector declined sharply between 1950, when it was the largest single source holding 43 per cent of all outstanding mortgage debt, and 1969, when it held only an estimated 23 per cent despite the inclusion of the fast growing pension fund holdings in this category. Second, the proportion of outstanding mortgage debt held by private financial institutions rose from 42 per cent in 1950 to 50 per cent in 1960 with the sharpest increase occurring during the mid-1950s after the chartered banks entered the mortgage field.

TABLE XI
PERCENTAGE SHARE OF OUTSTANDING MORTGAGE DEBT BY PRINCIPAL SECTORS, 1936–69*

	1936	1940	1945	1950	1955	1960	1965	1969
Financial institutions	42%	43%	42%	42%	48%	50%	51%	50%
Government and government agencies	10	12	11	15	14	18	16	21
Corporate lenders	4	4	3	1	1	5	9	7
Personal sector	44	41	44	43	37	28	24	23

*These proportions required estimates of "personal sector" holdings (a large component in the "personal and non-institutional corporations" grouping) and are therefore subject to large errors. They do, however, reflect reasonably well the basic underlying trends.

Totals do not always add to 100 per cent due to rounding.

Source: calculated from Central Mortgage and Housing Corporation, *Economic Research Bulletin*, no. 77 (R) (Ottawa 1971), and Central Mortgage and Housing Corporation, *Canadian Housing Statistics* (1970), 63.

This increased relative importance of financial institutions was maintained during the sixties despite the virtual cessation of chartered bank lending between 1960 and 1967, as trust and mortgage loan company lending accelerated to pick up the slack. Third, the government, whose importance as a supplier of mortgage funds had declined with the termination of the joint lending programme in 1954, re-emerged as a prime supplier of credit in 1957 with the inauguration of large scale CMHC direct lending. The extent of government participation in the market is not truly reflected by the mortgage holding figures of Table XI because CMHC became a large net seller of NHA mortgages after 1961 in an attempt to develop a secondary market in government insured mortgages. The development of this market together with a sharp acceleration in non-institutional corporate lending contributed to the larger mortgage holdings of the non-institutional private sector after 1960.

The decline in the relative importance of the personal sector may be explained by a number of events. First, the more advantageous borrowing terms and reduced risk for investors lead to a sharp rise in the relative importance of the NHA as compared to conventional sector of the mortgage market, as Table III indicated, and only financial institutions and CMHC are authorized to initiate these mortgages. Since secondary market sales are still quite small and made in large blocks, usually $100,000 or more minimum, the small personal investor is eliminated from this market. Second, financial institutions were able to attract an increasing share of personal savings through their ability to provide management, diversification, and obligations attractive to the public. Third, mortgage investments became relatively more attractive to institutions because of government guarantees, the beginnings of a rudimentary secondary market in NHA mortgages, the use of fully amortized mortgages, a longer period of favourable mortgage lending experience and economies of scale that arose as mortgage operations increased. Fourth, federal legislation was introduced removing many restrictions on institutional participation in the mortgage market – such as allowing the chartered banks to participate in the market, and increasing the permitted loan to value ratios. Fifth, as the size of mortgage transactions increased and financial institutions opened more branches, the comparative advantage increased for financial institutions and large corporations in the acquisition and servicing of mortgage investments. Consequently, the personal sector lost ground steadily to both the institutional and corporate sectors. At the same time, government policy decisions to more vigorously participate in the financing of residential construction after 1956 explains their relative growth, and is another factor in the relative decline of the personal sector.

Concomitant with these intra-sectoral shifts were substantial variations within the institutional sector. The effects of these developments may be seen from Tables XII and XIII which show the percentage distribution of institutionally held mortgage debt and new institutional mortgage initiations respectively.

These tables indicate that life insurance companies dominated the market in the early fifties, holding 70 per cent of outstanding institutional mortgage debt and making 70 per cent of institutional mortgage initiations, but by 1969 they had relinquished their position of prominence, and were not even the major institutional supplier of new mortgage loans. The beginning of the relative decline of the life insurance companies coincided with the chartered banks entry into the mortgage market in 1954 and continued throughout the fifties as the chartered bank presence increased. This declining trend was temporarily reversed in 1960–1 when the chartered banks virtually withdrew from the market, but reappeared during the mid-sixties as trust and mortgage loan company mortgage lending accelerated. Toward the end of the sixties renewed competition from the chartered banks together with a growing disenchantment with long-term fixed yield mortgage investments as a result of the continuing inflation and introduction of a tax on life insurance company earnings[35] culminated in a sharp decline in the proportion of new in-

TABLE XII
PERCENTAGE DISTRIBUTION OF INSTITUTIONALLY HELD MORTGAGE DEBT, 1950-69

	1950-1	1952-3	1954-5	1956-7	1958-9	1960-1	1962-3	1964-5	1966-7	1968-9
Life insurance cos.	70.0	71.0	68.6	64.7	60.8	60.0	58.5	54.9	54.3	51.4
Mortgage loan cos.	19.6	18.4	15.8	13.0	12.1	12.8	14.4	16.9	16.9	16.8
Trust companies	8.5	7.9	7.6	7.0	7.6	9.2	12.9	17.1	19.4	21.1
Chartered banks	—	—	6.5	13.8	17.8	16.3	12.2	8.5	7.2	8.0
Other institutions	1.8	1.7	1.6	1.6	1.7	1.8	2.1	2.7	2.7	2.4

Source: Central Mortgage and Housing Corporation, *Economic Research Bulletin*, no. 77 (R), Table 3 (Ottawa 1971), and Central Mortgage and Housing Corporation, *Canadian Housing Statistics* (1970), 63.

TABLE XIII
PERCENTAGE DISTRIBUTION OF NEW INSTITUTIONAL MORTGAGE INITIATIONS, 1950-69

	1950-1	1952-3	1954-5	1956-7	1958-9	1960-1	1962-3	1964-5	1966-7	1968-9
Life insurance cos.	70.5	69.5	57.7	55.9	45.6	53.2	48.1	42.5	42.9	26.7
Mortgage loan cos.	18.6	19.6	13.6	12.8	14.0	21.2	20.5	24.1	18.1	15.9
Trust companies	9.2	8.8	9.3	9.6	13.9	19.5	28.1	29.8	29.0	37.8
Chartered banks	—	—	17.3	19.6	24.3	3.0	0.5	0.6	6.8	15.1
Other institutions	1.7	2.1	2.1	2.1	2.2	3.1	2.8	3.0	3.3	4.6

Source: Central Mortgage and Housing Corporation, *Economic Research Bulletin*, no. 77 (R), Table 6 (Ottawa 1971), and Central Mortgage and Housing Corporation, *Canadian Housing Statistics* (1970), 22.

TABLE XIV
PERCENTAGE DISTRIBUTION OF INSTITUTIONAL CONVENTIONAL AND NHA MORTGAGE INITIATIONS, 1935-69

	NHA						Conventional					
	1936-45	1946-53	1954	1955-9	1960-6	1967-9	1936-45	1946-50	1951-5	1956-60	1961-6	1967-9
Life insurance companies	100	95	73	40	51	24	58	60	61	64	47	32
Mortgage loan companies	—	5	1	2	4	7	26	26	25	21	24	19
Trust companies	—	—	1	5	44	34	13	12	12	12	25	37
Chartered banks	—	—	24	53	1	31	—	—	—	—	—	9
Other institutions	—	—	—	—	—	4	3	2	2	3	4	3

Source: Calculated from Central Mortgage and Housing Corporation, *Economic Research Bulletin*, no. 77 (R) (Ottawa 1971), and Central Mortgage and Housing Corporation, *Canadian Housing Statistics* (1970), 22 and 24.

stitutional mortgage approvals made by life insurance companies, their proportion of approvals falling to 23 per cent in 1969 and only 17 per cent in 1970.

The chartered banks by virtue of their extensive branch network and large pool of funds are able to move very quickly into a prominent position in most capital markets. In 1954 the chartered banks were authorized to participate in the mortgage market, in the NHA sector, for the first time and they quickly made their presence felt. By 1955 they accounted for 23 per cent of all institutional mortgage initiations and during the latter half of the fifties they maintained over 20 per cent of the market. Their participation in the NHA sector was even more dramatic, as Table XIV indicates, since they initiated 53 per cent of all new NHA mortgage initiations 1955 to 1959. However, their prominence was short-lived as rising yields on traditional investments together with an increase in the NHA mortgage rate beyond the nominal yield ceiling permitted on chartered bank loans which would have posed an impossible credit rationing problem and loss of goodwill had they attempted to continue lending at their 6 per cent ceiling,[36] led to their virtual withdrawal from the market in 1960. This cessation of bank lending lasted until 1967 when the nominal ceiling on banking lending rates was removed and the banks were authorized to participate in the conventional mortgage market. Thereafter, the banks again vigorously re-entered the mortgage market and in 1969-70 their proportion of new institutional mortgage initiations reached 17 per

TABLE XV
ANNUAL AVERAGE RATE OF GROWTH OF FINANCIAL INSTITUTIONS, 1935-69

	1935-45	1946-50	1951-5	1956-60	1961-5	1966-9
Life insurance cos.	6.5%	6.2%	6.7%	6.2%	7.8%	5.4%
Mortgage loan cos.	0.2	9.3	9.2	10.6	21.6	7.9
Trust cos.	1.7	10.6	10.1	12.5	21.5	13.8
Chartered banks	9.1	5.7	6.4	4.4	8.9	13.1

Source: Royal Commission on Banking and Finance, *Report*, 174; Bank of Canada, *Statistical Summary* (1969); and CMHC, *Canadian Housing Statistics* (1970), 62.

cent, and their proportion of new NHA mortgage initiations reached 35 per cent.

Throughout the postwar period the trust companies, and to a lesser extent mortgage loan companies, experienced a phenomenal growth rate, as Table xv indicates. On the strength of this trust companies grew steadily in importance in the mortgage market, especially after 1958. By 1962–3 their share of new institutional mortgage initiations reached 28 per cent, and in 1969 and 1970 their share reached over 41 per cent, making them the largest single institutional supplier of mortgage credit. During this period the market share of mortgage loan companies oscillated within relatively narrow limits, and at the end of the sixties their market share at 16 per cent was little changed from 1950.

6
Private Financial Institution Mortgage Investment Behaviour

The preceding chapter indicated the importance of private financial institutions in the mortgage market in general, and in the financing of new residential construction in particular. This chapter develops a theoretical model to explain the lending behaviour of these institutions and then examines the postwar investment activities of these institutions within the context of the model. Chaper 7 provides econometric estimates of the mortgage lending functions of each of these institutions.

A. A PORTFOLIO SELECTION MODEL OF FINANCIAL INSTITUTION INVESTMENT BEHAVIOUR

As mentioned in chapter 5, the major financial institutions are financial intermediaries who gather funds from the public in exchange for their obligations and invest these funds in other market obligations. Their profitability primarily depends upon their efficiency, taken as their non-interest costs per dollar invested, their costs of funds per dollar invested, and their scale of operations. Each intermediary's share in the total financial business is governed by the public's preferences for their debt instruments and the services they offer. Since the rates of interest offered on an institution's obligations relative to those offered on alternative investment forms influences the public's preferences for their obligations, institutions endeavour to manage their investment portfolios as efficiently as possible both to increase their net investment yield and to enable them to offer competitive rates for funds. At the same time institutions wish to minimize the risks, both short-run market and long-term capital asset risks, associated with their investment portfolios.

If we assume that all investment risks in some way affect the certainty of the expected return and summarize this in a single measure σ^2, the variance of the expected return, and that all yield considerations including acquisition and servicing costs and tax advantages may be expressed in a single measure μ, the net expected return, then we can define financial institution investment preferences in terms of an investment utility function with its arguments σ^2_p and μ_p, i.e., $U = f(\mu_p, \sigma^2_p)$.[1] This utility function exists not for individual securities, but for the entire investment portfolio,[2] so that securities are evaluated not in isolation but with respect to their effect upon the entire portfolio. Because institutions are not risk seekers, they will not accept a lower expected return (μ_p) in order to increase the variance of their expected return (σ^2_p). Consequently, their indifference curves between μ_p and σ^2_p slope upward to the right, and may be supposed to be concave to the south-east in the usual way (although this is not necessary to define an equilibrium solution).

At any given time, a variety of financial assets exist, each possessing their own properties and characteristics in terms of marketability, liquidity, capital risk, etc., which affect the variance of their expected return (σ^2), and carrying different coupon yields, acquisition and servicing costs, potential tax advantages, etc., which affect the expected return (μ). An institution with a given volume of funds to invest can therefore select a variety of portfolios, represented in Figure 7 by the set ABCDE, each possessing an expected return (μ_p) and expected variance on this return (σ^2_p)[3] according to the mix of potential investments it selects. Because an institution seeks to maximize μ_p for any given σ^2_p, or conversely minimize σ^2_p for any given μ_p it will confine its choice of portfolios to that subset of efficient portfolios which possess the properties on the CDE boundary. This subset, or investment opportunity curve, must slope upward to the right and be concave towards the northwest.[4]

Combining the institution's indifference map with its investment opportunity curve, as in Figure 7, we get an equilibrium solution at D which defines an optimum or desired portfolio possessing an expected return μ'_p and expected variance in this return $\sigma^{2'}_p$. If an institution's investible funds increase, the investment opportunity curve moves to the right and a new equilibrium is defined. If no scale effects arise, i.e., if the institution's indifference map is homogeneous to degree one, and there are no changes in the properties or yields of the various securities, the proportional distribution will be unaffected.[5] If there is a change in the actual or subjective evaluation of the attributes of various securities or a change in the relative yield structure,[6] the composition and shape of the investment opportunity curve will be altered and the optimum portfolio mix will change. Once an optimum portfolio is defined, investment flows will occur to reduce the discrepancy between the institution's actual and target portfolios.

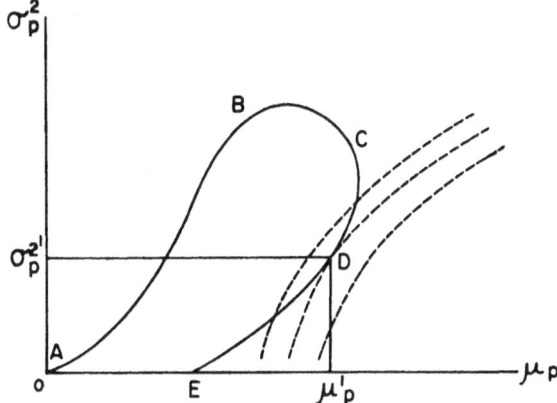

FIGURE 7 Investment opportunity frontier and institution's indifference map

Presented in this usual form the stock adjustment model describes a dynamic process in which market conditions and expectations prescribe portfolio targets desired for the next period. These targets, when compared with the actual portfolios existing in the present period, determine investment flows in the next period. If existing market yields, conditions, or anything that influences future expectations or subjective evaluations vary, new targets and imbalances are generated, and investment flows are altered.[7] However, investment flows in any period usually do not completely eliminate the discrepancy between an institution's actual and desired holdings. Failure for discrepancies to be quickly eliminated results from lags in the spread of information, the making of decisions and the execution of plans, and from comparisons of the costs of portfolio imbalance with the transactions cost of shifting into and out of securities and the opportunity investment costs arising from failure to manage portfolios efficiently.[8]

Maintenance of an imbalanced portfolio involves an institution in some costs in terms of lower expected yields and increased portfolio risk. These costs increase with the degree of portfolio imbalance and place institutions under considerable pressure to adjust their portfolios when imbalances are large. On the other hand, institutions usually prefer to adjust their portfolios out of current flows rather than by liquidating existing holdings since stock liquidations incur extra transactions costs which may be considerable, especially when dealing in securities with underdeveloped secondary markets.[9] These costs are incurred because institutions must repurchase their previously liquidated security once portfolio balance is achieved in order to maintain their newly acquired balance as their portfolios grow.

If an institution has a portfolio of 30 per cent mortgages and 70 per cent bonds, and desires to obtain a target portfolio of 50 per cent mortgages, 50 per cent bonds, it can approach this target either by liquidating bonds and shifting into mortgages, by investing all its gross inflow of funds into mortgages, or by some combination,[10] assuming gross inflows are positive. Since the costs associated with liquidating and purchasing securities are largely independent of the size of the portfolio imbalance, while the costs associated with the imbalance decline as the imbalance is reduced, the pressure to reduce portfolio imbalance via stock liquidations declines as the imbalance declines. The extent to which stocks will be liquidated for portfolio balancing purposes depends upon the comparison of the costs of the imbalance and the costs associated with moving into and out of excessive securities. Therefore, where the degree of portfolio imbalance is quite large, so that the costs of maintaining a temporarily[11] larger imbalance exceed the transactions costs associated with the liquidation procedure, institutions tend to liquidate securities to approach their desired balances. When this cost relationship is reversed institutions tend to approach their desired balances out of current gross flows.

The proportion of its gross flows that an institution will devote to relieving portfolio imbalance in any period is limited by its need to stay "open for business" in all or most security markets. If an institution were to devote a substantial proportion of its current gross flow to relieving portfolio imbalance, it must necessarily severely restrict its new purchases of securities in which its holdings are excessive. If these markets are imperfect in the sense that securities are allocated not solely on price considerations, but on traditional, personal, or other bases – as often occurs in direct bond placements, mortgages and real estate investments – then failure to stay open for business in these security markets may be extremely costly since it often damages goodwill and strains dealer relationships developed over years, as dealers and brokers are forced to look elsewhere for funds. In such a situation an institution may find it much more difficult to obtain future attractive investments in these securities until favourable dealer relationships can be re-established. Consequently, institutions tend to set some proportion of their funds aside for purchasing new securities in markets where the cultivation of goodwill and favourable relationship is essential for the acquisition of desirable investments. Therefore, some limits are placed upon the proportion of gross flows of funds that may be invested in a security in any given period.

Finally, the time path the stock adjustment process follows depends upon the relative yield desirability of investing in a security in one investment period compared to another, since relative interest rates affect not only the desired portfolio but also the speed of adjustment.

As mentioned earlier relative yields affect investment flows, in the first instance, as a determinant of the desired portfolio. This is illustrated in Figure 8, which shows portfolio selection between two assets (i.e., the optimum amount of each asset in the portfolio) rather than the selection of the optimum characteristics of the portfolio, as in Figure 7. In this formulation institutional preferences for asset characteristics are specified directly as a preference for the asset which enables the portfolio to take on those characteristics, and these preferences are summarized in the institution's indifference map. For portfolio balance reasons the indifference curves are convex to the origin. If security A is plotted on the x-axis and security B on the y-axis, for a given portfolio size an income line $a_0 b_0$ may be plotted such that b_0 is the total net investment income arising from a portfolio fully in-

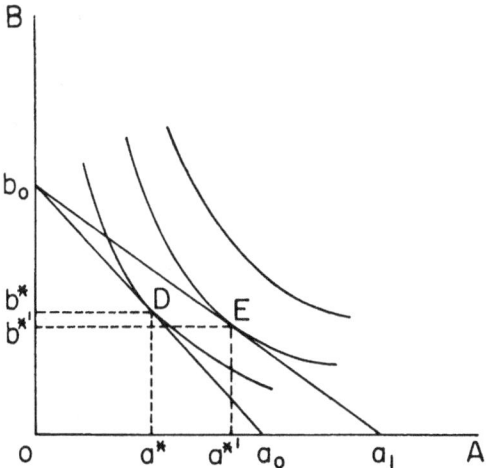

FIGURE 8   Portfolio selection choice between two assets, A and B

vested in B, and a_0 is the total net investment income arising from a portfolio fully invested in A. a_0b_0 is a straight line since scale effects, in the form of lower acquisition costs as funds devoted to a given investment form increase, are ignored. By combining the indifference map and income line, we define an optimum portfolio mix and a desired stock of A and B such that the net revenue from investment in B is b^* and from investment in A is a^*. If relative net investment yields change such that the net yield on A increases and B remains constant, the slope of the income line a_1b_0 becomes flatter and, with normal indifference curves, a new optimum portfolio is defined at E in which the proportion of asset A is increased. This may be seen from Figure 8 since the net revenue from asset B declines to b^{*1} although the net yield on B remains unchanged. Consequently a change in relative yields alters the optimum portfolio and influences investment flows.

However, institutions seek not only to obtain a desired portfolio, but endeavour to manage their portfolios so as to realize as high a yield as possible on any given portfolio. To accomplish this they attempt to purchase securities when their yields relative to other alternative security investments are attractive compared with some long-run normal expected yield relationship,[12] since failure to do so would result in a lower average expected yield associated with a given portfolio. Thus, temporary fluctuations in interest yield spreads can also affect institutional investment flows through their speeds of adjustment.

This is illustrated by a simple numerical example. Assume that an institution, which has a constant net inflow of funds but no capital repayments in the period under consideration, is able to invest in only two securities, mortgages and bonds; that it wishes to invest in these securities so as to maintain a long-run portfolio balance (which it now possesses) of 50 per cent mortgages and 50 per cent bonds; that mortgages and bonds have a long-run normal yield differential of 2 per cent; and that mortgage and bond yields fluctuate over the next nine periods as indicated in Table XVI. If the institution were to invest 50 per cent of its net inflow in each security in order to maintain its desired portfolio balance continuously, it

TABLE XVI
HYPOTHETICAL MORTGAGE AND BOND INTEREST RATES, IN PER CENT

Period	Mortgage yield	Bond yield	Differential	Average yield on investments arising from net inflow of funds if funds invested	
				50-50 in each period	100% in relatively attractive security
1	9.0	7.0	2.0	8.0	8.0
2	9.0	7.5	1.5	8.25	7.5
3	9.5	7.5	2.0	8.5	8.5
4	9.5	8.0	1.5	8.75	8.0
5	10.0	8.0	2.0	9.0	9.0
6	10.5	8.0	2.5	9.25	10.5
7	10.5	8.5	2.0	9.5	9.5
8	10.5	8.0	2.5	9.25	10.5
9	10.0	8.0	2.0	9.0	9.0
Average	9.833	7.833	2.0	8.833	8.944

would obtain an 8.833 per cent average yield on its new investments during this period, whereas, if it were to invest 100 per cent of its net inflow in a security which was relatively attractive in each investment period compared to its normal yield differential, the institution would obtain an investment yield on new investments of 8.944 per cent, while maintaining its desired long-run portfolio balance with only temporary deviations.[13]

Consequently, relative interest rates influence investment flows both through their effect upon the institution's selection of its optimum portfolio target and through their effect upon the relative attractiveness of investment in a security in one period compared to other periods, which affects the speed of portfolio adjustment.

This discussion is summarized in functional form in conjunction with the derivation of estimating equations for institutional mortgage supply functions in chapter 7. For now suffice it to say that financial institution investment in a security is a function of the relationship between its actual and desired holdings of this security, where its desired holdings depend upon the size of the investment portfolio and the relative price and non-price attributes associated with investment in this security vis-à-vis alternative investments, constrained by the size of its gross inflows of funds and the relative yield desirability of investing in this security in this period as opposed to future periods.

B. CHARACTERISTICS AND HISTORICAL PROFILE OF
FINANCIAL INSTITUTION INVESTMENT BEHAVIOUR

In order to enable a better understanding of mortgage supply functions estimated for the major lending institutions in Chapter 7, this section presents a brief discussion of the characteristics and historical profile of the general investment behaviour of each of these institutions during the postwar period.

During the immediate postwar period financial institution investment behaviour was dominated by portfolio balancing considerations. As indicated in Figure 9, Canadian intermediaries entered this period with extremely unbalanced portfolios, consisting mainly of government securities accumulated by funnelling the bulk of their investible funds into government loans during the war.[14] Government securities, which normally accounted for 10–15 per cent of life insurance company portfolios, 20–30 per cent of trust company portfolios and 10–12 per cent of mortgage loan company portfolios, in 1946 accounted for 60 per cent, 40 per cent, and 26 per cent of these institutions' portfolios respectively, while their mortgage holdings were correspondingly depressed. Institutions, therefore, endeavoured to liquidate their excess holdings of low yielding government debt and shift into higher yielding private securities, especially mortgages.[15]

Prior to November 1950, this stock adjustment process was greatly facilitated by the Bank of Canada's bond price support programme, which sought to maintain long-term government bond yields at $2\frac{1}{2}$ per cent. This programme, which artificially sustained the government securities' market, enabled financial institutions to make a virtually costless transfer of investments in any volume they wished, since they were certain that cash could be raised regardless of the level of mortgage

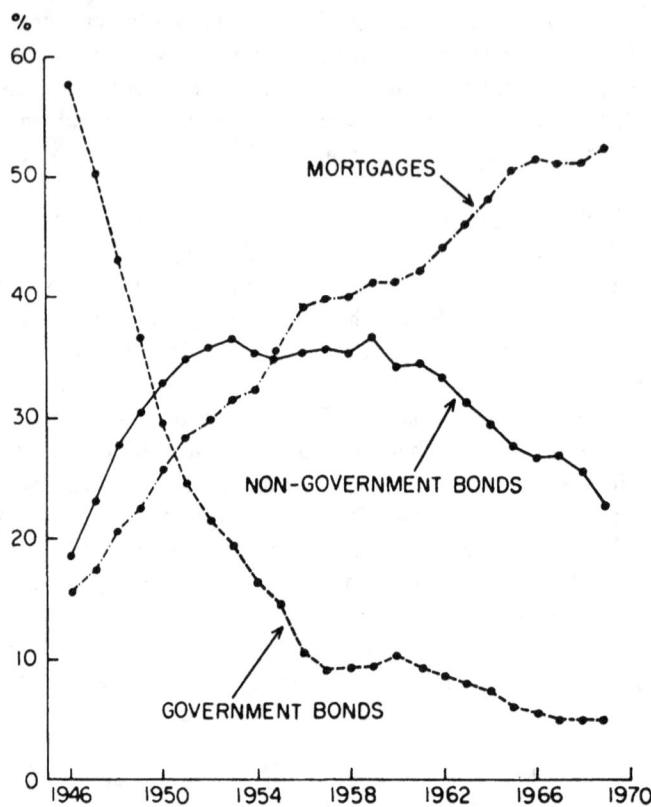

FIGURE 9 Percentage distribution of selected assets of non-bank financial institutions, 1946–69

commitments, without absorbing capital losses or by-passing attractive government security investments. These institutions, however, were constrained in this adjustment process by their ability to obtain attractive mortgage investments, since shortages of building materials, skilled labour and insufficient industrial capacity severely hampered the volume of residential construction and the creation of new mortgage debt. As the period progressed these bottlenecks were eliminated, industrial capacity expanded and the volume of mortgage lending increased. By the early to mid-1950s financial institutions had eliminated excessive distortions in their portfolios and short-run relative yield and gross flow considerations assumed a greater importance in institutional investment decisions. However, for the next decade the proportion of mortgages in investment portfolios continued their upward trend, not levelling off until the mid-sixties.

(a) Life insurance companies

As mentioned above, life insurance companies were the dominant force in the Canadian mortgage market for most of the postwar period. This resulted from their size – they held almost 22 per cent of institutionally held assets in 1969 – and their liability structure, which is particularly well suited for mortgage investment. Unlike other financial intermediaries which usually offer their obligations in exchange for a single payment, life insurance companies obtain most of their funds by way of life contingency contracts involving a series of payments stretching into the future.[16] This provides a high degree of stability in life insurance company inflows which, together with the basically actuarially predictable nature of their payments (abstracting from policy loan outflows), and premium incomes exceeding benefit payments, makes life insurance companies well suited to make the advance mortgage commitments which are essential for new construction projects.

Because most of their contingent liabilities are long term and their present premium income exceeds their benefit payments life company investment managers need not worry about liquidity considerations and can move with safety into long-term investments. Long-term investments typically not only carry higher yields than similar short term assets, but they also provide life companies with a hedge against declining interest rates by allowing a closer matching of maturity terms of assets and liabilities which enables life companies to minimize the variation in their expected return.[17]

If a financial intermediary's assets have a longer term than its liabilities an increase in interest rates adversely affects the intermediary, since it is forced either to go into the market and offer new securities on itself at higher interest rates or to sell some of its securities at a capital loss in order to meet its maturing liabilities. This forces an intermediary either to pay more for funds without receiving a corresponding increase in yields, or to absorb capital losses. On the other hand, falling interest rates have the opposite favourable effects so that, in effect, intermediaries with assets of longer maturities than their corresponding liabilities are speculating on falling interest rates. Conversely, if an intermediary's assets have a shorter maturity than its liabilities, an increase in interest rates allows it to reinvest its funds obtained at a fixed rate at higher yields providing additional returns. A fall in interest rates would cause the intermediary to suffer losses upon the reinvestment at lower yields of its funds obtained at the previous rate. Hence, intermediaries with assets of shorter maturities than liabilities are speculating on increasing interest rates. When the maturity terms of its assets and liabilities are equal, an intermediary has hedged its position, and is earning its return solely on the yield differential between its assets and obligations. Therefore, life insurance companies seek long-term investments within asset classifications although this exposes them to the uncertainties such as default risk associated with such investments.

While the maturity structure of life insurance company investment preferences is clear cut, their preferences between asset classifications are not. These depend upon the usual trade-off between expected yield and the variance in this yield.

Mortgages, which were the major investment outlet for life insurance companies throughout most of the postwar period, increasing from 12 per cent of life company assets in 1946 to over 45 per cent in 1970,[18] are a highly desirable form of investment because of their long-term and relatively low capital risk. This is especially true for NHA mortgages which typically have a 25- to 35-year term and are government insured against virtually all capital and interest loss, although they do provide a slightly lower yield than conventional mortgages. The illiquidity of mortgages because of the lack of a well functioning secondary market does not pose a serious problem for life companies, nor does the steady return of capital via amortization payments which reduces the effective term of a mortgage investment and necessitates a constant re-investing of funds, since these companies must undertake a minimum volume of new mortgage business in order to maintain their business contacts. A more serious problem stems from the statutory right of individuals to repay conventional mortgages after 5 years and NHA mortgages after 3 years upon payment of a bonus of 3 months interest. This places long-term lenders in the unenviable position of facing the possibility of substantial prepayments in periods of declining interest rates when investments cannot so satisfactorily be replaced, without the option of improving their investment position in periods of rising yields. However, in actuality, since most of their lending is to corporate borrowers who do not have this advantage and since short-term cyclical declines in interest rates have not been sufficient to make refinancing attractive throughout most of the postwar period this has not caused major difficulties. Moreover, somewhat offsetting this is the recent tendency for life companies to seek participation in the form of a percentage of gross revenue on revenue-producing properties they finance, which has the effect of increasing returns in inflationary periods.

Bonds, which are the major alternative form of investment for life insurance companies, have the advantage of providing a long-term low risk outlet for funds. Unfortunately, they also carry the lowest gross and net rates of return of all investment classes forcing investment managers to sacrifice yield in order to minimize risks. According to the Canadian Life Insurance Officers' Association *Submission to the Royal Commission on Banking and Finance*, gross yields on life company bond investments ran 155 to 172 basis points below gross mortgage yields, 86 to 142 basis points below gross real estate investment returns and 113 to 241 basis points below gross stock yields during the 1951 to 1960 period, and net bond yields ran 76 to 128 basis points below net mortgage yields.[19]

Within the bond classification government bond yields run below other yields, being approximately 30 basis points below provincial bond yields, 50 basis points below high grade corporate bond yields, and 70–75 basis points below municipal bond yields,[20] but are more marketable, virtually riskless, and free from undesirable call provisions. Because of the relatively high return that high grade corporate bonds provide within the bond classification, the willingness of corporations to tailor their security issues to lender requirements, the size of life company portfolios, and life company willingness to engage in direct placements, life insurance companies play a major role in the corporate bond market, holding 34 per cent of outstanding corporate bonds held in Canada in 1968. This compared to holdings of 15 per cent of municipal bonds, 10 per cent of provincial bonds and only 1.3 per cent of government bonds. In portfolio terms, as Table 17 indicates, non-government securities accounted for 33.8 per cent of all assets in 1969. Within this category corporate bonds accounted for 19.4 per cent, provincial bonds 2.6 per cent, municipal bonds 4.7 per cent, and foreign bonds 2.1 per cent of life insurance company investment portfolios in 1969.

The remainder of life insurance company portfolios consists of real estate, 4.5 per cent, policy loans, 4.6 per cent, and stocks, 6.8 per cent. Real estate investments, which are increasing both directly through outright purchases and indirectly via participation in consideration for supplying mortgage finance are a highly desirable form of investment because of their long-term nature, fairly good net return, possibility of capital gain, and inflationary hedge. However, because low risk investments are very difficult to obtain (except when participation is a bonus for the provision of mortgage finance) large real estate portfolios tend to become somewhat risky.

Stocks have tended to provide relatively high returns for life companies but until recently have occupied a minor role in their portfolios. The main reasons appear to be life insurance companies' view that fixed value assets provide greater capital security, legal restrictions limiting purchases to stocks with a good dividend record over periods of 5 to 7 years which often prevents the purchase of stocks when they are attractively priced, and fear of technical insolvency since stocks must be reported at market value.[21] However, expectations of increasing inflation and the imposition of a tax on their earnings have recently increased the desirability of equity investment in both stocks and real estate.

Policy loans are a unique form of investment in the sense that they arise passively as far as life companies are concerned because life insurance companies are obligated to advance these funds at the request of their policy holders. Consequently, policy loans should not be considered to form part of life insurance company investment portfolios in the usual sense.

As Table XVII indicates, the composition of life insurance company investment portfolios varied considerably during the postwar period with a dramatic upsurge in mortgage investments and decline in government securities. Life companies entered the postwar period with highly unbalanced portfolios consisting of 60 per cent government securities, 20 per cent other bonds and only 10 per cent mortgages as a consequence of the war and reduced construction activity during the 1930s. The immediate postwar years were spent rectifying this imbalance by liquidating government bonds and initiating new mortgage loans. Between 1948 and

TABLE XVII
PERCENTAGE DISTRIBUTION OF SELECTED ASSETS HELD BY ALL LIFE INSURANCE COMPANIES AS AT DECEMBER 31, 1935-69

	1935	1946	1950	1954	1957	1960	1963	1966	1969
Government securities	14.9	59.3	31.1	16.1	8.3	8.7	6.7	3.6	3.1
All other bonds	31.5	19.4	36.8	42.1	41.8	39.7	39.7	37.1	33.8
Mortgage loans:	19.0	10.3	19.2	29.1	36.4	37.6	40.7	45.2	44.9
NHA	—	1.4	7.3	15.7	19.8	17.9	19.4	14.5	14.2
Conventional	19.0	9.9	11.9	13.4	16.6	19.7	21.3	30.7	30.7
Real estate	4.2	1.2	1.5	2.6	3.4	3.6	3.2	3.5	4.5
Stock	8.6	2.1	3.3	3.3	3.3	3.1	3.1	4.3	6.8
Policy loans	13.1	5.2	4.4	4.6	4.5	4.3	3.9	3.7	4.6

Source: Derived from data in Canadian Life Insurance Officers' Association, *Submission to the Royal Commission on Banking and Finance* (Toronto 1962), 44; Bank of Canada, *Statistical Summary, 1969 Supplement*, 115; Central Mortgage and Housing Corporation, *Economic Research Bulletin*, no. 77 (R) (Ottawa 1971); and Central Mortgage and Housing Corporation, *Canadian Housing Statistics* (1970), 22, 24, and 62.

1951 life companies were extremely large net sellers of government bonds, and even after the bond price support programme ended these sales continued, although at reduced rates.[22] By 1957 government bond holdings had declined to 8.3 per cent of investment portfolios, and non-government bonds and mortgages had risen to 41.8 per cent and 36.4 per cent respectively. After 1956 considerable year to year variations in investment portfolios occurred but the relative long-run relationship between asset classifications remained fairly steady, although government and other bond holdings gradually declined in importance and mortgages continued to increase. After 1967, equity investments in stocks and real estate also began to increase.

(b) Trust companies
Canadian trust companies fit the classical description of a financial intermediary, borrowing funds from the public by way of deposits and guaranteed investment certificates (GICs) and investing these funds in financial assets – primarily mortgages and bonds. Trust companies also act as professional trustees administrating portfolios whose beneficial ownership belongs to others. Trust companies play an important role in the capital markets because of their size, in 1969 they held approximately 9 per cent of institutionally held assets in their intermediary capacity and administered considerably more than double this amount in their trustee capacity, their rapid rate of growth during the sixties, and their strong position in the mortgage market.

GICs are fully registered term certificates issued in various amounts – usually with a $100 or $500 minimum – for terms of 30 days to 10 years, with one to five years being most common. Deposits are usually payable on demand and carry a variety of chequing privileges. Because of the relatively short-term nature of their liabilities – 38 per cent are payable on demand and the remainder are issued for an average term of $2\frac{1}{2} - 3$ years[23] – and the sensitivity of their net inflows of funds to general market conditions – withdrawals increase and the percentage of GICs reinvested upon maturity decreases in periods of rising interest rates – trust companies must be mindful of their liquidity position. On the other hand, withdrawals are reasonably predictable and the maturity date of GICs known so that trust companies have considerable investment freedom.

Trust companies play a major role in the mortgage market where they have an advantage in acquiring and servicing mortgage investments because of the local character of their business and associations developed through their estate, trust and agency business. This advantage allows these institutions (and mortgage loan companies and banks) to obtain new mortgage investments at a lower acquisition cost than institutions who rely on agents or correspondents (as is common for life insurance companies).[24] This reduced acquisition cost can be thought of as flattening the slope of the income line in Figure 8 if asset A is taken to be mortgage investments, (i.e., increasing the relative net yield on mortgage investments), so that these institutions would have a higher proportion of mortgages in their portfolios than other institutions with identical preference functions.[25] Reinforcing this tendency is the cost advantage life insurance companies have in the non-government bond market, which steepens their income line, by virtue of their size and direct placements. On the other hand, the liquidity requirements for trust companies make mortgages a less desirable form of investment (the slope of their indifference curves are flatter along a given ray from the origin) than for life companies so that the equilibrium proportion of mortgages in both institutions' portfolios are quite close.[26]

Trust companies devote approximately 55 per cent of their investment portfolios to mortgages, with the bulk being in conventional mortgages although they continuously increased their NHA lending between 1954 and 1963. However, NHA mortgages were a relatively less desirable investment than conventional mortgages for trust companies because of the longer term on NHA mortgages prior to April 1969, when the minimum term of an NHA mortgage was reduced from 25 to 5 years, which subjected trust companies to the risks associated with increasing interest rates when the maturity term exceeds the term of their liabilities, the possibility of prepayment after three years, and the lower yields that NHA mortgages carry. Conventional mortgages, in addition to their higher yields, are usually written for a term of 5 to 10 years which enables trust companies to hedge their position by a closer matching of asset and liability maturity structures.[27] The preference for conventional mortgages on the basis of the shorter maturity term was eliminated in 1969 by the reduction in the minimum NHA term to 5 years.

Bonds provide the major alternative form of investment for trust companies and government bonds accounted for 10 per cent, provincial bonds 5 per cent, municipal bonds 2 per cent, and corporate and institutional bonds 6 per cent of trust company investment portfolios in 1969. Additional liquidity is provided by cash, deposits, and term certificates in other financial institutions and short-term notes which in total account for another 10 per cent of trust company assets.

The variation in the composition of trust company investment portfolios during the postwar period, shown in Table XVIII, is quite similar to that shown by the life insurance companies, although it is less pronounced. Trust companies were relatively slow in building their mortgage portfolios and by 1954 had only increased their proportion of mortgages to 28.1 per cent from 23.2 per cent in 1946 despite a reduction in government securities from 40.2 per cent to 26.1 per cent. After the

TABLE XVIII
PERCENTAGE DISTRIBUTION OF SELECTED ASSETS HELD BY TRUST COMPANIES AS AT DECEMBER 31, 1946-69

	1946	1950	1954	1957	1960	1963	1966	1969
Government securities	40.2	34.2	26.1	17.3	20.6	14.1	11.2	10.3
All other bonds	13.5	21.5	28.1	28.7	28.8	24.1	15.2	12.3
Mortgage loans:	23.2	25.9	28.1	35.3	36.4	48.3	55.3	56.6
NHA	0.4	0.5	0.6	4.5	6.6	13.0	12.6	10.3
Conventional	22.8	25.4	27.5	30.8	29.8	35.3	42.7	46.3
Stock	6.8	5.0	4.1	4.9	3.7	3.0	2.5	2.9
Cash	5.5	5.4	5.2	4.9	3.2	3.0	2.2	4.0

Source: Bank of Canada, *Statistical Summary, 1969 Supplement,* 110-1, and earlier issues, and Central Mortgage and Housing Corporation, *Economic Research Bulletin,* no. 77 (R) (Ottawa 1971), Tables 3, 4, and 5.

1954 revision of the National Housing Act they began a shifting into NHA mortgages which continued until 1963 when NHA mortgages reached 13.0 per cent of their portfolio. After 1960 NHA mortgages became a relatively more attractive investment as the NHA mortgage rate increased relative to the conventional rate and as CMHC attempted to increase the liquidity of NHA mortgages by developing a secondary market in these securities. During this period the relatively attractive NHA mortgage yield brought into the market funds from lenders such as pension funds and foreign institutions who were not authorized to initiate NHA loans, and trust companies (and to a lesser extent mortgage loan companies) began initiating NHA mortgages for future sale to these lenders. Because this mortgage banking operation entails the building up of inventories before the portfolio is transferred to the investor, trust company NHA mortgage holdings also increased at this time.

A by-product of this rapid increase in NHA activity was an increase in the desirability of conventional mortgage investments vis-à-vis other securities since the increased mortgage volume increased efficiency and reduced processing and administrative costs.[28] After 1963 trust companies moved more heavily into conventional mortgages as the net yields on these securities increased in attractiveness. By 1969, mortgages accounted for over 56 per cent of trust company investment portfolios, with conventional mortgages alone being 46 per cent.

(c) Mortgage loan companies

Mortgage loan companies are traditional financial intermediaries who are essentially specialty shops in the sense that over 75 per cent of their investment portfolio is devoted to mortgage investments. Despite their relatively small size (in 1969 they accounted for only 5 per cent of institutionally held assets) they account for over 16 per cent of institutional total mortgage initiations and 25 per cent of institutional new residential conventional mortgage initiations. Mortgage loan companies obtain funds by borrowing from the public by way of long-term notes and debentures, which accounted for 60 per cent of their liabilities (these have an issued maturity term centring around five years), and deposits which accounted for another 13 per cent of liabilities in 1969.

The bulk of mortgage loan company lending is in conventional mortgages which provide high yields and enable a close matching of asset and liability maturity terms. Abstracting from investments in affiliated companies which account for 8 per cent of their investments, most non-mortgage investments are undertaken to provide liquidity or a temporary haven for funds pending distribution into mortgages, although some companies regard their non-government bond holdings as permanent investments made for diversification.[29] Mortgage loan companies satisfied their liquidity requirements, which are quite small because of the matching of asset and liability maturities, by the continuous inflow of funds via amortization and mortgage repayments, their lines of credit with the chartered banks, recourse to CMHC as a lender of last resort, and by holding 4 per cent of their portfolio in government securities, 3 per cent in non-government bonds and 2 per cent in cash and deposits in other financial institutions in 1969.

The variation in mortgage loan company investment portfolios during the post-

TABLE XIX
PERCENTAGE DISTRIBUTION OF SELECTED ASSETS HELD BY MORTGAGE LOAN COMPANIES AS AT DECEMBER 31, 1946-69

	1946	1950	1954	1957	1960	1963	1966	1969
Government securities	25.9	12.0	11.8	8.3	8.1	7.1	4.9	4.1
All other bonds	6.2	6.5	5.0	4.5	5.3	4.3	3.0	2.8
Mortgage loans:	52.5	69.5	74.9	77.0	75.6	77.0	75.9	76.2
NHA	0.4	3.8	6.2	8.4	6.2	5.9	5.0	6.4
Conventional	52.1	65.7	68.7	68.6	69.4	71.1	70.9	69.8
Stock	7.3	5.7	2.1	2.6	3.3	3.3	2.4	2.5
Cash	4.2	4.4	2.8	3.0	1.7	1.5	1.2	1.0

Source: Bank of Canada, *Statistical Summary, 1969 Supplement*, 112-3, and earlier issues, and Central Mortgage and Housing Corporation, *Economic Research Bulletin*, no. 77 (R) (Ottawa 1971), Tables 3, 4 and 5.

war period, shown in Table XIX, is quite small compared to the variations in life insurance and trust company portfolios since they began with relatively large mortgage holdings, but it exhibits the same general trends of sharply declining government bond holdings and rising mortgage holdings.

(d) Chartered banks

By virtue of their vast pool of loanable funds and extensive branch system, the chartered banks are a potentially dominant force in the mortgage market. However, with the exception of the mid-1954 to 1959 period when the banks were major originators of NHA mortgages, and the post-1967 period when they re-entered the mortgage market, chartered banks' influence was largely confined to their role as a supplier of short-term construction credit.[30]

Prior to the March 1954 amendment to the Bank Act which authorized the chartered banks to participate in the NHA sector of the mortgage market but not the conventional sector, the chartered banks were prohibited from initiating mortgage loans. After their lending restrictions were eased the chartered banks entered the mortgage market with enthusiasm and began building mortgage portfolios. Between 1955 and 1959 the banks virtually dominated the NHA sector, originating over 50 per cent of all privately initiated NHA mortgages, and by the end of 1959 NHA mortgages accounted for 7 per cent of their investment portfolios. However, at the end of 1959 and beginning of 1960 the banks virtually ceased mortgage lending. At this time (and until 1967) the chartered banks were constrained in their investments by a nominal 6 per cent interest ceiling. During 1959 monetary conditions tightened and interest rates crept upward culminating in a sharp $\frac{3}{4}$ per cent hike in the NHA interest ceiling (which was also the effective lending rate) to $6\frac{3}{4}$ per cent in December. This placed the NHA rate three-quarters of one per cent above the nominal maximum bank lending rate. Rather than face an impossible credit rationing problem had they continued to lend at their 6 per cent ceiling when the equilibrium rate was considerably higher the banks withdrew from the mortgage market.[31] This cessation of lending lasted until 1967 when an amendment to the Bank Act removed the interest ceiling on bank lending rates and authorized the banks to participate in the conventional as well as NHA sector of the mortgage market.

TABLE XX
PERCENTAGE DISTRIBUTION OF SELECTED ASSETS HELD BY CHARTERED BANKS AS AT DECEMBER 31, 1946-69

	1946	1950	1954	1957	1960	1963	1966	1969
Government securities (excluding treasury bills)	46.1	34.3	28.4	14.8	14.6	14.8	10.3	9.6
Other bonds	9.2	11.2	7.6	7.8	6.9	6.3	5.2	4.7
Mortgage loans:	—	—	.7	4.7	6.8	4.9	3.5	4.3
NHA	—	—	.7	4.7	6.8	4.9	3.5	3.2
Conventional	—	—	—	—	—	—	—	1.1
Loans	24.2	34.1	39.3	43.5	45.9	46.6	46.3	48.0
Bank of Canada notes and deposits	10.8	9.4	7.6	7.0	7.0	6.9	6.9	5.3
Treasury bills	2.1	1.4	3.4	6.4	6.8	7.2	6.9	6.7

Source: Bank of Canada, *Statistical Summary, 1969 Supplement,* 22-3, and earlier issues.

The composition of chartered bank investment portfolios during the postwar period is shown in Table XX and indicates many of the trends observed in other institutions as well as some unique features. In a manner similar to the life insurance, trust and mortgage loan companies, the banks ran down their government bond holdings after the war from 46 per cent in 1946 to 14.8 per cent in 1957 and 9.6 per cent in 1969, primarily replacing these securities with treasury bills and general loans. Bank mortgage holdings rose from nil in 1953 to 7.2 per cent of total major assets in 1959, before declining to 3.5 per cent in early 1967 as a consequence of their withdrawal from the market. In 1969 mortgages rebounded slightly to 4.3 per cent of total assets, with NHA mortgages accounting for 3.2 per cent and conventional mortgages 1.1 per cent.

(e) Other lending institutions

Other lending institutions refer to Quebec savings banks, mutual benefit and fraternal societies.[32] These institutions do not exert much influence upon the national mortgage market, but they do exercise considerable influence in selected local and regional markets and in 1968-9 they held 2.4 per cent of outstanding institutionally held mortgage debt and initiated 4.6 per cent of new institutional mortgage loans. As a group these institutions have devoted approximately 40 per cent of their portfolios to mortgages since 1965, up from just over 20 per cent in 1961.

The most important institutions in this group are the Quebec savings banks which held 79 per cent of the mortgages and 69 per cent of the assets in the group in 1969. In 1969, 50.0 per cent of their investment portfolio was devoted to mortgages, 48.5 per cent to conventional mortgages, up from 2.0 per cent in 1952 and 29.7 per cent in 1963. During this period their holdings of government securities fell steadily from 43.8 per cent to 6.4 per cent and their holdings of all other bonds from 40.9 per cent to 22.7 per cent.

7
Econometric Analysis of the Mortgage Market

A. FINANCIAL INSTITUTION MORTGAGE SUPPLY FUNCTIONS

(a) The model

The model of financial institution investment behaviour described in the first section of chapter 6 may be summarized in functional form with respect to mortgage lending as follows.[1] At any given time a financial institution is assumed to have some desired mortgage portfolio target (M^*), and it makes investments so as to reduce the discrepancy between its desired mortgage holdings (M^*) and its actual mortgage holdings (M). The rate at which it reduces this discrepancy, or its speed of adjustment, is γ.[2]

(1) $\quad M - M_{t-1} = \gamma(M^* - M_{t-1})$.

Since an institution's portfolio target (M^*) is not directly observable, the target is generally assumed to depend upon the yield (RM) and other attributes (ZM) of mortgage investments compared to the yield (RB) and other attributes (ZB) of alternative security investments, and the size of the institution's investment portfolio (A). Because bonds are the major alternative to mortgage investments for the non-bank financial institutions included in this study, accounting for an average of approximately 77 per cent of life insurance company non-mortgage assets, 70 per cent of trust company non-mortgage assets and 51 per cent of mortgage loan company non-mortgage assets 1950–69, our model is further simplified by assuming bonds represent the alternative investments to mortgages.

(2) $\quad M^* = f(\text{RM, RB, ZM, ZB, A})$.

Substituting equation 2 into equation 1, gives equation 3.

(3) $\quad M - M_{t-1} = \gamma f(\text{RM, RM, ZM, ZB, A}) - \gamma M_{t-1}$.

This model is an incomplete representation of the mortgage investment process because it ignores the forward commitment procedure whereby mortgages are negotiated many months in advance of the actual disbursement of funds.[3] The introduction of this process necessitates the respecification of the model in terms of decision variables which respond to current economic considerations, i.e., in terms of variables representing the actual commitment of funds, or the reformulation of the lag patterns to reflect the time lag between the commitment and disbursement of funds.[4] In order to avoid the specification of the long and variable lag between commitments and disbursements and because it is the commitment or mortgage approval which most directly influences the construction decision, financial institution mortgage lending behaviour is represented by the volume of their mortgage approvals (MA).

Because the volume of mortgage approvals is a gross rather than a net concept, the use of mortgage approvals as the dependent variable necessitates a respecification of the model to allow for expected principal repayments (PR^e). Expected principal repayments enter the investment decision since an institution must not only approve a sufficient volume of mortgages to close the gap between its desired and existing mortgage holdings, but also to replenish the portion of its existing holdings that will be repaid in the current period. Hence, the investment function becomes

(4) $\quad MA = \gamma(M^* - M_{t-1}) + \delta PR^e.$

A further complication arising from the forward commitment procedure is the existence of outstanding mortgage commitments, i.e., mortgages previously approved and not yet disbursed.[5] These outstanding commitments may enter the investment decision at the portfolio determination stage if investment managers seek to obtain some stock of mortgage commitments to generate future mortgage flows sufficient to reach their portfolio targets. In this case mortgage approvals arise both to generate optimum mortgage holdings after accounting for principal repayments and the takedown of previously committed but undisbursed funds (which is a function of past outstanding commitments), and to generate the desired stock of outstanding commitments (COM*) after accounting for the disbursement of past commitments. Consequently, we get a new investment function in equation 5

(5) $\quad MA = \gamma(M^* - M_{t-1}) + \delta PR^e - \beta COM_{t-1} + a(COM^* - COM_{t-1}) + \beta COM_{t-1}.$

If we assume outstanding commitments are desired to provide the optimum mortgage stock in the future, then the target outstanding commitments is a function of the desired mortgage stock, the actual mortgage stock, and the expected principal repayments.

(6) $\quad COM^* = g(M^* - M_{t-1}) + p\, PR^e.$

Because quarterly repayment and disbursement data are not available except for life insurance companies further assumptions are required with respect to expected repayments and outstanding commitments. Expected mortgage repayments are assumed to be proportional to existing mortgage holdings for an institution. Studies by Pesando on the flows of funds into United States life insurance companies, for which good data are available, suggest that the mortgage rate is also of significance in affecting repayments, especially repayments in full,[6] but that the size of their existing mortgage holdings is the most important influence.[7] To avoid further complications our specification ignores this interest sensitivity.

(7) $\quad PR^e = \theta\, M_{t-1}.$

Outstanding mortgage commitments may be treated in a variety of ways, the two simplest being to assume they are a constant, and their influence is reflected in the intercept, or that they increase in proportion to existing mortgage holdings. The latter procedure is more realistic, hence, outstanding mortgage commitments are assumed to be proportional to existing mortgage holdings.[8]

(8) $\quad \text{COM} = \phi \, M_{t-1}.$

Substituting equations 2, 6, 7, and 8 into equation 5 gives

(9) $\quad \text{MA} = f(\gamma + ag)[\text{RM, RB, ZM, ZB, A}] - [(\gamma - \delta\theta) + a(g - p\theta)]M_{t-1} - a\phi M_{t-2}.$

Because institutions can alter their outstanding mortgage commitments much more quickly than stock of mortgages the discrepancy between COM* and COM_{t-1} is likely to be small.[9] For simplicity, if we assume this variable (COM* − COM_{t-1}) approximates zero, equation 9 reduces to

(10) $\quad \text{MA} = f\gamma[\text{RM, RB, ZM, ZB, A}] - (\gamma - \delta\theta)M_{t-1}.$

Although the interpretation of the coefficients vary slightly, the basic functional relationship of equations 9 and 10 is

(11) $\quad \text{MA} = f'(\text{RM, RB, ZM, ZB, A}, M_{t-1}).$

assuming the coefficient on M_{t-2} approximates zero.

Re-writing equation 11 in linear form, impounding ZM and ZB in a disturbance μ and expressing interest rates in differential form to alleviate multicollinearity gives equation 12, the basic estimating equation.

(12) $\quad \text{MA} = a + b_1 (\text{RM} - \text{RB}) + b_2 A - b_3 M_{t-1} + M_t.$

(b) The estimated regressions

(i) Total and residential mortgage approvals

In most security markets the multiplicity of debt instruments considerably complicates the selection of the appropriate rate for empirical work, and the mortgage market is no exception. As discussed previously there are two major categories of mortgages in Canada, National Housing Act (NHA) mortgages which are government-insured mortgages with lending terms and yields under government control, and conventional mortgages which do not have government insurance and are essentially free of direct government controls. In order to account for these somewhat different debt instruments two procedures were followed. In this section separate regressions are presented for life insurance company, mortgage loan company and trust company total mortgage approvals and residential mortgage approvals using a mortgage rate variable (RM) which is the average of the conventional (RC) and NHA (RNHA) mortgage rates, i.e., RM = (RC + RNHA)/2. This allows variations in either the conventional or NHA mortgage rate to influence the total mortgage lending activity of an institution. In the next section the conventional and NHA segments of the mortgage market are separated, and regressions are presented for conventional residential and NHA mortgage approvals of each institution. Because the chartered banks were empowered to participate only in the NHA sector of the market during our estimation period only an NHA equation is presented for them.

Alternative non-mortgage investment opportunities (the opportunity cost of mortgage investment) for non-bank financial intermediaries are represented by a bond yield variable (RB) which is a weighted average of the long-term government bond yield and the McLeod, Young, Weir 40 bond average. The weights for the long-term government of Canada, provincial, corporate, municipal, and public utility bonds are approximately in proportion to bonds outstanding, namely 0.5, 0.125, 0.125, 0.125, and 0.125 respectively.[10] Alternative investment opportunities for the chartered banks are represented by the long-term government of Canada bond yield (RLT) although loans are their major alternative investment because of the nominal yield ceiling imposed on bank lending rates during our estimation period and because government bonds represent their major class of bond investment. To allow for lagged interest rate responses our interest rate variables were introduced currently, lagged and in distributed lag form using Almon variables,[11] and the best results selected.

Because life insurance company policy loans vary in response to borrower demands rather than investor preferences, life insurance company portfolio targets are specified in terms of total assets less policy loans (A-PL). Chartered bank and trust company portfolio targets are specified in terms of total assets, and the mortgage loan company target is specified in terms of deposit and debenture liabilities (DEB).[12]

Finally, a dummy variable ADV, taking the values of the asset size of each institution (or DEBDV taking the values of the deposit size for mortgage loan companies) for 1Q'66 to 4Q'67 and zero elsewhere, was introduced to represent the shift in the desired proportion of mortgages to assets that institutions wished to hold after 1966. A number of factors, some applicable to all institutions and others to specific institutions, were responsible for the shifts. These factors include the tying of the NHA mortgage ceiling to the long-term government bond yield in 1966 and formula revision for this tie in 1967, the Bank Act revision in early 1967, the Amendments to the Canadian-British Insurance Companies Act in 1965, the Amendments to the Trust Companies Act and Loan Companies Act in 1965, and the growing concern with inflation by investment managers during this period.

Because it is not theoretically clear whether an additive (linear) or multiplicative (logarithmic) model is the more appropriate specification for financial institution lending behaviour, our model was estimated in both forms. The results for the linear model are presented here because they do not differ significantly from the logarithmic results and they are more easily interpreted.

Table XXI presents the regression results for total institutional mortgage approvals (MA) and Table XXII presents the regression results for institutional residential mortgage approvals (RMA) for life insurance companies, trust companies, and mortgage loan companies using quarterly data 1Q'55 to 4Q'67 and for chartered banks using quarterly data 2Q'54 to 4Q'59. Because our model has properties similar to a distributed lag model, the lagged mortgage stock variable being similar to a lagged dependent variable since the MA variable approximates $\triangle M$, the absence of serial correlation cannot be indicated by the Durbin-Watson statistic.[13]

TABLE XXI
TOTAL MORTGAGE APPROVAL REGRESSION RESULTS (MA)

	Constant	Q1	Q2	Q3	ADV	DEBDV	PL_{t-1}	$(A-PL)$	A	DEB	M_{t-1}	$(RM-RB)_{t-i}$								R^2	$\bar{R}^2$	DW	ρ
												$i=0$	$i=1$	$i=2$	$i=3$	$i=4$	$i=5$	$i=6$	$i=7$				
Life insurance companies																							
21.1a	−381.4	−0.24	62.76	26.66	−0.014			0.095			−0.099	18.12	15.85	13.59	11.32	9.06	6.79	4.53	2.26				
	(4.62)	(0.02)	(5.55)	(2.38)	(7.75)			(2.91)			(1.67)	(2.83)	(2.83)	(2.83)	(2.83)	(2.83)	(2.83)	(2.83)	(2.83)	0.82	0.78	1.38	
21.1b	−412.6	−5.03	56.57	22.75	−0.014			0.187			−0.276	6.54	5.72	4.90	4.09	3.27	2.45	1.63	0.82				
	(2.71)	(0.64)	(6.22)	(2.91)	(4.01)			(3.46)			(2.96)	(0.61)	(0.61)	(0.61)	(0.61)	(0.61)	(0.61)	(0.61)	(0.61)			2.25	0.593
21.1c	−97.76	−7.74	56.61	25.01	−0.019		−2.09		0.180		−0.168	28.35											
	(1.41)	(0.83)	(6.08)	(2.71)	(10.65)		(5.93)		(6.31)		(3.66)	(1.85)								0.88	0.85	1.94	
21.1d	−101.2	−7.77	56.48	24.91	−0.019		−2.09		0.183		−0.172	28.00											
	(1.41)	(0.85)	(6.06)	(2.74)	(10.28)		(5.72)		(6.17)		(3.63)	(1.78)										2.01	0.037
Trust companies																							
21.2a	−128.8	−3.06	27.62	13.94	−0.025				0.151		−0.134	6.84	5.99	5.13	4.28	3.42	2.57	1.71	0.86				
	(3.27)	(0.31)	(2.89)	(1.51)	(5.20)				(4.58)		(2.21)	(1.71)	(1.71)	(1.71)	(1.71)	(1.71)	(1.71)	(1.71)	(1.71)	0.90	0.89	2.22	
21.2b	−128.8	−2.36	28.21	14.33	−0.027				0.146		−0.122	6.94	6.07	5.20	4.33	3.47	2.60	1.73	0.87				
	(3.66)	(0.23)	(3.02)	(1.47)	(5.96)				(4.85)		(2.22)	(1.96)	(1.96)	(1.96)	(1.96)	(1.96)	(1.96)	(1.96)	(1.96)			2.10	−0.128
Mortgage loan companies																							
21.3a	−32.48	12.02	34.51	7.36		−0.023				0.317	−0.240	9.90											
	(1.76)	(2.03)	(5.75)	(1.25)		(3.86)				(5.53)	(4.04)	(1.14)								0.85	0.84	1.89	
21.3b	−32.32	11.98	34.48	7.35		−0.023				0.317	−0.240	9.97											
	(1.71)	(2.06)	(5.75)	(1.26)		(3.74)				(5.40)	(3.95)	(1.12)										1.92	0.034
Chartered banks																							
21.4a*	−528.7	−15.53	38.88	31.78					0.055		−0.165	29.65											
	(4.77)	(1.41)	(3.72)	(3.14)					(5.05)		(3.95)	(1.95)								0.81	0.65	1.87	
21.4b*	−524.2	−15.47	38.94	31.80					0.055		−0.164	29.01											
	(4.59)	(1.43)	(3.72)	(3.20)					(4.87)		(3.82)	(1.86)										1.92	0.039

*The interest rate variable used in these regressions is (RNHA−RLT).

TABLE XXVI
FINANCIAL INSTITUTION NET INFLOW REGRESSION RESULTS

	Constant	Q1	Q2	Q3	A	W	A_{t-1}	DEB_{t-1}	$(A-PL)_{t-1}$	PL_{t-1}	RLT	RLT_{t-1}	$(RPS-R03)$	$(RPS-R03)$	$(R1GIC-R90)$	$(RCH-RPS)_{t-1}$	$(RCH-R90)_{t-1}$	R^2	$\bar{R}^2$	DW	ρ
Life insurance cos. $\Delta(A-PL)$																					
26.1a	−1421.9	105.1	24.7	−19.7		0.60			−0.22			−61.35						0.31	0.25	1.87	
	(2.48)	(2.14)	(0.48)	(0.41)		(2.56)			(2.29)			(1.37)									
26.1b	−1717.8	108.1	32.8	−20.6		0.71			−0.27			−67.13								2.01	0.114
	(2.79)	(2.33)	(0.65)	(0.45)		(2.88)			(2.63)			(1.35)									
26.1c ΔPL	14.0	0.066	1.54	1.63	0.0036					−0.190		4.93						0.62	0.59	1.07	
	(5.19)	(0.10)	(2.56)	(2.59)	(6.91)					(6.99)		(6.20)									
26.1d	12.1	0.18	1.60	1.63	0.0032					−0.171		4.62								2.08	0.477
	(2.83)	(0.40)	(3.15)	(3.61)	(4.32)					(4.62)		(4.40)									
Trust cos.																					
26.2a ΔA	−920.5	121.6	39.1	21.4		0.25	−0.184	−0.074			−78.37				22.11	161.76		0.67	0.53	1.65	
	(3.58)	(6.06)	(1.95)	(1.06)		(3.44)	(3.02)	(1.42)			(2.69)				(0.97)	(1.56)					
26.2b	−1181.9	118.5	41.0	18.9		0.32	−0.249	−0.079			−101.70				27.68	220.57				2.01	0.270
	(3.90)	(6.83)	(2.14)	(1.08)		(3.80)	(3.58)	(1.47)			(2.98)				(1.05)	(2.01)					
Mortgage loan cos. ΔDEB																					
26.3a	−193.8	−17.9	−12.0	−15.6		0.071					−26.85				6.07	26.94		0.44	0.40	1.88	
	(2.05)	(1.92)	(1.30)	(1.69)		(2.33)					(2.14)				(0.58)	(1.86)					
26.3b	−200.2	−17.7	−11.8	−15.5		0.073					−27.62				6.51	25.13				1.97	0.048
	(2.04)	(1.95)	(1.28)	(1.71)		(2.32)					(2.12)				(0.61)	(1.69)					
Chartered banks ΔA																					
26.4a	−457.4	−275.7	−88.9	−154.7		0.35	−0.022				−188.21		93.04	285.68				0.55	0.48	1.99	
	(1.14)	(3.13)	(1.01)	(1.76)		(1.47)	(0.32)				(1.93)		(1.77)	(1.67)							
26.4b	−450.0	−275.9	−89.0	−154.8		0.35	−0.020				−187.08		93.29	283.61						1.98	−0.007
	(1.13)	(3.12)	(1.01)	(1.75)		(1.46)	(0.30)				(1.93)		(1.78)	(1.66)							

Consequently, a Hildreth-Lu transformation was performed for each regression, and the results are presented below the untransformed regressions.[14]

These regressions indicate that Canadian financial institutions generally exhibit considerable interest rate responsiveness in their mortgage investments. This enables them to play an important role in transmitting monetary influences to the residential construction sector. Considerable variability exists in the interest sensitivity of the investment decisions of these institutions, with the chartered banks and life companies being most interest sensitive, trust companies next, and mortgage loan companies least sensitive. In terms of elasticities taken at the means, life insurance companies[15] have an interest elasticity of 0.67, trust companies 0.52, and mortgage loan companies 0.22 for total mortgage approvals, and 0.85, 0.61, and 0.39 respectively for residential mortgage approvals. The chartered banks have an elasticity of 0.92 for residential mortgage approvals.

The ranking of these institutions in terms of relative interest rate responsiveness is not surprising since it is consistent with the traditional view that institutions will be more responsive to varying economic conditions the freer they are from legal, liquidity, and traditional investment constraints. The chartered banks had considerable investment freedom in this period since they were just entering the mortgage market and consequently were not constrained by portfolio balancing or liquidity concerns since their mortgage activities represented only a minor proportion of their total investment activities. A more pertinent constraint for the banks was obtaining the required expertise and market contacts, but since their lending was confined to the government-insured sector their risks were considerably reduced, and their branch network and other activities provided instant contacts. Life insurance companies were also essentially free from legal and liquidity constraints because of their large net cash flows and the long-term nature of life contingency obligations. However, these institutions become concerned about liquidity when rising interest rates increase their policy loan demand, and the negative coefficient greater than one on the PL variable suggests rising loan demand generates extrapolative expectations and a corresponding liquidity build up. When policy loans are included as a separate independent variable the expectational effects it picks up substantially reduce the interest elasticity to 0.24 for total and 0.42 for residential mortgage approvals. These elasticities are likely downward biased because of the collinearity between the policy loan and interest rate variables. At the other extreme, mortgage loan companies, whose investments are virtually confined to mortgages, are likely to be least influenced by varying yields except to the extent that they delay placement of funds, speculating on rising mortgage rates. Trust companies, who have considerable investment freedom but also liquidity constraints, fall in between these positions.

Somewhat more surprising is the fact that for each institution the interest sensitivity for their residential mortgage lending was considerably larger than for their total mortgage lending.

If some assumptions are made concerning the proportion of expected repayments that institutions plan to reinvest in mortgages (δ), the proportion of an institution's mortgage portfolio expected to be repaid in the current period (θ), and if the discrepancy between COM* and COM_{t-1} is assumed to be very small on the grounds that institutions can alter their outstanding commitments quite quickly and that the desired stock of commitments is not growing very quickly, the stock adjustment coefficients in our regressions can be calculated. If we assume that institutions plan to reinvest all their mortgage repayments in mortgages (i.e., $\delta = 1$), that institutions can within a quarter adjust their actual outstanding commitments to their desired level so that the (COM* − COM_{t-1}) variable approaches zero, as in equation 10, and that the chartered banks receive mortgage repayments each quarter equivalent to 2.0 per cent, life insurance companies receive repayments equivalent to 2.1 per cent, trust companies receive repayments equivalent to 4.4 per cent and mortgage loan companies receive repayments equivalent to 3.2 per cent of their total mortgage portfolios (i.e., $\theta = 0.020, 0.021, 0.044,$ and 0.033 respectively),[16] then the chartered banks have a stock adjustment coefficient (γ) of 0.185, the life insurance companies of 0.120, using equation 21.1a, and 0.189 using equation 21.1c, the trust companies of 0.178, and the mortgage loan companies of 0.272 using the ordinary least squares (OLS) estimates.[17] These figures imply that mortgage loan companies require just over 2 quarters, trust companies and the chartered banks approximately 3 quarters, and life insurance companies between 3 and 5 quarters using the estimates from equations 21.1a and 21.1c respectively to remove half the discrepancy between their desired and actual mortgage holdings. These figures also imply an equilibrium desired proportion of mortgages to total assets of 30 per cent for the chartered banks, 85 per cent for the trust companies, between 79 per cent using equation 21.1a and 95 per cent using equation 21.1c for the life insurance companies, and 93 per cent for mortgage loan companies once an adjustment is made to reflect the fact that debentures and deposits were approximately 80 per cent of mortgage loan company total assets over the estimation period.[18] To the extent that (COM*−COM_{t-1}) does not approach zero and $\alpha(g-p\theta)$ is positive, the calculated speeds of adjustment are biased upward and the equilibrium desired proportion of mortgages to total assets is biased downwards.

Because these companies were adjusting their desired proportion of mortgages upward during much of the estimation period, the desired stocks derived from this estimation period are probably an over-estimate and should not be extrapolated into the future without adjustment. Some adjustment is provided by the inclusion of the (ADV) and (DEBDV) dummy variables since their significant negative coefficients indicate that the desired proportion of mortgages to assets (debentures and deposits for mortgage loan companies) declined significantly after 1965. For 1966 and 1967 these proportions became 71 per cent for the trust companies, between 68 and 85 per cent for life insurance companies, and 86 per cent of assets for mortgage loan companies.

(ii) Conventional residential and NHA mortgage approvals
The model developed in equation 12 can also be used to explain financial institution conventional residential and NHA mortgage lending activity. To do so, the model requires modification to reflect the fact that the relevant interest rate variable

representing the relative desirability of conventional mortgage investment compared to bond investment is the conventional mortgage-bond yield differential (RC − RB), and representing the relative desirability of NHA mortgage investment to bond investment is the NHA mortgage-bond yield differential (RNHA − RB). Moreover, since conventional and NHA mortgages are investment substitutes for each other, the conventional mortgage–NHA mortgage yield differential (RC − RNHA) should be included in both the conventional and NHA functions. If these modifications are made the basic conventional residential mortgage approval (CRMA) and NHA mortgage approval (NHAMA) estimating equations become equations 13 and 14 respectively.

(13) $\quad \text{CRMA} = a + b_1(\text{RC}-\text{RB}) + b_2(\text{RC}-\text{RNHA}) + b_3 A - b_4 M_{t-1}.$

(14) $\quad \text{NHAMA} = a + b_1(\text{RNHA}-\text{RB}) - b_2(\text{RC}-\text{RNHA}) + b_3 A - b_4 M_{t-1}.$

Ideally, the lagged mortgage stock variable in these equations should be the institution's conventional residential and NHA lagged mortgage holdings. However, these data are not available quarterly for the estimation period and consequently the assumption was made that the non-yield investment properties were sufficiently similar that institutional portfolio targets were expressed in terms of total mortgage holdings, thus permitting the use of lagged total mortgage holdings in both equations.

The estimated regressions for conventional residential mortgage approvals are presented in Table XXIII and for NHA mortgage approvals in Table XXIV. All regressions were estimated using quarterly observations 1Q'55 to 4Q'67.

These regression results indicate that financial institution conventional residential and NHA mortgage lending were influenced by the yield differential between conventional and NHA mortgages as well as by variations in the relative yield between mortgages and alternative bond investments. The opposite sign of the conventional–NHA mortgage yield differential in the non-bank financial institution conventional and NHA regressions indicates the substitutability of these mortgage investments for one another, and the importance of their relative yields in the investment process. The higher negative coefficient on this yield differential in the NHA regressions indicates that there is not a "one to one" shifting between these classes of mortgages. This suggests that some shifting takes place between NHA and conventional non-residential mortgage investment when this yield spread shifts. The insignificance of this yield differential, although it has the appropriate sign, in the mortgage loan company conventional mortgage approval regression is not surprising in view of the relatively minor role that NHA mortgages play in their investment portfolios. NHA mortgages averaged only 6 per cent of total mortgage loan company investment portfolios during the estimation period compared to almost 70 per cent for conventional mortgages. The small proportion of NHA mortgages in mortgage loan company portfolios probably also explains the failure of the stock adjustment specification in the transformed mortgage loan company NHA regressions, equations 24.3b and 24.3d.

The significance of the conventional–NHA mortgage yield spread in the allocation of funds between these categories of mortgage investments was further tested by

TABLE XXIII
CONVENTIONAL RESIDENTIAL MORTGAGE APPROVAL REGRESSIONS (CRMA)

	Constant	Q1	Q2	Q3	ADV	DEBDV	(A−PL)	A	DEP	M_{t-1}	RC−RNHA	\multicolumn{8}{c}{$(RC-RB)_{t-i}$}	R^2	$\bar{R}^2$	DW	ρ
												$i=0$	$i=1$	$i=2$	$i=3$	$i=4$	$i=5$	$i=6$	$i=7$				
Life insurance companies																							
23.1a	−279.4	−0.82	26.25	14.18	−0.0098		0.044			−0.022	22.63	10.16	8.89	7.62	6.35	5.08	3.81	2.54	1.27	0.83	0.82	1.60	
	(3.33)	(0.10)	(3.05)	(1.69)	(5.74)		(1.65)			(0.48)	(1.40)	(1.93)	(1.93)	(1.93)	(1.93)	(1.93)	(1.93)	(1.93)	(1.93)				
23.1b	−265.8	−2.20	24.06	12.93	−0.0092		0.066			−0.068	20.10	6.46	5.65	4.85	4.04	3.23	2.42	1.62	0.81			2.01	0.319
	(2.34)	(0.30)	(2.94)	(1.82)	(4.02)		(1.92)			(1.15)	(1.11)	(0.95)	(0.95)	(0.95)	(0.95)	(0.95)	(0.95)	(0.95)	(0.95)				
23.1c	−203.0	−0.65	27.37	14.22	−0.0089		0.048			−0.039	32.95	12.49								0.81	0.80	1.43	
	(2.64)	(0.07)	(3.07)	(1.63)	(5.15)		(1.77)			(0.83)	(2.12)	(0.81)											
23.1d	−216.9	−2.75	23.37	12.34	−0.0085		0.078			−0.097	21.66	4.75										2.03	0.430
	(2.04)	(0.39)	(2.91)	(1.80)	(3.39)		(2.00)			(1.46)	(1.20)	(0.24)											
Trust companies																							
23.2a	−94.4	0.51	17.22	11.84	−0.013			0.064		−0.041	9.65	5.43	4.75	4.07	3.39	2.71	2.03	1.36	0.68	0.86	0.85	1.59	
	(2.72)	(0.08)	(2.91)	(2.05)	(3.92)			(2.02)		(0.78)	(0.78)	(1.97)	(1.97)	(1.97)	(1.97)	(1.97)	(1.97)	(1.97)	(1.97)				
23.2b	−85.7	0.25	16.88	11.53	−0.011			0.067		−0.050	10.26	4.52	3.96	3.39	2.83	2.26	1.70	1.13	0.57			1.90	0.237
	(2.12)	(0.04)	(2.93)	(2.24)	(2.99)			(2.20)		(0.93)	(0.80)	(1.34)	(1.34)	(1.34)	(1.34)	(1.34)	(1.34)	(1.34)	(1.34)				
Mortgage loan companies																							
23.3a	−42.1	7.49	25.32	7.33		−0.018			0.215	−0.152	1.71	10.55								0.83	0.81	1.98	
	(2.14)	(1.45)	(4.88)	(1.47)		(3.37)			(3.86)	(2.66)	(0.19)	(1.34)											
23.3b	−42.7	7.53	25.34	7.34		−0.018			0.216	−0.152	1.87	10.69										1.96	−0.021
	(2.21)	(1.45)	(4.89)	(1.46)		(3.44)			(3.93)	(2.70)	(0.21)	(1.38)											

TABLE XXIV
NHA MORTGAGE APPROVAL REGRESSIONS (NHAMA)

	Constant	Q1	Q2	Q3	(A−PL)	A	DEP	M_{t-1}	RC−RNHA	$(RNHA-RB)_{t-i}$								R^2	$\bar{R}^2$	DW	ρ
										$i=0$	$i=1$	$i=2$	$i=3$	$i=4$	$i=5$	$i=6$	$i=7$				
Life insurance companies																					
24.1a	32.87	−3.47	28.46	11.57	0.014			−0.029	−44.21		18.46							0.80	0.67	1.42	
	(1.66)	(0.70)	(5.68)	(2.37)	(1.43)			(1.60)	(5.69)		(2.68)										
24.1b	44.24	−3.86	28.56	11.91	0.013			−0.029	−47.56		14.98									2.01	0.318
	(1.79)	(0.93)	(6.07)	(2.92)	(1.15)			(1.35)	(5.33)		(1.91)										
Trust companies																					
24.2a	−12.43	−3.96	4.89	1.64		0.060		−0.084	−27.67	1.91	1.67	1.43	1.19	0.95	0.72	0.48	0.24	0.53	0.51	2.08	
	(0.39)	(0.53)	(0.65)	(0.22)		(2.22)		(1.84)	(1.81)	(0.69)	(0.69)	(0.69)	(0.69)	(0.69)	(0.69)	(0.69)	(0.69)				
24.2b	−16.83	−3.82	5.00	1.48		0.064		−0.090	−24.53	1.98	1.73	1.48	1.24	0.99	0.74	0.49	0.25			1.97	−0.085
	(0.57)	(0.49)	(0.67)	(0.19)		(2.48)		(2.07)	(1.66)	(0.78)	(0.78)	(0.78)	(0.78)	(0.78)	(0.78)	(0.78)	(0.78)				
24.2c	−50.1	−5.33	5.22	0.94		0.089		−0.133		13.85								0.50	0.49	2.17	
	(3.25)	(0.69)	(0.69)	(0.13)		(4.57)		(3.92)		(1.54)											
24.2d	−48.4	−5.02	5.33	0.87		0.090		−0.134		12.33										2.01	−0.109
	(3.38)	(0.62)	(0.71)	(0.11)		(5.07)		(4.36)		(1.49)											
Mortgage loan companies																					
24.3a	1.43	−0.19	2.57	1.40			0.003	−0.002	−4.02	0.46	0.40	0.34	0.29	0.23	0.17	0.11	0.06	0.43	0.24	1.19	
	(0.43)	(0.21)	(2.84)	(1.53)			(0.34)	(0.29)	(2.36)	(1.30)	(1.30)	(1.30)	(1.30)	(1.30)	(1.30)	(1.30)	(1.30)				
24.3b	−8.28	−0.61	3.27	2.26			−0.029†	0.029†	3.83†	1.89	1.66	1.42	1.18	0.95	0.71	0.47	0.24			2.00	0.900
	(1.06)	(1.21)	(5.72)	(4.39)			(2.52)	(2.50)	(2.09)	(2.13)	(2.13)	(2.13)	(2.13)	(2.13)	(2.13)	(2.13)	(2.13)				
24.3c	−3.52	−0.31	2.91	1.89			0.014	−0.013		0.71	0.62	0.53	0.44	0.35	0.27	0.18	0.09	0.35	0.14	0.93	
	(1.27)	(0.33)	(3.10)	(2.01)			(1.82)	(1.71)		(2.01)	(2.01)	(2.01)	(2.01)	(2.01)	(2.01)	(2.01)	(2.01)				
24.3d	−5.17	−0.31	3.02	1.86			−0.021†	0.022†		1.20	1.05	0.90	0.75	0.60	0.45	0.30	0.15			1.93	0.754
	(0.91)	(0.58)	(4.99)	(3.59)			(1.81)	(1.93)		(1.56)	(1.56)	(1.56)	(1.56)	(1.56)	(1.56)	(1.56)	(1.56)				

*This variable is lagged one quarter in the mortgage loan company equations – equations 24.3a – 24.3d.
†This variable has the wrong sign.

regressing the ratio of conventional residential to NHA mortgage approvals against this yield differential, as specified in equation 15.

(15)   CRMA / NHAMA = f(RC-RNHA).

The regression results are presented in Table XXV and indicate that this yield spread is clearly significant for life insurance companies and trust companies, and is significant at the 10–15 per cent confidence level for mortgage loan companies. The model was also specified to include the lagged bond rate on the hypothesis that when economic activity increases conventional residential mortgage lending also increases relative to NHA lending because lenders expect the NHA rate will shortly be adjusted upward, and NHA mortgages will become relatively more attractive in the future.

The preceding analysis indicates that both the yield spread between mortgages and non-mortgage alternative security investments and between the conventional and NHA categories of mortgage investments significantly influence financial institution conventional and NHA mortgage investment decisions.

B. FLOWS OF FUNDS INTO FINANCIAL INSTITUTIONS

(a) The model

Because the asset size of financial institutions exerts a highly significant influence on the volume of mortgage lending activity undertaken by these institutions, the factors affecting asset size are examined briefly in this section. Our interest here is not to develop a complete model of the allocation of financial savings, but rather to examine the interest sensitivity of inflows of funds into financial institutions engaged in mortgage lending in order to determine the interest sensitivity of mortgage flows.[19]

The basic approach in this section is to assume that the net change in asset size ($\triangle$A), and hence the asset size, of a financial institution depends upon the willingness of the public to hold the obligations issued by an institution. This demand for an institution's obligations is assumed to be characterized by a typical stock adjustment model and to depend upon the wealth of the public (W), represented by permanent real disposable income calculated by applying an 8 quarter geometrically declining moving average, the yield offered by an institution on its obligations (RI) relative to the yield on competing securities (RJ), and the amount of this obligation held by the public at the end of the previous period.[20]

(16) $\triangle$A = f(RI, RJ, W, A$_{-1}$).

Because the inflow variable in the mortgage loan company mortgage regressions is debentures and deposit liabilities, a change in debenture and deposit liabilities ($\triangle$DEB) equation is specified for mortgage loan companies.

In addition to a net change in asset equation for life insurance companies, a change in policy loan equation is also shown since policy loans are the most interest sensitive component of life insurance company net change in assets, and since policy loans appear as a separate variable in equation 21.1c. Because the

TABLE XXV
RATIO OF CONVENTIONAL RESIDENTIAL TO NHA MORTGAGE APPROVAL REGRESSIONS (CRMA/NHAMA)

	Constant	Q1	Q2	Q3	(RC–RNHA)	RB$_{t-1}$	R^2	$\bar{R}^2$	DW	ρ
Life insurance companies										
25.1a	1.96 (1.11)	−2.16 (1.60)	−2.99 (2.20)	−2.68 (2.01)	5.71 (2.83)		0.26	0.15	0.86	
25.1b	−0.84 (0.41)	−1.34 (1.63)	−2.25 (2.39)	−2.54 (3.28)	9.68 (4.29)				2.21	0.650
25.1c	−12.95 (4.09)	−1.48 (1.37)	−2.26 (2.07)	−2.30 (2.17)	7.48 (4.54)	2.62 (5.26)	0.54	0.47	1.30	
25.1d	−14.38 (3.19)	−1.28 (1.49)	−2.03 (2.08)	−2.27 (2.74)	9.10 (4.61)	2.66 (3.57)			2.00	0.387
Trust companies										
25.2a	−10.98 (1.41)	9.02 (1.52)	2.61 (0.44)	−0.65 (0.11)	23.12 (2.59)		0.16	0.13	1.80	
25.2b	−10.64 (1.31)	9.05 (1.59)	2.55 (0.43)	−0.66 (0.12)	22.65 (2.39)				2.00	0.096
25.2c	−22.18 (1.26)	9.54 (1.58)	3.16 (0.52)	−0.37 (0.06)	24.44 (2.67)	1.97 (0.71)	0.17	0.14	1.80	
25.2d	−22.59 (1.18)	9.55 (1.66)	3.13 (0.52)	−0.36 (0.06)	24.08 (2.48)	2.10 (0.69)			2.00	0.093
Mortgage loan companies										
25.3a	21.16 (0.51)	11.24 (0.35)	−38.06 (1.18)	−20.87 (0.66)	55.31 (1.15)		0.09	0.03	1.56	
25.3b	15.28 (0.33)	12.58 (0.44)	−36.89 (1.20)	−20.73 (0.75)	63.27 (1.17)				1.98	0.225
25.3c	−103.49 (1.12)	16.95 (0.53)	−31.96 (1.00)	−17.75 (0.57)	70.07 (1.45)	21.90 (1.50)	0.13	0.07	1.62	
25.3d	−108.86 (0.99)	17.11 (0.59)	−31.20 (1.00)	−17.66 (0.63)	76.26 (1.41)	22.05 (1.25)			1.96	0.190

ability of the public to obtain policy loans depends upon the cash surrender value of their insurance in force, which is assumed to vary proportionately with life company assets, variations in policy loan holdings (PL) are assumed to depend upon existing life insurance company assets (AL), the interest rate on alternative sources of funds (RJ), and the amount of outstanding policy loans at the end of the preceding period. No policy loan cost variable was included in the specification because the policy loan borrowing rate was fixed at 6 per cent.

(17) $\quad \triangle \text{PL} = f(\text{AL}, \text{RJ}, \text{PL}_{t-1})$.

(b) The estimated regressions
The regression results for the change in asset size for life insurance companies, trust companies, and chartered banks, the change in debenture and deposit size for mortgage loan companies, and change in policy loans for life insurance companies are shown in Table XXVI. Regressions using both ordinary least squares and the Hildreth-Lu transformation procedure are shown for all regressions. All regressions used quarterly data 1Q'1955 to 4Q'1967.

The interest rates used in these regressions are as follows:
(1) Life insurance companies: (RLT), the long-term government of Canada bond yield was used in both the net change in asset and policy loan regressions. No other rates were included since the rate implicit in life contingency contract premiums is unobtainable, and since the rate on policy loans was a constant.
(2) Trust companies: (RCH – RPS), the trust and mortgage loan company chequable deposit rate minus the chartered bank personal savings deposit rate; (R1GIC –R90), the one-year GIC and debenture rate minus the chartered bank 90-day term deposit rate; and (RLT), the long-term government bond yield.
(3) Mortgage loan companies: (R1GIC – R90), the one-year GIC and debenture rate minus the chartered bank 90-day term deposit rate; (RCH – R90), the trust and mortgage loan company chequable deposit rate minus the chartered bank 90-day term deposit rate; and (RLT), the long-term government bond yield.
(4) Chartered banks: (RPS – R03), the chartered bank personal savings deposit rate minus the zero-to-three-year government bond rate; (R90 – R03), the chartered bank 90-day term deposit rate minus the zero-to-three-year government bond rate; and (RLT), the long-term government bond yield.

These regression results indicate that the inflows of funds into financial institutions are sensitive to monetary conditions. The life insurance company regressions indicate that net inflows of funds and policy loan demand are influenced by the return on alternative investments (in the asset equation) and the cost of alternative sources of funds (in the policy loan equation), where these alternative rates are represented by the long-term bond yield. The trust company regression indicates that the demand for trust company obligations is significantly influenced by the rates paid by trust companies for deposits and guaranteed investment certificates relative to the chartered bank personal savings deposit and 90-day term deposit rates and other market yields represented by the long-term government bond yield. The mortgage loan company regression indicates that the demand

TABLE XXVI
FINANCIAL INSTITUTION NET INFLOW REGRESSION RESULTS

	Constant	Q1	Q2	Q3	A	W	A_{t-1}	DEB_{t-1}	$(A-PL)_{t-1}$	PL_{t-1}	RLT	RLT_{t-1}	(RPS–R03)	(R90–R03)	(R1GIC–R90)	(RCH–RPS)$_{t-1}$	(RCH–R90)$_{t-1}$	R^2	$\bar{R}^2$	DW	ρ
Life insurance cos. $\Delta(A-PL)$																					
26.1a	−1421.9	105.1	24.7	−19.7		0.60			−0.22			−61.35						0.31	0.25	1.87	
	(2.48)	(2.14)	(0.48)	(0.41)		(2.56)			(2.29)			(1.37)									
26.1b	−1717.8	108.1	32.8	−20.6		0.71			−0.27			−67.13								2.01	0.114
	(2.79)	(2.33)	(0.65)	(0.45)		(2.88)			(2.63)			(1.35)									
26.1c ΔPL	14.0	0.066	1.54	1.63	0.0036					−0.190		4.93						0.62	0.59	1.07	
	(5.19)	(0.10)	(2.56)	(2.59)	(6.91)					(6.99)		(6.20)									
26.1d	12.1	0.18	1.60	1.63	0.0032					−0.171		4.62								2.08	0.477
	(2.83)	(0.40)	(3.15)	(3.61)	(4.32)					(4.62)		(4.40)									
Trust cos. ΔA																					
26.2a	−920.5	121.6	39.1	21.4		0.25	−0.184	−0.074			−78.37			22.11	161.76			0.67	0.53	1.65	
	(3.58)	(6.06)	(1.95)	(1.06)		(3.44)	(3.02)	(1.42)			(2.69)			(0.97)	(1.56)						
26.2b	−1181.9	118.5	41.0	18.9		0.32	−0.249	−0.079			−101.70			27.68	220.57					2.01	0.270
	(3.90)	(6.83)	(2.14)	(1.08)		(3.80)	(3.58)	(1.47)			(2.98)			(1.05)	(2.01)						
Mortgage loan cos. ΔDEB																					
26.3a	−193.8	−17.9	−12.0	−15.6		0.071					−26.85			6.07		26.94		0.44	0.40	1.88	
	(2.05)	(1.92)	(1.30)	(1.69)		(2.33)					(2.14)			(0.58)		(1.86)					
26.3b	−200.2	−17.7	−11.8	−15.5		0.073					−27.62			6.51		25.13				1.97	0.048
	(2.04)	(1.95)	(1.28)	(1.71)		(2.32)					(2.12)			(0.61)		(1.69)					
Chartered banks ΔA																					
26.4a	−457.4	−275.7	−88.9	−154.7		0.35	−0.022				−188.21		93.04	285.68				0.55	0.48	1.99	
	(1.14)	(3.13)	(1.01)	(1.76)		(1.47)	(0.32)				(1.93)		(1.77)	(1.67)							
26.4b	−450.0	−275.9	−89.0	−154.8		0.35	−0.020				−187.08		93.29	283.61						1.98	−0.007
	(1.13)	(3.12)	(1.01)	(1.75)		(1.46)	(0.30)				(1.93)		(1.78)	(1.66)							

for their obligations is influenced by the rates paid on deposits and debentures relative to the chartered bank 90-day term deposit rate and other market rates represented by the long-term government bond yield. Finally, the chartered bank regression indicates that the demand for their obligations depends upon their personal savings deposit and 90-day term deposit rates relative to alternative rates represented by the zero-to-three-year and long-term government bond yields.[21]

C. CONVENTIONAL MORTGAGE YIELD DETERMINATION

The supply functions for individual financial institutions can be combined into an aggregate mortgage supply function and equated with the demand function for mortgage credit to determine the mortgage interest rate. Because the NHA mortgage rate was administratively set until November 1966 and then tied (at two different levels) to the long-term government bond yield in 1967 and 1968, this rate is taken to be a government policy variable. The mortgage variable (RM) used in this study is the average of the conventional (RC) and NHA (RNHA) mortgage rates.

(18) $\quad \text{RM} = (\text{RC} + \text{RNHA}) / 2,$

and hence its behaviour partly reflects direct government policy on the NHA component and free market forces on the conventional component. Our attention in this section focuses upon the market determination of the conventional mortgage rate and thereby, for a given government NHA mortgage rate, the mortgage rate.

The total supply of conventional mortgage credit (SCM) can be assumed to vary proportionately with the sum of the supply from the major conventional lending institutions, the life insurance companies, trust companies, and mortgage loan companies. Summing the supply functions of these institutions gives equation 19.

(19) $\quad \text{SCM} = a \sum_{i=1}^{3} \text{CMA}^i = s(\text{RC}, \text{RNHA}, \text{RB}, \sum_{i=1}^{3} \beta_i A^i, \sum_{i=1}^{3} \gamma_i M^i_{-1}),$

where the individual conventional supply functions are given by equation 13 and superscript i refers to the three major lending institutions.[22]

The demand for conventional mortgage credit for residential construction is directly related to the demand for this construction, and is primarily influenced by the same variables as the demand for housing.[23] In addition, the demand for conventional mortgage credit depends upon the cost of this credit relative to the cost of alternative sources of funds, including the opportunity cost of equity financing. This is represented by the cost of NHA financing (RNHA) and the bond yield (RB). For estimation purposes the demand for conventional mortgage credit (DCM) may be summarized as a function of permanent real family disposable income (YD/FAM), the per family stock of dwelling units (SH/FAM), the cost of conventional mortgage credit (RC), and the cost of alternative funds represented by (RNHA) and (RB), as in equation 20

(20) $\quad \text{DCM} = d(\text{YD/FAM}, \text{SH/FAM}, \text{RC}, \text{RNHA}, \text{RB}).$

Equating equations 19 and 20 and solving for RC gives equation 21.

(21) $\text{RC} = r(\text{RB}, \text{RNHA}, \text{YD/FAM}, \text{SH/FAM}, \sum_{i=1}^{3} \beta_i \text{A}^i, \sum_{i=1}^{3} \gamma_i \text{M}^i_{t-1})$.

Because institutions wish to invest different proportions of their investment portfolios in mortgages, a total institutional investment portfolio variable (ALTM) was created by weighting each institution's assets[24] by the average of the coefficients on the institution's portfolio variable in the ordinary least squares (OLS) and Hildreth-Lu regressions presented in Table XXIII.[25] For consistency, these weights were also applied to the mortgage stock variable (MLTM). The total institutional investment portfolio and mortgage stock variables are the weighted sums of life insurance company (L), trust company (T), and mortgage loan company (M) asset and mortgage holdings. The chartered banks are excluded since they did not participate in the conventional mortgage market until 1967.

(22) $\text{ALTM} = 0.055 \,(\text{AL} - \text{PL}) + 0.065 \,\text{AT} + 0.215 \,\text{DEPM}$.

(23) $\text{MLTM} = 0.055 \,\text{ML} + 0.065 \,\text{MT} + 0.215 \,\text{MM}$.

The regression results using ordinary least squares and the Hildreth-Lu procedure with quarterly observations 1Q'55 to 4Q'67 are presented in equations 24 and 25

(24) $\text{RC} = 17.33 - 16.85 \,(\text{SH/FAM})_{t-1} + 3.11 \,(\text{YD/FAM}) - 0.0036 \,\text{ALTM}$
   (7.50)   (7.22)   (2.95)   (3.14)

   $+ 0.0057 \,\text{MLTM}_{t-1} + 0.24 \,\text{RNHA}_{t-1} + 0.54 \,\text{RB}_{t-1}$
   (4.17)   (3.02)   (8.21)

SEE = 0.117, $R^2 = 0.96$, DW = 1.28.

(25) $\text{RC} = 17.97 - 16.84 \,(\text{SH/FAM})_{t-1} + 2.70 \,(\text{YD/FAM}) - 0.0023 \,\text{ALTM}$
   (5.60)   (5.08)   (2.13)   (1.75)

   $+ 0.0043 \,\text{MLTM}_{t-1} + 0.17 \,\text{RNHA}_{t-1} + 0.53 \,\text{RB}_{t-1}$
   (2.52)   (1.89)   (7.02)

SEE = 0.109, $\rho = 0.461$, DW = 1.94.

The significance of the included variables indicates the appropriateness of the specified model for the determination of the conventional mortgage rate. However, despite its nice structure and interpretation, for predictive purposes a simple model in which the conventional mortgage rate is solely a function of the lagged bond rate and change in that rate performs almost as well, although its ordinary least squares standard error of estimate (SEE) is much larger.

(26) $\text{RC} = 3.57 + 0.66 \,\text{RB}_{t-1} + 0.51 \,\triangle \text{RB}$
   (19.43) (18.57)   (3.46)

SEE = 0.198, $R^2 = 0.88$, DW = 0.30.

(27) $\text{RC} = 3.03 + 0.77 \,\text{RB}_{t-1} + 0.40 \,\triangle \text{RB}$
   (5.99) (8.88)   (5.34)

SEE = 0.098, $\rho = 0.476$, DW = 1.54.

D. INTEREST SENSITIVITY OF INSTITUTIONAL MORTGAGE FLOWS

The above analysis indicates the adjustment mechanism by which monetary influences are transmitted to the residential construction sector via the mortgage investment behaviour of mortgage lending institutions. This sensitivity to monetary influences occurs both in the actual portfolio adjustments of and in the flows of funds into these institutions.

In order to obtain an indication of the over-all sensitivity of each institution's mortgage flows to changes in monetary conditions two simulation experiments were run combining the equations for inflows and mortgage approvals. The mortgage approval equations used were the ordinary least squares estimates presented in Table XXI for total mortgage approvals. (The life insurance equation was equation 21.1a.) The inflow equations used were the ordinary least squares estimates presented in Table XXVI for net changes in assets or debentures and deposit liabilities. (The life insurance equation was equation 26.1a for net change in assets minus policy loans.) In addition, the mortgage rate (RM) determination equation was derived from the conventional mortgage rate equation (equation 24) and the mortgage rate identity (equation 18) as

(28) $\text{RM} = 8.67 + 0.50 \text{ RNHA} + 0.12 \text{ RNHA}_{t-1} + 0.27 \text{ RB}_{t-1} - 0.0018 \text{ ALTM}$
$+ 0.0029 \text{ MLTM}_{t-1} - 8.43 \text{ (SH/FAM)}_{t-1} + 1.56 \text{ (YD/FAM)}.$

To complete the model two further relationships were required. First, the relationship between thrift institution obligation rates and the yield on government securities was obtained by regressing the interest rate or interest rate differential appearing in each institution's inflow equation (Table XXVI) upon the current and lagged short-term (zero-to-three-year) government bond yield (R03). The results of these regressions are presented in Table XXVII in a form which indicates the adjustments in thrift institution obligation rates and in RLT and RB to a once and for all increase of two per cent (200 basis points) in the short-term government bond yield. The R^2 in Table XXVII is the R^2 obtained when the obligation rate or rate spread was regressed upon the short-term government bond yield.

TABLE XXVII
ASSUMED AND DERIVED INTEREST RATE ADJUSTMENTS FOR SIMULATION EXPERIMENTS

Yield or yield spread	Period 1	2	R^2
RCH–R90	−0.20	0.20	0.19
RCH–RPS	−0.08		0.69
R1GIC–R90	−0.22	0.04	0.21
RPS–R03	−1.84	0.12	0.86
R90–R03	−2.80		0.06
RLT	0.46	0.30	0.75
RB	0.46	0.30	0.74
R03	2.00		
RNHA experiment 1	0	0.60	
experiment 2	0	0	

Second, a mortgage stock adjustment equation was estimated for each institution to transform mortgage approvals into mortgage holdings. The equation estimated is of the form

$$(29) \quad M - (1-\theta) M_{t-1} = \sum_{i=0}^{n} \beta_i MA_{t-i}.$$

Because values for the parameter θ, the proportion of an institution's mortgage holdings repaid in a period, can be determined outside the model, the model was estimated in the constrained form shown in equation 29. Values of θ for life insurance companies, trust companies and mortgage loan companies were taken as one quarter of the gross annual decrease in the mortgage holdings of each institution less NHA mortgages sold by each institution, divided by the average annual mortgage holdings of each institution over the period 1955 to 1967.[26] The θs so calculated were 0.021 for life insurance companies, 0.044 for trust companies, and 0.032 for mortgage loan companies. The value θ for the chartered banks was set at 0.020, just below that for life insurance companies, since chartered bank repayment experience during this period was not representative because of their lack of mortgage holdings at the beginning of the period.

Equation 29 indicates that the stock of mortgages held by an institution increases with the disbursement of previously approved mortgage loans, and decreases with mortgage repayments. Because of the use of the forward commitment procedure in the mortgage market mortgage disbursements lag mortgage approvals. In the case of new construction loans the lag may be considerable as funds are disbursed in stages during the construction period. Consequently, a distributed lag formulation was used to represent the disbursement of mortgage funds (and hence increase of mortgage stock) arising from mortgage approvals. The coefficients on the current and lagged mortgage approval variables represent the proportion of mortgage approvals made in period $t-i$ disbursed in period t.[27] The distributed lag for mortgage approvals was estimated by the Almon technique

TABLE XXVIII
FINANCIAL INSTITUTION MORTGAGE STOCK ADJUSTMENT REGRESSIONS (DEPENDENT VARIABLE M)

	MA_{t-i}									
	$i=0$	$i=1$	$i=2$	$i=3$	$i=4$	M_{t-1}	R^2	DW	$\Sigma \beta_i$	Average lag
28.1 Life insurance companies	0.261 (3.43)	0.289 (36.95)	0.231 (6.91)	0.133 (4.71)	0.041 (3.93)	0.979	0.80	1.28	0.955	1.38
28.2 Trust companies	0.303 (5.25)	0.341 (18.21)	0.227 (7.60)	0.076 (5.85)		0.956	0.93	1.33	0.947	1.08
28.3 Mortgage loan companies	0.211 (3.43)	0.520 (13.84)	0.237 (9.37)			0.968	0.92	1.01	0.968	1.03
28.4 Chartered banks	0.146 (2.34)	0.553 (14.76)	0.260 (10.84)			0.980	0.79	1.31	0.959	1.12

using second and third degree Almon variables. The estimated results using ordinary least squares are presented in Table XXVIII.[28] The non-bank financial institution equations were estimated over the period 1Q'56 to 4Q'67, and the chartered bank equation was estimated over the period 1Q'56 to 4Q'59.

Since a variety of lag formulations were tried and the statistically "best" presented, the results indicate that there is a somewhat different mortgage disbursement-mortgage approval pattern for each institution. For each institution the proportion of funds disbursed peaks in the quarter after they were approved and then declines. Life insurance companies have the longest average lag, while the other institutions have shorter and approximately the same average lag. The sum of the coefficients of the mortgage approval variables ($\Sigma \beta_i$) represents the proportion of mortgage approvals disbursed. In every case this is less than 1.0, which indicates that not all mortgage approvals generate disbursements. The mortgage attrition rates implied by the regressions in Table XXVIII are 4.5 per cent for life insurance companies, 5.3 per cent for trust companies, 3.2 per cent for mortgage loan companies, and 4.1 per cent for the chartered banks. These rates are highly sensitive to the value of θ, such that $\partial \beta / \partial \theta > 0$, and must be accepted with caution.

The above model is shown in the flow diagram in Figure 10. The feedbacks in the system, all of which involve one-period lags, are indicated by dashed lines. Although the recursive structure of the model simplified its solution, the existence of lagged effects complicates the dynamic structure so that a simple one-period impact multiplier is not very useful by itself. Thus, simulations were run over 8 quarters to illustrate the effect of changes in monetary conditions.

The model simulated consists of the ordinary least squares estimates for (1) financial institution mortgage approvals (Table XXI; the life insurance company equation was 21.1a); (2) financial institution inflow of funds (Table XXVI); (3) the mortgage rate determination equation (equation 28, chapter 7); (4) thrift institution obligation rates and the yield on government securities (Table XXVII); and (5) the mortgage stock (Table XXVIII). In the simulations only monetary effects are considered and no feedbacks are introduced from the real sector.

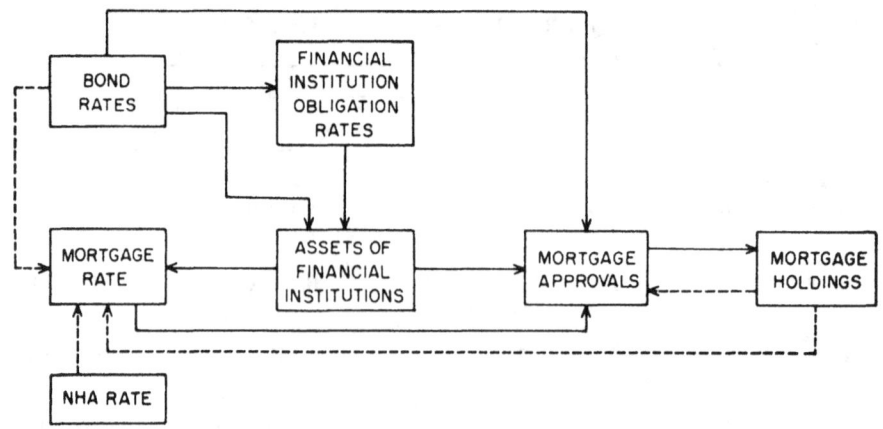

FIGURE 10 Flow diagram of mortgage market model

In chapter 8 simulations are conducted with feedbacks arising in the housing sector.

The model was simulated under two sets of assumptions. In the first simulation the short-term government bond yield was assumed to shift upward by 200 basis points, generating an increase in the long-term government (RLT) and average bond (RB) yields of 46 basis points in the first period and 30 basis points in the second period, and inducing an upward revision in the NHA mortgage rate of 60 basis points in the second period (Table XXVII, experiment 1). In the second simulation the same increases in the bond yields were assumed, but it was assumed there was no change in the NHA mortgage yield (Table XXVII, experiment 2).

The simulation results are presented in Table XXIX. The first set of results, under probably the more realistic assumptions, shows the successive quarter to quarter changes in the mortgage rate and mortgage approvals resulting from the one-shot increase in the short-term government bond rate and subsequent increases in the long-term government and NHA mortgage rates. The impact effects are a reduction in approvals of $72.11 million for the chartered banks, $8.15 million for life insurance companies, $9.27 million for trust companies, and $4.34 million for mortgage loan companies. Life insurance company mortgage approvals decline for three periods and trust company and mortgage loan company approvals for two periods before part of their reductions are reversed, while chartered banks show a quarter to quarter increase in their approvals in the second period. The lagged increases occur as a result of the rise in the mortgage rate and feedbacks from the lagged stock. The different timing in the pattern of adjustments for each institution results from the different lag structures of their portfolio responses to changing investment yields and from different lag structures in the response of the public to changes in their obligation rates. Ultimately, variations in each institution's approval pattern will approach zero.

The first year effects (sum of the cumulative effects of four quarters) of these rate changes are a reduction in approvals of $225.2 million for the chartered banks, $57.8 million for life insurance companies, $50.6 million for trust companies, and $29.0 million for mortgage loan companies. These reductions correspond to approximately a 99 per cent decline in chartered bank average annual mortgage approvals during their estimation period, a 7.9 per cent decline in life insurance company average annual mortgage approvals, a 14.3 per cent decline in trust company average annual mortgage approvals, and a 10.5 per cent decline in mortgage loan company average annual mortgage approvals. Although the chartered bank decline seems unreasonably high, it must be remembered that chartered bank mortgage lending occurred in only six years prior to 1967, and during this period was extremely volatile. Chartered bank mortgage lending rose from zero before the second quarter of 1954 to $327 million in 1955, fell by more than 50 per cent in 1956 to $159 million, and was only $3 million in the first quarter of 1957 as alternative security yields rose, rebounded again in 1958 to $303 million, then fell to $176 million in 1959 and virtually nothing thereafter as alternative security yields rose again. Because of the extreme volatility and unusual circumstances surrounding chartered bank mortgage lending in the nineteen fifties when

TABLE XXIX
MORTGAGE APPROVAL SIMULATION RESULTS, QUARTER TO QUARTER CHANGES

Assumptions	Period	Average mortgage rate (basis points)	Chartered banks ($ million)	Mortgage approval changes		
				Life insurance cos. ($ million)	Trust cos. ($ million)	Mortgage loan cos. ($ million)
Simulation 1						
Change R03 200 basis points	1	1.0	-72.11	-8.15	-9.27	-4.34
	2	43.4	12.59	-7.17	-5.64	-8.01
Change RNHA 60 basis points	3	14.6	7.94	-1.91	1.28	4.48
	4	-0.9	9.58	0.17	0.88	3.45
	5	-0.9	7.89	0.39	1.27	1.72
	6	-0.7	6.32	0.87	1.20	0.88
	7	-0.5	4.91	1.21	1.13	0.41
	8	-0.4	3.78	1.50	1.07	0.29
Simulation 2						
Change R03 200 basis points	1	1.0	-72.11	-8.15	-9.27	-4.34
	2	13.4	-5.21	-12.61	-7.70	-8.01
No change RNHA	3	7.3	8.38	-7.83	-0.93	1.51
	4	-1.1	11.61	-4.64	-0.85	2.86
	5	-1.3	10.56	-3.24	0.04	2.25
	6	-1.2	8.67	-1.55	0.47	1.59
	7	-1.1	6.82	-0.12	0.82	1.02
	8	-1.0	5.28	1.20	1.12	0.61
Annual total change from base period						
Simulation 1	1-4	58.1	-225.21	-57.76	-50.56	-28.98
	5-8	55.6	-103.88	-60.15	-38.99	-7.05
Simulation 2	1-4	20.6	-265.70	-90.73	-62.89	-35.51
	5-8	16.0	-142.15	-149.57	-70.67	-15.50

they first entered the mortgage market, caution must be exercised in interpreting the chartered bank results and in extrapolating these results into the future.

It is interesting to note that, including the feedback effects from the lagged stock variable, changes in institutional investment preferences arising from changing yield differentials accounted for only 10.3 per cent of the first year and 4.7 per cent of the second year chartered bank decline in mortgage approvals, 72.5 per cent of the first year and 68.0 per cent of the second year life insurance company decline in mortgage approvals, 34.9 per cent of the first and 42.7 per cent of the second year trust company decline in mortgage approvals, and 28.0 per cent of the first year and 8.5 per cent of the second year mortgage loan company decline in mortgage approvals. These percentages are shown in Table xxx. In each case the balance of the adjustment arises from the institution's net change in asset or deposit and debenture size.

The second set of simulation results in Table xxix shows the successive quarter to quarter changes in mortgage approvals resulting from the one-shot increase in the short-term government bond rate and the subsequent increases in the long-term government bond yield and financial institution obligation rates, but with the NHA mortgage rate held constant. The simulation results indicate that the first year effects of these changes would be a reduction of chartered bank mortgage approvals of $265.7 million, or approximately 117 per cent of their average annual approvals during their estimation period, a reduction of life insurance company mortgage approvals of $90.7 million or 12.4 per cent of their average annual approvals, a reduction of trust company mortgage approvals of $62.9 million or 17.7 per cent of their average annual approvals, and a reduction of mortgage loan company mortgage approvals of $35.5 million or 12.8 per cent of their average annual mortgage approvals.

Finally, these simulation experiments can be used to derive the simulated elasticities for each institution's mortgage approvals with respect to interest rate changes by comparing each institution's percentage change in their average annual mortgage approvals with the change in the relevant interest yield expressed in terms of the percentage change from its mean. These elasticities are shown in Table xxxi, and indicate that chartered bank mortgage lending is by far the most interest elastic. Trust company mortgage lending is next most interest elastic with respect to bond yield changes, but life insurance company lending is next with respect to NHA mortgage yield changes. Since life insurance companies devote the

TABLE XXX
PROPORTION OF MORTGAGE APPROVAL CHANGES FROM BASE YEAR ARISING FROM CHANGING INVESTMENT YIELDS*

Assumptions	Year	Chartered banks	Life insurance cos.	Trust cos.	Mortgage loan cos.
Simulation 1	1	10.3	72.5	34.9	28.0
	2	4.7	68.0	42.7	8.5
Simulation 2	1	27.7	89.2	48.6	41.2
	2	30.4	92.7	67.9	58.0

*The balance of the adjustment for each institution arises from the changes in their asset size or their deposit and debenture liability size.

TABLE XXXI
SIMULATED MORTGAGE APPROVAL ELASTICITIES OVER TIME WITH RESPECT TO VARIOUS INTEREST RATES

With respect to	Year	Chartered banks	Life insurance cos.	Trust cos.	Mortgage loan cos.
Average bond yield (NHA mortgage yield varies 80% of change in RB)	1	−6.80*	−0.55	−1.01	−0.75
	2	−3.26*	−0.59	−0.79	−0.18
Average bond yield (NHA mortgage yield constant)	1	−8.40*	−0.88	−1.27	−0.92
	2	−4.49*	−1.46	−1.43	−0.40
NHA mortgage yield	1	2.54	0.77	0.59	0.38
	2	1.84	1.42	1.03	0.34

*With respect to long-term government bond yields.

highest proportion of their funds to NHA mortgage lending amongst the non-bank financial intermediaries, the latter result seems reasonable. Life insurance company mortgage lending shows the least interest elasticity with respect to bond yield changes in the first year despite their high investment elasticity because their net inflows of funds are the least interest sensitive.

From the analysis of this chapter it is clear that monetary influences have a substantial influence upon the volume of Canadian financial institution mortgage approvals, influencing both the inflow of funds and portfolio investment decisions of financial institutions. The chartered banks appear to be most strongly influenced both in percentage and absolute terms since both their portfolio decisions and availability of funds are strongly influenced by relative yields. Trust companies who are similarly influenced both through their portfolio decisions and availability of funds rank second in proportionate changes in mortgage approvals although their smaller size means their absolute lending adjustments are slightly less than life insurance companies. Both life insurance companies, whose interest sensitivity is reflected primarily in their investment decisions, and mortgage loan companies, whose interest sensitivity shows primarily in their net inflows, are also quite interest sensitive in their mortgage lending behaviour although they rank behind the other institutions in the proportionate change in their mortgage approvals.

D
Housing and government policy

8
Impacts of Monetary and Fiscal Policy upon Residential Construction

A. INTRODUCTION

Part B of this study examined the structure and operation of the Canadian housing market and indicated the sensitivity of this sector to monetary influences. Part C described the structure and operation of the Canadian mortgage market and analysed the availability and cost mechanisms by which monetary influences are transmitted to the residential construction sector. This part of our study now turns to an examination of the effects of government policy on residential construction. Since most government policies operate via financial variables, much of the discussion is concerned with government impacts on the mortgage market. This chapter focuses upon the implications for housing of general monetary and fiscal policy, and the next chapter focuses upon the implications of the two major government direct housing programmes, the federal loan guarantee and insurance programme and the Central Mortgage and Housing Corporation direct lending programme.

B. CYCLICAL BEHAVIOUR OF RESIDENTIAL CONSTRUCTION

As mentioned in chapter 1, residential construction exerts a significant impact upon the economy through its size, it accounts directly for approximately 4.8 per cent of gross national expenditure and indirectly for an additional 2.5 per cent via induced service investment and consumer durable production, and through its anti-cyclical behaviour. This anti-cyclical behaviour may be seen from Figure 11 which plots a 4 quarter moving sum of total housing starts and privately financed housing starts (i.e., excluding CMHC financed housing starts[1]) against a four quarter moving average of the unemployment rate. Figure 11 indicates that almost all periods of declining housing starts coincided with or occurred shortly after declines in the unemployment rate and with the exception of the 1961 to 1965 expansion in housing starts, virtually all periods of rising housing starts coincided with periods of rising unemployment. The major exception to this anti-cyclical pattern, the 1961 to 1965 expansion in housing starts which occurred during a period of falling unemployment and increasing economic activity, nevertheless took place in a relatively stagnant economy when the unemployment rate averaged approximately 5 ½ per cent. When economic activity recovered to the point where unemployment de-

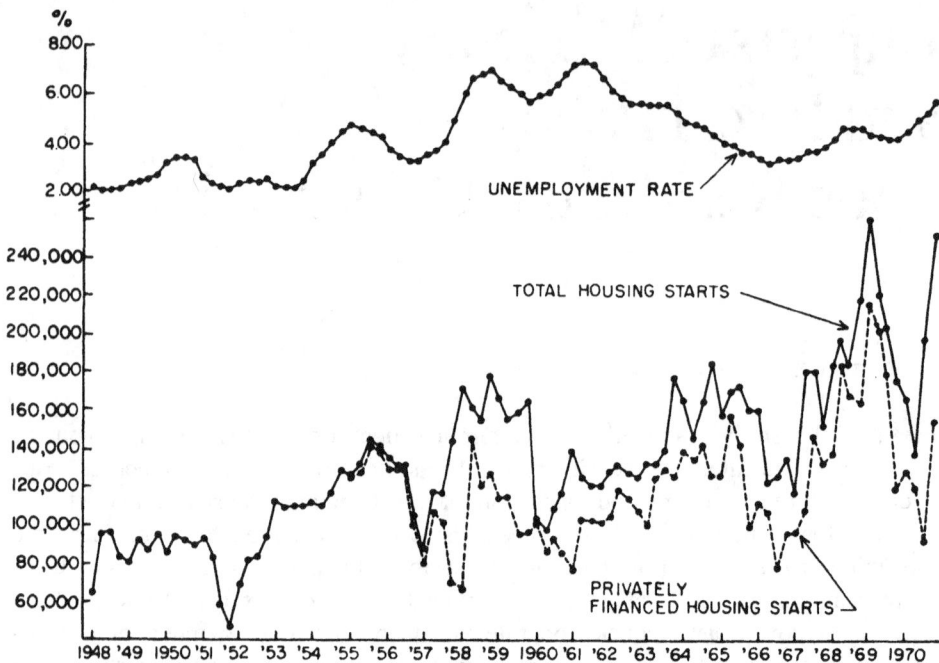

FIGURE 11   Total housing starts, privately financed housing starts, and the unemployment rate, four quarter moving sum, 1948–70

clined to four per cent in 1965–6, housing starts plunged dramatically.

The explanation for this marked anti-cyclical performance of the housing sector has been alluded to in the previous chapters and may be summarized as follows: when economic activity expands the demand for investible funds exerts upward pressures on interest rates. This upward pressure adversely affects the availability of private funds for residential construction both because financial institutions experience a slowdown in their net inflow of funds and because the demand for funds from competing sectors reduces the mortgage-alternative investment yield spread causing financial institutions to reduce the proportion of new investments flowing to the housing sector. At the same time, rising mortgage rates and tightening non-price credit terms reduce the demand for new construction since the demand for residential construction is more interest elastic than is the demand in many competing sectors. These anti-cyclical monetary forces usually outweigh the pro-cyclical income forces causing residential construction to have a tendency to fluctuate in an anti-cyclical fashion. This tendency may be reinforced, retarded or even possibly reversed by discretionary economic policy.

C. MONETARY POLICY

Although monetary policy is not usually designed specifically to influence the volume of residential construction activity, residential construction activity is profoundly influenced by it. In fact, residential construction is probably the sector most significantly affected by monetary policy and it provides one of the major arteries, if not the major one, by which monetary policy is transmitted to the economy.

Monetary policy can significantly influence residential construction by reinforcing or ameliorating existing monetary influences. As mentioned above, residential construction activity generally declines in periods of rising economic activity. This occurs because rising economic activity is usually accompanied by a stronger demand for funds in competing sectors which raises the general level of interest rates, reduces the mortgage yield-bond yield spread, and restrains the flow of funds into financial intermediaries for any given monetary policy. If, during this upswing, the monetary authorities were to follow an expansionary monetary policy the increasing demand for funds by competing sectors could more readily be satisfied, relieving the upward pressure on interest rates and the decline in financial institution mortgage commitments. If, on the other hand, the monetary authorities were to follow a contractionary monetary policy, the upward pressure on interest rates and decline in mortgage commitments would be intensified, contributing to a sharper and more prolonged contraction in residential construction activity. Analogously, in periods of declining or stagnant economic activity the usual expansion in residential construction activity can be intensified by a policy of monetary ease and dampened by a policy of monetary restraint.

In order to obtain an indication of the impact of monetary policy on residential construction and the housing market two simulation experiments were run using the aggregate housing model estimated in chapter 4 and the mortgage market model estimated in chapter 7. The model simulated consists of the ordinary least squares estimates for (1) housing starts (equation 9, chapter 4); (2) housing prices (equation 6, chapter 4); (3) the stock of houses (equation 5, chapter 4); (4) construction costs (equation 11, chapter 4); (5) the mortgage rate (equation 28, chapter 7); (6) financial institution mortgage approvals (Table XXI, the life insurance company equation was 21.1a); (7) financial institution inflow of funds (Table XXVI); (8) the interest rate relationships shown in Table XXVII; and (9) the mortgage stock (Table XXVIII). In addition, to complete the model, an investment in residential construction (IRC) equation (equation 1), was taken from an earlier study,[2] and two identities, equations 2 and 3, were added.

(1) $\text{IRC} = 119.28 + 4.56 \text{ HS} + 1.86 \text{ HS}_{t-1} + 1.01 \text{ HS}_{t-2}$
    (7.11) (17.91)   (7.83)   (3.91)

   1Q'54 – 4Q'67, $R^2 = 0.88$, DW $= 1.06$.

(2) $\triangle \text{YD} \equiv 0.046 \triangle \text{IRC}$.

(3) $\triangle \text{PGNE} \equiv 0.046 \triangle \text{PH}$.

Because CLC and FAM appear in the denominator of ratios, initial values for these variables were required. These variables were initialized at their average values for the estimation period. FAM, average hourly earnings in construction, land costs, CMHC constant dollar lending and the deviation of investment in non-residential construction from its trend were assumed to be exogenous variables and held constant.

In the first simulation monetary restraint was assumed to increase the zero-to-three-year government bond yield by 200 basis points in the first period, generating an increase in the bond yield average (RB) of 46 basis points in the first period and 30 basis points in the second period, and inducing an upward revision in the NHA mortgage rate of 60 basis points in the second period (as in simulation 1, chapter 7). In the second simulation monetary restraint was assumed to cause the same increases in the zero-to-three-year government bond yield and bond yield average, but it was assumed that the NHA mortgage rate was held constant. The results of the simulation experiments for quarter to quarter changes in the average mortgage rate (RM), the price of houses (PH), housing starts (HS) and investment in residential construction (IRC) are presented in Table XXXII.

The first set of simulation results indicates that this more stringent monetary policy together with the increase in the NHA mortgage rate would lead to 16,190 fewer housing starts in the first year and 26,070 fewer starts in the second year compared to the base year. These reductions correspond to a decline of 11.3 per cent and 18.2 per cent respectively in the annual average number of starts during the estimation period. The second set of simulation results indicates that this more stringent monetary policy together with a constant NHA mortgage rate would lead to 13,160 fewer housing starts in the first year and 19,620 fewer starts in the second year compared to the base year. These reductions correspond to a decline

TABLE XXXII
HOUSING MODEL SIMULATION RESULTS, QUARTER TO QUARTER CHANGES

Assumptions	Period	Mortgage rate (basis points)	Housing prices (% change)	Housing starts (thousands)	Investment in residential construction ($ million)
Simulation 1					
Change R03 200	1	1.0	0.0	0.0	0.0
basis points	2	43.4	0.04	−2.80	−12.77
Change RNHA 60	3	14.7	0.16	−3.68	−21.99
basis points	4	−0.6	0.26	−0.43	−11.63
	5	−0.5	0.24	0.26	−3.33
	6	−0.4	0.13	0.14	0.69
	7	−0.4	0.03	0.05	0.75
	8	−0.4	−0.01	0.01	0.28
Simulation 2					
Change R03 200	1	1.0	0.0	0.0	0.0
basis points	2	13.4	0.04	−2.80	−12.77
No change RNHA	3	7.4	0.14	−2.31	−15.74
	4	−0.8	0.20	−0.14	−7.77
	5	−1.0	0.17	0.21	−1.63
	6	−1.0	0.08	0.12	0.80
	7	−1.1	0.01	0.06	0.70
	8	−1.0	0.01	0.06	0.50
		Annual total change from base period			
Simulation 1	1-4	59.5	0.46	−16.19	−93.92
	5-8	57.8	0.85	−26.07	−195.03
Simulation 2	1-4	21.0	0.38	−13.16	−77.56
	5-8	16.9	0.55	−19.62	−147.34

of 9.2 per cent and 13.7 per cent respectively in the annual average. If the simulations were carried further, the third year would show a slight recovery in housing starts compared to the second year as a result of rising house prices caused by the previous contraction in housing starts. If all the variables in our model were treated as endogenous variables in the simulations, the decline in housing starts beginning around period three would be slightly less as reduced non-residential construction activity and land costs would generate a decline in construction costs not captured in our simulations, and thereby boost residential construction activity. Both sets of simulation experiments indicate that monetary policy has a small effect upon housing prices, since housing prices rise 0.46 per cent in simulation 1 and 0.38 per cent in simulation 2 after one year, and 0.85 and 0.55 per cent in simulations 1 and 2 respectively after two years.

The simulation experiments can also be used to derive the elasticity of housing starts with respect to interest rate changes. Because the change in the bond yield average was fourteen per cent of the average bond yield average during the estimation period, housing starts have a simulated elasticity calculated at the means of -0.81 in the first year and -1.30 in the second year assuming the NHA mortgage rate is increased by 60 basis points in the second period, and -0.65 in the first year and -0.98 in the second year assuming no change in the NHA mortgage rate. The second year elasticities are larger absolutely because of the time lags before the full impacts are felt. In both cases the third and following years' elasticities decline successively. Because the increase in the NHA mortgage rate was 9.28 per cent of its average level during the estimation period and housing starts declined by 3030 units or 2.12 per cent in the first year and 6450 units or 4.52 per cent in the second year after the NHA rate was increased, the simulated housing start elasticities are -0.23 in the first year and -0.49 in the second year with respect to the NHA mortgage rate, calculated at the means. These elasticities are all consistent with the simulated mortgage lending elasticities shown in the Table XXXI.

These simulation results indicate that the residential construction sector has been strongly influenced by monetary policy. Under the realistic assumption that the NHA mortgage rate would be adjusted with a lag to changes in monetary conditions, housing starts have an average two-year elasticity of -1.06 with respect to changes in long-term bond yields.

Before we can extrapolate this elasticity into the future we must consider the impact, if any, of the 1969 change in the National Housing Act which allowed the NHA mortgage rate to fluctuate freely and be determined by market forces. This contrasts with the situation during our estimation period when the NHA rate was essentially administratively set by way of an interest ceiling or, after November 1966, tied by a formula to the long-term bond average.

One explanation given by a number of economists for the past anti-cyclical behaviour of residential construction and high sensitivity of this sector to monetary policy is that the interest ceiling on government insured mortgages was responsible for the relative desirability of new mortgage investments, and hence the availability of mortgage credit, varying with monetary conditions and monetary policy.[3] If this argument were correct the removal of the interest ceiling would substantially weaken the relationship between new residential construction and monetary policy. Recent evidence, however, suggests that the interest rate ceiling did not play such a pivotal role in the transmission of monetary policy for three main reasons.[4]

First, the demand for new residential construction is sensitive to the cost and terms of mortgage credit as well as to the availability of mortgage credit. This may be seen from the aggregate housing start equation (equation 9 in chapter 4) since the negative coefficient on the mortgage cost variable is not only highly significant, but its absolute value exceeds that on the credit availability variable. This means that an increase in mortgage rates would have a net negative impact on total housing starts, the negative demand effects outweighing the positive availability effects. A possible explanation for the difference between our results and the fixed rate hypothesis is that single-family dwellings were relatively more important in residential construction during the fifties, when the fixed rate hypothesis was raised. The single housing start equation (equation 31 in chapter 4) shows a larger absolute value of the positive coefficient on the credit rationing variable than the absolute value of the negative coefficient on the mortgage cost variable, indicating that rising mortgage rates have a net positive effect on single dwelling housing starts and that freeing the NHA rate reduces the responsiveness of single dwelling construction to monetary policy. On the other hand, the multiple dwelling housing start equation (equation 32 in chapter 4) shows that the negative mortgage cost effects are much greater than the positive availability effects so that freeing the NHA rate accentuates the responsiveness of multiple starts to monetary policy. On balance, as the aggregate start equation indicates, it appears that the responsiveness to monetary policy may be accentuated slightly by freeing the NHA rate.

Second, institutional impediments in the mortgage market have retarded the speed of adjustment and amplitude of conventional mortgage rate fluctuations even though this rate has been free of interest ceilings.[5] Since it is likely that a free NHA rate will experience the same impediments as the conventional rate, the relative desirability of new mortgage investments is still likely to vary with monetary policy even in the absence of a yield ceiling, although this variability will be less than if a ceiling were operative. Empirical evidence for the smaller amplitude and lagged speed of adjustment of the conventional mortgage rate may be seen from the comparision of interest rates in Figure 2, and from the conventional mortgage rate determination equation (equation 24 in chapter 7) in which the sum of the average bond rate and NHA mortgage rate coefficients are only 0.78 and appear with a one quarter lag. This suggests that if a change in long-term bond yields were fully reflected in the same quarter in the NHA rate, the conventional mortgage rate would adjust by only 78 per cent of the change in bond yields after one quarter. Our simulations indicate the rate will continue to adjust upward through feedback effects, but that over-all the adjustments in this rate lag and have a smaller amplitude than adjustments in bond yields.

Third, it appears that the interest rate ceiling on government insured mortgages did not increase the sensitivity of non-bank financial institution mortgage lending to variations in monetary policy as much as the fixed rate hypothesis implies because of offsets in the conventional sector. These offsets arise because of the tendency for the ceiling to shift the allocation of credit between the conventional and NHA sectors of the mortgage market rather than entirely away from mortgages and into alternative security investments. This is discussed in more detail in the section on the federal loan guarantee and insurance programme in chapter 9.[6]

This analysis suggests that the net effect of the removal of the yield ceiling on NHA mortgages for the effectiveness of monetary policy is likely to be very small, and that if any effect does arise it is likely to be in the direction of increasing the overall sensitivity of residential construction to monetary policy. By sectors, single family construction is likely to be somewhat sheltered and multiple dwelling construction more exposed to monetary policy. Consequently, monetary policy should continue to have a highly significant impact upon residential construction.

D. FISCAL POLICY

Fiscal policy in the form of adjustments in the over-all tax rate and/or expenditure levels has a much smaller impact on residential construction than monetary policy. However, government tax and expenditure policies can and do exert a significant influence upon housing.

Fiscal policy operating by way of a change in the personal tax rate effects residential construction in a number of ways. First, a tax change, by altering personal disposable income, changes the demand for housing services. This alters the price of housing services and thereby the ratio of housing prices or rents to construction costs, affecting the volume of residential construction. Some idea of the magnitudes involved as a result of a given tax change can be deduced from our model. Our model indicates that a one per cent change in per family personal disposable income will generate a 0.83 per cent increase in housing prices and this in turn will increase housing starts by approximately 3 per cent. If we define a typical fiscal policy change as a 5 per cent tax change, i.e., equivalent to a 5 per cent surtax, it is unlikely that a typical policy change will alter housing starts by more than 3 per cent, since a 5 per cent tax change will alter family personal disposable income by 1.03 per cent for a family with $10,000 taxable income and $2500 deductions, and alter family personal disposable income by 1.29 per cent for a family with $15,000 taxable income and $2500 deductions.[7] Second, to the extent that a given policy change is effective, it will influence non-residential construction activity and thereby increase construction costs (equation 11 in chapter 4). If we assume that a 5 per cent tax cut increases construction costs by 0.5 per cent, the net increase in housing starts is reduced to only 1.15 per cent, assuming that rising construction costs do not generate price expectations sufficient to stimulate construction activity and ignoring the feedback effects of increased residential construction activity on construction costs. Third, rising incomes not only increase the demand for housing units, but also the quality of dwelling demanded and, consequently, the impact of fiscal policy must be adjusted upward. In chapter 3 we concluded that the over-all demand elasticity for housing services with respect to income was between 0.6 and 1.0. Since our model (equation 7 in chapter 4) indicates a stock demand elasticity in units of 0.3, the expenditure effects indicated by our model should be increased by approximately $2\frac{1}{2}$ times. Hence, we can conclude that a 5 per cent personal tax cut would increase housing starts by slightly over one per cent, and residential construction expenditures by approximately $2\frac{1}{2}$ per cent.

Fiscal policy operating by way of a change in corporate tax rates also effects residential construction in a number of ways. First, by increasing gross business savings, a tax reduction enables corporations to more easily finance multiple-dwelling construction. Second, by stimulating non-residential construction activity it tends to increase construction costs and thereby retard new housing construction. No separate estimates of the effects of corporate tax changes are included, but they are unlikely to be large unless accompanied by personal tax changes.

Fiscal policy may also operate from the expenditure side through changes in government spending. However, unless these expenditures are direct housing expenditures the effects of the policy operate upon housing via changes in personal disposable income and construction costs and via their monetary effects as described above. Direct government housing expenditures will, of course, have a significant impact upon residential construction activity, but they have been very rare in peacetime as most government housing programmes operate via CMHC direct loans to builders, final users or non-profit and limited dividend groups, or via the federal loan guarantee or insurance programme. Between 1960 and 1970, for example, direct government housing construction averaged only 1415 units a year or 1 per cent of total starts.

In addition to traditional adjustments, fiscal policy can exert a significant influence upon residential construction in a variety of ways. First, changes in capital cost allowance provisions would significantly affect the after tax cash flows and yield of real estate investments vis-à-vis alternative securities and thereby affect residential construction activity from the alternative investment viewpoint.[8] By altering cash flows it would also affect the ability of development companies and investors to undertake new projects. Second, changes in the proportion of municipal revenues raised by realty taxes would affect residential construction activity by changing the relative cost of housing services vis-à-vis other consumer goods and services, thereby affecting the demand for housing services. Third, variations in the sales tax on building materials significantly affect construction costs (equation 11, chapter 4) and thereby residential construction activity. Finally, direct subsidies, as in the winter works programme of 1963–5 which gave a $500 payment per unit to builders of one to four unit dwellings which were substantially completed between December 1 and March 31, can exert a very significant impact on residential construction. According to our aggregate housing start equation (equation 9, chapter 4), the winter works programme was responsible for an additional 8880 housing starts each winter, or an additional 5.5 per cent of total starts annually, if this programme did not shift starts from other periods into the winter.[9]

From this discussion it is evident that residential construction is influenced much more significantly by a typical monetary policy shift than a typical fiscal policy shift, although fiscal policy has an affect upon residential construction activity. If we assume that a typical shift in fiscal policy is represented by a 5 per cent tax change, i.e., a 5 per cent surtax, and a typical shift in monetary policy is represented by a 10 per cent change in the long-term government bond yield, a typical fiscal policy change has approximately one-tenth the impact on housing starts that a typical monetary policy change has.

9
Impacts of Government Direct Housing Programmes[1]

A. FEDERAL LOAN GUARANTEE AND INSURANCE PROGRAMME

(a) *Programme features*
A federal mortgage guarantee or insurance programme has existed in various forms in Canada since 1935. The programme was originally introduced to stimulate residential construction by making mortgage credit available on greatly liberalized terms (lower interest rates, longer amortization periods, and higher loan to value ratios) to stimulate demand. To ensure that adequate funds would be forthcoming under these terms a new debt instrument, the NHA mortgage, was created. The principal features of this instrument were that the federal government would: (*a*) make loans jointly, on a 25–75 per cent basis, with authorized lending institutions; (*b*) provide an interest subsidy and capital guarantee which virtually eliminated all risk of capital and interest loss on funds advanced by institutions; and (*c*) have the right to set the lending terms and conditions under which funds would be advanced.

The main aspects of this programme remained intact until 1954, when the format was radically altered. In that year a National Housing Act revision eliminated the joint loan technique, interest subsidies, and government guarantee, and replaced them with a system of federal loan insurance.[2] Since the government retained the right to determine lending terms that qualified for insurance it remained in a position to exercise considerable influence over the willingness of lenders and borrowers to participate in this market. On November 22, 1966, in response to criticism over its management of lending terms, the government relinquished some of its discretionary authority and tied the NHA interest ceiling $1\frac{1}{2}$ per cent above the yield on long-term government of Canada bonds in the previous quarter.[3] In September 1967 this yield spread was raised to $2\frac{1}{4}$ per cent and on June 27, 1969 the NHA mortgage rate was freed to find its own level in the market. Consequently, what remains is a federal loan insurance programme with the insurance charge lower than institutions would impute for self insurance, and where the government determines the maximum loan amount per dwelling, the maximum loan to value ratio, the maximum and minimum term and amortization period, and the relationship between the borrower's income and gross debt service that qualify for insurance, but not the interest rate that may be charged on such a loan.

Some idea of the subsidy provided by this programme may be seen by comparing the cost of the NHA insurance fee with the present value of the difference in NHA and conventional mortgage interest costs after the NHA mortgage rate was market determined, since the interest spread represents the risk differential or self insurance cost of conventional lending. During 1970 the NHA mortgage rate on home ownership loans was an average of 39 basis points below the prime conventional rate, so that the present value of this differential on a 5-year term mortgage amortized over 25 years was approximately 160 basis points, and on a 25-year term mortgage amortized over 25 years was approximately 270 basis points. Since 58 per cent of NHA mortgages were for 5-year terms, with most of the balance for 25-year terms, there was an average interest saving of approximately 2.24 per cent of the loan amount compared to an insurance fee of 1.0 per cent, and therefore a subsidy of approximately $1\frac{1}{4}$ per cent of the loan amount.

(b) Supply impacts

(i) Long run
The supply of private mortgage credit for new residential construction comes primarily from financial institutions and, as discussed in part C, depends to a large extent upon the desirability of mortgages as an investment compared with alternative investment opportunities. By creating a virtually risk free investment and setting the charge for absorbing these risks below what lenders would normally incorporate in their calculation for making an uninsured loan, the loan guarantee and insurance programmes have greatly increased the long run desirability of mortgage investments. From 1946 to 1970 the proportion of mortgages in non-bank financial institution investment portfolios rose from just under 18 per cent to over 55 per cent, and NHA mortgage holdings rose from one per cent to over 12 per cent.

Of course not all this increase in NHA lending represents a net addition to mortgage availability because of the investment substitutability that exists between NHA and conventional mortgages. However, NHA and conventional mortgages are not perfect substitutes for one another, as is demonstrated in Table XXXIII by the different inter-institutional time patterns for NHA and conventional mortgage investment. From 1946 to 1956 life insurance companies strongly preferred NHA to conventional mortgage investments and their NHA holdings rose from 1.6 per cent to 19.8 per cent of total assets while conventional holdings rose only from 10.4 per cent to 20.7 per cent. From 1962 to 1970 their preferences strongly shifted to conventional mortgages which rose from 24.7 per cent in 1962 to 36.6 per cent of total assets in 1970, while NHA mortgages declined from 19.5 per cent to 13.8 per cent. Trust companies who, in contrast, showed very little interest in NHA mortgages prior to the National Housing Act revision of 1954, demonstrated a strong preference for NHA mortgages from 1954 to 1963, and their NHA holdings rose from 0.6 per cent of total assets to 13 per cent while conventional holdings rose only from 27.5 per cent to 35.3 per cent. After 1962 they also shifted toward conventional mortgages as their conventional mortgage holdings rose from

TABLE XXXIII
MORTGAGE HOLDINGS OF NON-BANK FINANCIAL INSTITUTIONS AS A
PERCENTAGE OF TOTAL ASSETS, 1946-70

Year	Life insurance companies*			Trust companies			Mortgage loan companies		
	NHA	Conv.	Total	NHA	Conv.	Total	NHA	Conv.	Total
1946	1.6	10.4	12.0	0.3	22.5	23.2	0.4	52.1	52.5
1950	7.2	15.6	22.8	0.5	25.2	25.9	3.8	65.7	69.5
1954	15.7	17.2	32.9	0.6	27.5	28.1	6.2	68.7	75.0
1956	19.8	20.7	40.5	4.5	31.7	36.2	7.4	70.7	78.1
1958	18.9	23.4	42.3	5.6	30.2	35.8	7.9	68.8	75.7
1962	19.5	24.7	44.2	11.2	33.4	44.6	6.0	70.1	76.1
1966	16.0	34.6	50.6	12.7	43.0	55.7	5.0	71.4	76.4
1968	13.8	37.7	51.5	11.0	43.7	54.7	5.1	70.0	75.1
1970	13.8	36.6	50.4	10.4	47.9	58.3	9.1	64.2	73.3

*Prior to 1960, figures are based on 12 life insurance companies
Source: Central Mortgage and Housing Corporation, *Economic Research Bulletin*, no. 77 (R) (Ottawa 1971); CMHC, *Canadian Housing Statistics* (1970), 62-3; and Bank of Canada, *Statistical Supplement* (1968), 106-14.

33.4 per cent to 47.9 per cent of total assets while the proportion of their NHA holdings declined slightly from 11.2 per cent to 10.4 per cent. Mortgage loan companies failed to demonstrate a strong preference for NHA mortgages until the 1968–70 period[4] when their NHA holdings rose from 5.1 per cent to 9.1 per cent of total assets while their conventional holdings declined from 70.0 per cent to 64.2 per cent.

Since all institutions faced the same relative yield opportunities between NHA and conventional mortgages,[5] the different timing of each institution's NHA and conventional investment indicates that these mortgages were not perfect substitutes. Rather, each instrument possessed certain non-yield properties which enabled it to satisfy specific institutional investment objectives at specific times. Hence, it is reasonable to assume a substantial proportion of funds invested in NHA mortgages would, in the absence of such a debt instrument, have gone into non-mortgage investments.

Furthermore, the increased desirability of mortgage investment arising from this programme was not confined to the NHA sector. Because substantial economies of scale exist in mortgage lending, increased lending activity arising from the creation of NHA mortgages increased the desirability of conventional mortgages relative to non-mortgage investments. From 1951 to 1956, for example, life company initiating and servicing costs declined from 1.02 per cent to 0.54 per cent for capital invested in mortgages while these costs for other security investments remained unchanged at 0.09 per cent,[6] increasing the relative yield attractiveness of mortgage investments in general, for a given gross yield spread.

Finally, the reduction in risks, greater standardization in mortgage quality, and government assistance in developing a secondary market under this programme, have combined to open the vast resources of the trust and pension funds to the mortgage market. Since 1954, trust and pension funds have accounted for one-third of all NHA secondary market purchases, thereby augmenting the available supply of capital for mortgage lending.

When all these influences are considered there is little doubt that the mortgage guarantee and insurance programmes have substantially increased the flow of funds into residential construction during the postwar period. The crucial question, however, is whether this increase in the availability of funds has increased the volume of residential construction or simply increased pressure on demand without a corresponding increase in supply, thereby increasing land and building costs. To the extent that an increase in the flow of funds into mortgages occurred at a time of full employment of resources when the constraints upon the volume of residential construction were shortages of suitable materials, labour, and building capacity, as in the 1946–52 period,[7] the effect appears to have been primarily on prices. During this seven-year period, institutional mortgage lending increased over 130 per cent, mostly in the NHA sector, while housing starts rose only 30 per cent. Over this same period residential construction costs and prices of NHA single detached homes rose 60 per cent faster than the consumer price index.

Although the increase in the availability of funds that arose from the government guarantee and joint loan programme was not largely transformed into an increase in the real level of residential construction activity in the 1946–52 period, it would be wrong to assume that the programme was solely responsible for the relatively faster rise in housing prices than in the consumer price index. Given the extent to which institutions wished to rebuild their depleted mortgage portfolios during the early postwar period and the tremendous backlog of housing demand (as evidenced by the fact that 30 to 35 per cent of all Canadian families were in need of new housing accommodation even as late as 1951),[8] probably much of this inflation would have occurred even in the absence of the government housing programme. However, when construction is limited by lack of materials, labour or building capacity, more liberal credit is more likely to push up costs and prices than increase production.[9]

After 1953, when lack of funds, one of the conditions the insurance programme was designed to alleviate, was the constraint upon the volume of residential construction activity, the programme had a considerable effect upon the real volume of residential construction. In regressions run over the 1953 to 1963 period, a very high correlation was found between changes in the value of mortgage approvals and changes in housing starts, and no significant correlation was found between changes in the value of mortgage approvals and housing prices or construction costs.[10] Similarly, the housing model estimated in chapter 4 for the 1957 to 1967 period indicates that the mortgage availability variables had a very significant impact upon the volume of housing starts, while it failed to detect any significant relationship between the credit availability variables and housing prices. Therefore, it appears that during periods when building material and labour markets functioned normally and when the availability of funds was a constraint upon residential construction, the loan insurance programme led to an increase in the real volume of residential construction and did not contribute to inflation.[11]

(ii) Short run

Theoretically, the federal loan insurance programme should also have exerted a strong cyclical influence upon residential construction through the imposition of an interest yield ceiling on NHA mortgages, since this ceiling could alter the relative yield desirability of mortgage investment by affecting the yield spread between mortgages and alternative investments. This could happen either directly through changes in the NHA ceiling or indirectly through the maintenance of the existing ceiling when yields on alternative investments fluctuate.

However, as mentioned in chapter 8, the impact of the NHA ceiling on total residential construction activity and the over-all availability of mortgage credit was much less than is usually supposed. In order to analyse this impact a housing model was developed to explain separately the volume of conventional and NHA financed housing starts. The resultant conventional financed housing start (HSC) and NHA financed housing start (HSNHA) equations are presented in functional form in equations 1 and 2, where NHA financed housing starts include CMHC as well as private institutionally financed starts.

(1) $\quad$ HSC $= h($PH/CLC, RC, RC $-$ RB, RNHA $-$ RB, CMHC$)$

(2) $\quad$ HSNHA $= h'($PH/CLC, RNHA, RNHA $-$ RB, CMHC$)$.

These equations are similar to the aggregate housing start equation developed in chapter 4, but have been modified to reflect special conventional and NHA financing features as follows: (a) the average mortgage rate variable (RM) was replaced by the conventional mortgage rate variable (RC) in the conventionally financed housing start equation and by the NHA mortgage rate variable (RNHA) in the NHA financed housing start equation; (b) the private credit rationing variable, the yield differential between mortgages and bonds (RM$-$RB), was replaced by the yield differential between conventional mortgages and bonds (RC$-$RB) in the conventional housing start equation: and by the yield differential between NHA mortgages and bonds (RNHA$-$RB) in the NHA housing start equation; and (c) the private and public NHA credit rationing variables, the yield differential between NHA mortgages and bonds (RNHA$-$RB), and the volume of Central Mortgage and Housing Corporation direct lending (CMHC) respectively, were included in the conventional equation to represent the extent to which unsatisfied NHA demand spills over into the conventional sector. Since NHA financing is available at lower cost and more liberal non-price lending terms than conventional credit, NHA credit is usually preferred by those eligible for it and, hence, an increase in the availability of private institution or CMHC NHA credit is likely to cause a reduction in the volume of conventionally financed housing starts.[12]

These equations were estimated by ordinary least squares using quarterly observations 1Q'1957 to 4Q'1967 and the results are presented in equations 3 and 4. The coefficients on the CMHC variables were estimated using first degree Almon variables.

(3) $\quad$ HSC $= -46.88 - 11.01$ Q1 $+ 8.15$ Q2 $+ 6.88$ Q3 $+ 7.50$ WW
$\quad\quad\quad\quad\;\;\,(2.59)\;\;(7.23)\quad\;(5.33)\quad\;(4.39)\quad\;(2.91)$
$\quad\quad\quad\quad + 112.94$ (PH/CLC) $- 7.76$ RC$_{t-1}$ $- 6.95$ (RNHA$-$RB)$_{t-1}$ $+ 7.41$ (RC$-$RB)$_{t-1}$
$\quad\quad\quad\quad\;\;\;\;(5.20)\quad\quad\quad\quad\;\;\,(3.42)\quad\quad\;\;\,(2.92)\quad\quad\quad\quad\quad\;(2.51)$
$\quad\quad\quad\quad - 1.21$ (CMHC/PH) $- 0.61$ (CMHC/PH)$_{t-1}$.
$\quad\quad\quad\quad\;\;\;\;(1.22)\quad\quad\quad\quad\;\;(1.22)$

$\quad$ R$^2 = 0.90$, $\bar{\bar{R}}^2 = 0.63$, DW $= 1.96$.

(4) $\text{HSNHA} = 9.00 - 8.29 \, \text{Q1} - 1.10 \, \text{Q2} - 0.40 \, \text{Q3} + 17.54 \, (\text{PH}/\text{CLC})_{t-1}$
   $(0.77) \quad (7.33) \quad (0.93) \quad (0.36) \quad (1.13)$
   $- 3.70 \, \text{RNHA}_{t-1} + 6.00 \, (\text{RNHA} - \text{RB})_{t-1} + 5.33 \, (\text{CMHC}/\text{PH})$
   $(2.49) \quad\quad\quad (4.43) \quad\quad\quad\quad\quad (7.72)$
   $+ 2.66 \, (\text{CMHC}/\text{PH})_{t-1}$
   (7.72)

$\text{R}^2 = 0.84$, $\bar{\text{R}}^2 = 0.69$, $\text{DW} = 1.92$.

These regression results reconfirm the appropriateness of our housing model and indicate the basic similarity between the conventional and NHA-financed sectors. Both conventional and NHA housing starts are strongly influenced by their respective costs of mortgage credit, the yield spread between mortgage and bond investments (which indicates that significant credit rationing takes place in both sectors), and the ratio of housing prices to construction costs, although the influence of this last variable is considerably weaker in the NHA sector. The coefficients on the RNHA – RB and CMHC variables have the opposite sign in the conventional regression than they have in the NHA regression indicating that some people rationed out of the NHA sector shift to conventional financing.[13]

In terms of the impact of the ceiling on the NHA mortgage rate, the conventional housing start regression indicates that a one per cent increase in the NHA mortgage rate would reduce conventional starts by 6950 units as funds are shifted to the NHA sector and borrowers take advantage of the generally more liberal NHA borrowing terms. The NHA rate increase would also increase NHA starts by 2300 units (the net of the RNHA coefficients) as the positive availability effects outweigh the negative cost effects of the higher NHA mortgage rates, leaving a net decline in total starts of 4650 units. If these estimates are correct, they mean that a policy of administratively maintaining the NHA rate slightly below its equilibrium market level actually increases housing starts, and that the effect of adjusting this rate upward actually reduces housing starts, just the opposite of the fixed rate hypothesis.

Confirmation of our results can be found in the behaviour of housing starts and mortgage approvals after administrative changes in the NHA ceiling. Between March 1954, when the federal loan insurance programme was introduced, and November 1966, when the NHA mortgage rate was tied to the long-term government bond yield, there were nine administrative changes in the NHA yield maximum. Of these nine changes, only one, after the ceiling was raised from 6 per cent to 6¾ per cent in December 1959, was followed by a change in seasonally adjusted institutional mortgage approvals in the same direction (i.e., was an increase in the NHA ceiling accompanied by an increase in mortgage approvals) and in no case was this change accompanied by a change in seasonally adjusted housing starts in the same direction, although the increase in the NHA rate in November 1966 was followed by an increase in housing starts two quarters later.[14] In all other cases changes in the NHA yield ceiling failed to prevent changes in institutional mortgage approvals and housing starts from varying in the *opposite* direction. Moreover, in the one case in December 1959 when mortgage approvals did rise after an increase in the NHA ceiling, this increase coincided with a very rapid decline in the long-term government bond yield of 65 basis points in less than six months, which no doubt contributed to part of the mortgage lending adjustment.

Our results contradict the fixed rate hypothesis because of the offsets generated in the conventional sector of the mortgage and housing markets. The conventional and NHA mortgage approval regressions indicate that mortgage lending activity in both sectors is significantly influenced by the conventional-NHA mortgage yield differential. The regression results in Tables XXIII and XXIV indicate that 37 per cent of the steady-state increase in the availability of NHA mortgage credit generated by an increase in the NHA mortgage rate is offset by a decline in the availability of conventional residential mortgage credit for life insurance companies, and 28 per cent of the steady-state increase is similarly offset for both trust companies and mortgage loan companies, ignoring the feedback effects on the conventional mortgage rate. Similarly, equations 3 and 4 indicate that although NHA housing starts increase with an increase in the NHA mortgage rate, as the fixed rate hypothesis suggests, this increase is more than offset by the concomitant decline in conventionally financed housing starts. Consequently, although institutional NHA mortgage lending and NHA financed housing starts do vary according to the fixed rate hypothesis, these variations are ameliorated by offsetting variations in the conventional sector, so that the net effect for the market as a whole is relatively small. On the other hand, our analysis does indicate that the yield ceiling had a very significant effect upon the mix of NHA and conventional institutional mortgage lending, and upon the mix of NHA and conventionally financed housing starts.

(c) Demand impacts

(i) Long run

The mortgage insurance programme has a significant effect upon the aggregate demand for residential construction by putting housing within the reach of many families who desire new homes but cannot afford the more stringent borrowing terms associated with conventional finance. The National Housing Act increased loan to value ratios from the 60 to 65 per cent that existed for conventional mortgages to over 80 per cent, lengthened amortization terms from 10 to 20 years to 25 years and lowered the interest rate, thereby substantially reducing downpayment requirements and monthly carrying charges. Many families who were previously excluded from the housing market because of insufficient savings to satisfy the downpayment requirement or insufficient current incomes to meet monthly payments were thus enabled to enter the market.

An indication of the importance of these variations may be seen from the Royal Commission on Banking and Finance "Consumer Survey" cited in chapter 3 which found that if, during the 1957–62 period, downpayment requirements had been 10 per cent higher, 15 per cent of families purchasing homes with mortgage credit (approximately 85 per cent of all home purchasers) would either have purchased no home (9 per cent) or a cheaper home (6 per cent). If monthly payments had been 10 per cent higher, 32 to 40 per cent would either have purchased no home (20–25 per cent) or a cheaper home (12–15 per cent).[15]

As would be expected from a programme of this sort, most benefit has accrued to middle-income families who purchase medium price homes and only secondary benefits have filtered to the lower income classes. For example, in 1970, as Table XXXIV indicates, only 4.2 per cent of NHA loans for new housing went to families with incomes below $7000 while 34.7 per cent of Canadian non-farm families had incomes below $7000; 31.4 per cent of these loans went to families with incomes between $7000 and $9999 while 26.4 per cent of non-farm families had incomes in this range; and 64.4 per cent of these loans went to families with incomes $10,000 or more while 38.9 per cent of non-farm families had incomes in this range.

To the extent that loan insurance has enabled middle income families to move into better accommodations some uplifting of lower income class housing standards was made possible as the previous dwellings of moving families became vacant. Through new construction and filtering the percentage of housing stock in need of major repair had fallen to 5.6 per cent in 1961, (although another 20 per cent was still in need of major repair). However, the degree to which filtering was responsible for this improvement is hard to ascertain because of very great data difficulties. For this process to have been effective some downward pressure would have had to be exerted on rents since 70 per cent of NHA borrowers previously lived in rental dwellings. Since 1952 the DBS rental index has risen more slowly than the index of the cost of home-ownership, the index of NHA new home prices and the MLS price index, but the index of average monthly rents has risen faster than all but the MLS price index, leaving the whole question unsettled and awaiting better statistics.

(ii) Short run

Not only has the mortgage insurance programme stimulated effective demand in the long run, but it has also been used to exert a strong cyclical influence upon the economy. In periods when there is not a substantial disequilibrium in the housing market arising from shortages in building capacity, materials or mortgage credit, a liberalization of lending terms will stimulate residential construction while a tightening of terms will curtail it. Appropriate variations in lending terms should, therefore, normally exert a significant stabilizing influence on the economy.

Between 1947 and 1970 the principal mortgage lending terms were adjusted

TABLE XXXIV
NON-FARM FAMILY INCOMES AND INCOMES OF NHA BORROWERS FOR NEW HOUSING, 1970

Family income ($)	Families borrowing under NHA (per cent)	All non-farm families (per cent)
0-4999	0.2	19.0
5000-6999	4.0	15.7
7000-9999	31.4	26.4
10,000-14,999	47.0	20.3
15,000+	17.4	18.6
Total	100.0	100.0

Source: CMHC, Canadian Housing Statistics (1970), 78.

on seven different occasions. Loan-to-value ratios were increased six times, in December 1949, March 1954, December 1957, December 1960, November 1966, and June 1969; and decreased once, in February 1951. The maximum amortization term was increased twice, in December 1960 and June 1969. It is interesting to note that with the sole exception of the February 1951 reduction in the loan to value ratio all changes in credit terms have been in the direction of greater ease. This is probably due to the reluctance of policy-makers to apply more stringent terms to such a politically sensitive area, and means that variations in lending terms have not exhibited the reversibility that proper stabilization techniques should follow.

This failure to tighten terms periodically is particularly important since it reduces the effectiveness of future liberalizing changes. As lending terms become more liberal subsequent easements of a similar magnitude become successively less effective, and a potentially powerful policy weapon is dissipated. This may be seen from Table v which indicates that successive increases in amortization terms result in diminishing reductions in monthly payments – for example, a 15-year extension in the amortization period on a 10-year, 8 per cent mortgage reduces monthly carrying costs by 37 per cent, while a similar extension on a 25-year mortgage reduces monthly carrying costs by only 12 per cent – and from the fact that downpayment requirements can be lowered only to zero.

Another method by which demand for residential construction can be affected is through variations in the size of the maximum loan permitted under this programme. Setting the loan maximum is a policy variable which may be implemented either by direct action or "conscious neglect." Maintenance of a given loan maximum per dwelling unit in a period of increasing home prices tends to make NHA financing undesirable by prohibiting a sufficiently large loan to permit the purchase of a home of the desired quality. This either forces the prospective home purchaser to shift to more expensive conventional financing, which has a lower loan to value ratio and results in less income generation per dollar downpayment, or to postpone his housing purchase, both of which reduce effective demand. Raising the loan maximum has the opposite effect of increasing the demand by enabling families who could not afford conventional financing but wished a more expensive home than the NHA maximum permitted to re-enter the market.

The NHA loan maximum does not appear to have been utilized either actively or passively for stabilization purposes in Canada. During the postwar period to the end of 1970 there were eight increases in the loan maximum[16] but these were essentially technical adjustments designed to keep pace with rising price levels and were not attempts to liberalize lending terms. With the exceptions of a large increase in March 1954 and a very large increase in the loan maximum for apartment units in February 1968, the percentage increases in the loan maximum did not significantly differ from the percentage increases in home prices.[17] Likewise, with the exception of the mid-1955 to 1957 period and the late 1960s prior to April 1969 when the home ownership loan maximum was increased to $25,000, all significant increases in housing prices were accompanied by a corresponding adjustment in the loan maximum, indicating the absence of this technique for stabilization purposes.

It should be added here, however, that the loan maximum may be used as a policy tool for other than stabilization purposes since variations in the relative loan maximum per unit for single and multiple dwellings can substantially affect the single and multiple mix of construction.

B. CENTRAL MORTGAGE AND HOUSING CORPORATION DIRECT LENDING

In addition to influencing the volume of residential construction activity indirectly by affecting the demand for or supply of mortgage credit through the loan insurance programme, the government can influence the housing sector directly through the lending powers of Central Mortgage and Housing Corporation. CMHC, a crown corporation established to administer federal housing programmes, was authorized in 1946 to make residential construction loans out of public funds when adequate private financing was not forthcoming. Although CMHC initially used this direct lending power sparingly, since 1957, when it began large-scale lending to stimulate building activity, it has financed approximately 420,000 new housing units, or almost 19 per cent of all new dwelling units constructed in Canada between 1957 and 1970. Seventy-one per cent (and prior to 1968, ninety per cent) of these loans were made under section 40, which enables CMHC to supply funds for general residential construction as opposed to low income housing. The balance of the loans were made under a variety of other programmes – Limited Dividend, Low Rental, Non-Profit, Public Housing, Student Housing, and Federal-Provincial Rental and Sales Housing programmes. The discussion that follows pertains primarily to section 40 CMHC direct lending, although some of the discussion is relevant for the other programmes as well.

The degree to which a direct lending programme increases the level of activity in a sector depends upon the extent to which these loans satisfy demands that the private sector would otherwise have met. Since CMHC borrowers under section 40 must, in most cases, demonstrate an inability, through at least two rejected loan applications, to obtain private mortgage credit on NHA terms, CMHC lending is usually considered to be of a "residual nature" providing a net addition to the supply of mortgage credit and the volume of residential construction.[18] However, since the NHA terms upon which CMHC lending usually takes place are much more favourable to the borrower than conventional terms (having lower interest rates, higher loan to value ratios, and a longer amortization period), the loan refusal requirement does not necessarily mean that private mortgage credit is unobtainable, but only that it is unobtainable upon NHA terms. Hence, the possibility exists that the increased availability of CMHC credit on NHA terms reduces the demand for private conventional financing and thereby reduces the volume of conventionally financed housing starts.

This possibility was examined by including the volume of CMHC direct lending

(CMHC) as a variable in the conventionally financed housing start equation as well as the NHA financed housing start equation estimated above in equations 3 and 4. These regressions indicate that an additional million dollars in constant 1957 dollars of CMHC lending will generate an additional 79.9 NHA financed housing starts (the average constant dollar mortgage loan being $12,500 per unit[19]), but will cause conventionally financed housing starts to be reduced by 18.2 units as demand that would otherwise be satisfied in the conventional market is satisfied by CMHC direct loans. This means that an additional million dollars of CMHC constant dollar lending would generate only 61.7 additional housing starts net, and that all CMHC direct lending under section 40[20] is not "residual" in the sense of providing a net addition to the volume of residential construction since reductions in the conventionally financed housing sector offset approximately 20 to 25 per cent (the regressions indicate 22.8 per cent) of the additional housing starts generated in the NHA financed sector.

In addition to the direct demand implications, two other secondary effects should also be considered. First, it is possible that in satisfying some potential or actual conventional demand an increase in the availability of CMHC funds will reduce the conventional mortgage rate and hence stimulate conventional housing starts. To examine this our conventional mortgage rate determination equation was modified in a variety of ways to include the volume of CMHC direct lending. However, in no case did the volume of CMHC lending have any significant influence upon the conventional mortgage rate.

Second, it is possible that additional government demand for funds to finance CMHC lending will raise bond rates and thus reduce the private availability of funds. The extent to which this is likely depends upon the method followed in funding the direct lending programme. If funds are raised via government security sales to financial institutions the ability or willingness of these institutions, who supply the vast majority of funds for new residential construction, to invest in mortgages may be diminished since additional government security sales tend to raise bond rates relative to mortgage rates.[21] If, on the other hand, the government obtains its financing by security sales to the central bank, the housing sector should experience secondary benefits from the resultant increase in the money supply. Finally, if funds come out of additional tax revenues or reduced spending on alternative programmes, the incidence of the tax or nature of the forgone expenditure will determine the extent of the offset in the housing sector. Although we cannot directly measure the funding mix, which largely determines the magnitude of the financial offsets, we suspect the mix has been such as to have little effect upon the housing sector. However, further study, probably along full economy stimulation lines, is required before any definite conclusions can be reached.

Another issue surrounding the direct lending programme is the extent to which it has a pro-cyclical bias since it is designed to alleviate private credit gaps, and these gaps arise only when funds are scarce because of excessive demands by other sectors or restrictive government policies, both of which occur in periods of accelerating economic activity. Between 1957 and 1970 there were nine major changes in

CMHC direct lending policies as seen by changes in the volume of its lending. On a seasonally adjusted basis large increases in lending occurred in late 1957 and early 1958, in late 1960, in late 1965, generally throughout the 1963 to 1967 period (especially late 1966 and early 1967), and in the second half of 1970; while substantial contractions took place in mid-1958, early 1960, mid-1961, and late 1967, and early 1968. Moreover, in 1963, CMHC began to use its direct lending authority to smooth seasonal fluctuations in residential construction, reducing its lending at the beginning and substantially increasing it toward the end of each year.

A comparison of CMHC lending with general economic and housing market conditions indicates that CMHC has conducted its direct lending more with an eye on stabilizing the residential construction sector than the economy in general. This may be seen by comparing CMHC lending with residential construction activity and measures of general economic activity such as industrial output, unemployment rates, and the rate of inflation, with appropriate time lags. However, the timing of variations in CMHC direct lending in 1968 and especially in 1970 indicates that general stabilizing objectives are also being considered. During this period CMHC performance in this area improved vastly, although it is too early to detect a shift in emphasis since appropriate policies for stabilizing the economy more or less coincided with policies appropriate for stabilizing the construction industry.

The appropriateness of a policy designed to stabilize the housing sector as opposed to the general level of economic activity depends upon the marginal social gains to be realized from an extra degree of stabilization influence compared to the gains from an immediate increment in housing accommodations. Unless the nation is experiencing a severe housing shortage the social benefits of general stabilization will probably outweigh those of additional housing expenditures and, therefore, CMHC must exercise extreme care to harmonize its lending policies more with general stabilization policies and the over-all needs of the economy than with the needs of the residential construction section alone. It should also be realized, however, that the direct lending programme provides an additional policy weapon and the option of exerting restraining influences upon the general economy while sheltering the housing sector when conditions warrant such selectivity.

C. HOUSING PRIORITIES AND STABILIZATION
PRIORITIES: A POLICY DILEMMA

The discussion of the last two chapters has exposed a major policy dilemma, namely the trade-off between socially desirable housing policy and socially desirable general economic stabilization policy. This trade-off arises because variations in residential construction activity exert a significant impact upon the general level of economic activity and because residential construction normally behaves in an anti-cyclical manner and is highly responsive to general economic policy.

In periods of increasing economic activity additional pressures are usually exerted on the nation's capital markets, reducing the availability of funds for residential construction and raising the cost of mortgage finance. The high sensitivity of housing expenditures to the availability and cost of credit causes downward pressure on construction activity, and means that residential construction will normally act counter-cyclically, reducing the degree of general economic instability. This counter-cyclical pressure may be accentuated or ameliorated by government policy, as the following examples illustrate.

If, during a general economic expansion, a policy of monetary restraint is followed, it will tend to restrain excessive expansion in aggregate economic activity, but will accentuate the amplitude of fluctuations in the housing sector by reinforcing existing market tendencies. On the other hand, an expansionary monetary policy, while mitigating the decline in housing activity and dampening cyclical fluctuations in this sector, will reinforce expansionary pressures in the general economy and increase over-all cyclical instability.

If, during a general economic expansion, CMHC direct lending is conducted so as to stabilize residential construction activity, it will generate additional spending power in the economy and reinforce general cyclical instability. On the other hand, if CMHC direct lending is contracted to restrain general economic demand and price pressures, it will reinforce the decline and instability in the residential construction sector.

If, during an economic expansion, the terms that qualify for federal loan insurance are tightened (or in the case of maximum loan amounts held constant), the affordability of new housing will be reduced and residential construction retarded, stabilizing the economy in general but amplifying instability in the housing sector. On the other hand, if these terms are eased, demand will be accentuated placing additional pressures on the economy.

Consequently, it is clear that during periods of excessive economic expansion a combination of monetary, direct lending and selective credit policies may be used to reduce aggregate economic pressures via residential construction by reducing the availability and increasing the cost of mortgage credit, and by tightening the conditions that qualify for NHA loan insurance. However, since residential construction is likely to stagnate or decline during an excessive economic expansion these policies will usually increase the amplitude of fluctuations and cyclical instability in the residential construction sector. If the objective is to reduce cyclical instability in residential construction just the opposite policies are required. Analogously, during periods of general economic stagnation, policies that are appropriate to stimulate general economic activity reinforce expansionary tendencies in residential construction, while those policies that restrain a rapid acceleration of housing expenditures further depress the level of general economic activity.

The problem, therefore, is which set of policies to follow; those policies that accentuate the counter-cyclical behaviour of residential construction so as to reduce general economic instability, or those policies that reduce the counter-cyclical behaviour of residential construction but accentuate general economic instability. Obviously, no definitive answer can be given since the appropriate policy depends upon the relationship of the economy at a given time to all its stabilization and social welfare goals. Hence, the answer reduces to the relative marginal social benefits of an additional expenditure for housing at a given time versus the marginal social costs of this expenditure in terms of reduced general economic stability and the reduced marginal social benefits of other expenditures.

In this connection two further points should be raised. First, it is possible that increased instability in the residential construction sector reduces efficiency in the industry and/or retards the growth of industrial capacity, thereby exerting extra inflationary pressure on construction costs in periods of accelerated construction activity. This pressure is shown to exist in the construction cost equation since construction costs vary with the level of construction activity relative to its industrial capacity. However, the importance of this instability is unlikely to be relatively large because of the strong seasonal pattern in construction which makes the cyclical pattern less important, the increasing substitutability of non-residential for residential construction activity on the part of the major developers, and the sensitivity of labour and material costs to conditions in the whole construction industry and not just the residential sector.

Second, it is possible that increased instability in residential construction reduces the long-run supply of houses and thereby the housing standards of the nation. However, this effect is unlikely since the monetary forces and demand restraining forces are reversible, i.e., increased availability of funds, lower costs of credit, and easier borrowing terms will stimulate construction during generally slack or stagnant economic periods replenishing the previously forgone housing stock. Consequently, while monetary and demand restraining policies may retard residential construction during one phase of the business cycle, thereby depressing housing standards for a short period of time, it is unlikely that over the full cycle (or over a 5- to 10-year period) the total number of housing units started will be lower, or housing standards reduced.[22]

From our analysis it would therefore appear that, unless the immediate housing shortage were critical, general stabilization priorities would usually outweigh short-term housing priorities.

Appendix: Summary of Symbols and Sources of Data

HOUSING STARTS AND STOCK VARIABLES

HS – total housing starts in thousands of units
HSC – conventionally financed housing starts in thousands of units
HSM – multiple dwelling unit housing starts (including duplex and row housing starts) in thousands of units
HSNHA – NHA financed (including CMHC financed) housing starts in thousands of units
HSS – single dwelling unit housing starts in thousands of units
SH – total stock of housing units in thousands
SH/FAM – total stock of housing units per family
SHOC – stock of owner-occupied housing units in thousands
SHOC/FAM – stock of owner-occupied housing units per family
SHR – stock of occupied rental housing units in thousands
SHR/POP – stock of occupied rental housing units per family

Sources
HS, HSM, HSS – Central Mortgage and Housing Corporation, *Canadian Housing Statistics* (1970), 2–3, 10
HSC, HSNHA – *ibid*, 14
SH, SHOC, SHR – annual data supplied by Central Mortgage and Housing Corporation. Quarterly data were estimated by the Bank of Canada by adding quarterly completions to annual estimates, and by substracting demolitions and adding conversions evenly distributed over the four quarters

PRICE, RENT AND COST VARIABLES

CC – construction cost index (1957 = 100), an index of average construction costs per square foot on new NHA single detached dwellings
CLC – construction and land cost index (1957 = 100), an index of average construction and land costs per square foot for new NHA single detached dwellings
L – index of land costs (1957 = 100) on land used for new NHA single detached dwellings
PGNE – implicit private GNE deflator (1957 = 100)
PH – housing price index (1957 = 100), calculated as an average of an index of the average price of Multiple Listing Service sales (PMLS) and an index of the average selling price of new NHA houses (PNHA), i.e., PH = (PMLS + PNHA)/2
PMLS – index of home prices (1957 = 100), calculated as a four quarter moving

average of the average monthly price obtained in real estate sales through Canadian real estate board Multiple Listing Service

PNHA – index of new NHA home prices (1957 = 100), calculated as the average selling price of new NHA single detached, semi-detached and row dwellings for owner occupancy

R – index of average rents paid for rental housing accommodation (1957 = 100)

WC – index of average hourly earnings of hourly rated construction workers (1957 = 100)

Sources

CC, CLC, L – Central Mortgage and Housing Corporation, *Canadian Housing Statistics* (1970), 70

PGNE – Dominion Bureau of Statistics, *National Accounts*

PMLS – the Canadian Association of Real Estate Boards, *The Canadian Realtor* (Don Mills, Ontario). See, for example, December 1968 issue, 13

PNHA – annual data, Central Mortgage and Housing Corporation, *Canadian Housing Statistics* (1970), 68. Quarterly data supplied by Central Mortgage and Housing Corporation, Research Department

R – data supplied by Dominion Bureau of Statistics, Prices Division, from Labour Force Survey

WC – Dominion Bureau of Statistics, *Man Hours and Hourly Earnings*, and Bank of Canada *Review* (Dec. 1971), s101.

CMHC LENDING VARIABLES

CMHC – CMHC direct mortgage approvals in millions of dollars

CMHC/PH – CMHC direct mortgage approvals in tens of constant 1957 dollars

CMHCM – CMHC direct mortgage approvals for multiple unit construction in millions of dollars

CMHCM/PH – CMHC direct mortgage approvals for multiple unit construction in tens of constant 1957 dollars

CMHCS – CMHC direct mortgage approvals for single unit construction in millions of dollars

CMHCS/PH – CMHC direct mortgage approvals for single unit construction in tens of constant 1957 dollars

Sources

CMHC, CMHCM, CMHCS – Central Mortgage and Housing Corporation, *Canadian Housing Statistics* (1970), 36, and supplied by Central Mortgage and Housing Corporation Research Department.

DEMOGRAPHIC, INCOME, AND EXPENDITURE VARIABLES

FAM – number of families in thousands

POP – population in thousands

YD – permanent real disposable income in millions of constant 1957 dollars

YD/FAM – permanent real disposable income in millions of constant 1957 dollars per thousand families

YD/POP – permanent real disposable income in millions of constant 1957 dollars per thousand population

W – a wealth variable represented by an eight quarter geometrically declining moving average of permanent real disposable income in millions of dollars
INRC – non-residential construction expenditure in millions of constant 1957 dollars
$\widehat{INRC}$ – estimated non-residential construction expenditure in millions of constant 1957 dollars, estimated from the equation

$$\widehat{INRC} = a + b_1 Q1 + b_2 Q2 + b_3 Q3 + b_4 T$$

IRC – residential construction expenditure in millions of constant 1957 dollars
$\widehat{IRC}$ – estimated residential construction expenditure in millions of constant 1957 dollars, estimated from the equation

$$\widehat{IRC} = a + b_1 Q1 + b_2 Q2 + b_3 Q3 + b_4 T$$

Sources
FAM, POP – annual estimates, Central Mortgage and Housing Corporation, *Canadian Housing Statistics* (1970), 92–3. Quarterly data supplied by Bank of Canada, POP by linear interpolation of annual data and FAM by interpolation using fixed weights assigned to each quarter based on behaviour of marriage data
YD – supplied by Bank of Canada as an eight quarter geometrically declining average of real personal disposable income divided by private GNE deflator
INRC, IRC – Dominion Bureau of Statistics, *National Accounts*, Table 9, lines 8 and 9

OTHER HOUSING VARIABLES

DVST – building materials sales tax dummy variable, taking the value one from the third quarter of 1963 to the end of 1965 and zero elsewhere
Q1, Q2, Q3 – seasonal dummy variables for the 1st, 2nd, and 3rd quarters respectively
T – time trend over the period 1Q'53 to 4Q'67
WW – winter housebuilding incentive programme dummy variable, taking the value one in the last quarters of 1963 to 1965 and zero elsewhere

INTEREST RATE VARIABLES

RB – bond interest yield, calculated as an average of the long-term government of Canada bond yield and the McLeod, Young, Weir 40 bond average.
RC – conventional mortgage interest rate
RCH – trust and mortgage loan company chequable deposit rate
RLT – long-term government of Canada bond yield
RM – mortgage interest rate, calculated as an average of the conventional (RC) and NHA (RNHA) mortgage rates
RNHA – actual NHA mortgage rate
RPS – chartered bank personal savings deposit rate
R03 – zero-to-three-year government of Canada bond yield
R1GIC – one-year trust company GIC and mortgage loan company debenture rate
R40 – McLeod, Young, Weir 40 bond yield average
R90 – chartered bank 90 day term deposit rate

Sources
RLT – Bank of Canada, *Statistical Summary, 1969 Supplement*, 77–85

RC, R90 – *ibid*, 86–7
RCH, RPS, R03, R1GIC – supplied by Bank of Canada, Research Department.
RNHA – Bank of Canada, *Statistical Summary, 1969 Supplement*, 86–7. Prior to October 1967 legal maximum rate was used except for 1955 when the actual lending rate fell below the ceiling as shown in J.V. Poapst, *The Residential Mortgage Market*, a study prepared for the Royal Commission on Banking and Finance (Ottawa 1962), 159–60
R40 – supplied by McLeod, Young, Weir, 40 King St W, Toronto

FINANCIAL INSTITUTION MORTGAGE APPROVAL
AND MORTGAGE STOCK VARIABLES

CRMA – conventional residential mortgage approvals in millions of dollars
MA – total mortgage approvals in millions of dollars
NHAMA – NHA mortgage approvals in millions of dollars
RMA – total residential mortgage approvals in millions of dollars
M – stock of mortgages in millions of dollars.
MLTM – weighted sum of mortgage holdings of trust, all life insurance, and mortgage loan companies. Weights are 0.065, 0.055 and 0.215 respectively

Sources
Separate data for each of the following institutions: life insurance companies, trust companies, mortgage loan companies, chartered banks
CRMA, MA, NHAMA, RMA – annual data, Central Mortgage and Housing Corporation, *Canadian Housing Statistics* (1970), 22, 24
RMA – quarterly data, *ibid.*, 28.
CRMA, MA, NHAMA – quarterly data supplied by Central Mortgage and Housing Corporation, Research Department
M – trust companies: Bank of Canada, *Statistcial Summary, 1969 Supplement*, 110–11
M – mortgage loan companies: *ibid.*, 112–13
M – chartered banks: *ibid.*, 22–3
M – life insurance companies, annual data: *ibid.*, 115. Quarterly data calculated by interpolation of annual data based upon quarterly mortgage investment transactions of 16 life insurance companies: *ibid.*, 118–19

FINANCIAL INSTITUTION ASSETS, DEBENTURES
AND POLICY LOAN VARIABLES

A – total assets of a financial institution in millions of dollars
ADV – asset dummy variable taking the value of the asset size of each institution in millions of dollars for 1Q'66 to 4Q'67 and zero elsewhere
ALTM – weighted sum of total assets of trust companies, assets minus policy loans of life insurance companies, and deposit and debenture liabilities of mortgage loan companies. Weights are 0.065, 0.055 and 0.215 respectively.
DEB – deposit and debenture liabilities of mortgage loan companies in millions of dollars
DEBDV – deposit and debenture liability dummy variable taking the value of the deposit and debenture liabilities of mortgage loan companies in millions of dollars for 1Q'66 to 4Q'67 and zero elsewhere.

158 RESIDENTIAL MORTGAGE MARKETS

PL – policy loans of all life insurance companies in millions of dollars

Sources

A – trust companies: Bank of Canada, *Statistical Summary, 1969 Supplement*, 110–11
 – chartered banks: *ibid.*, 22–3
 – life insurance companies, annual data: *ibid.*, 115. Quarterly data calculated by interpolation of annual data based upon quarterly investment transactions and asset size of 16 life insurance companies, *ibid.*, 118–19
DEB – mortgage loan companies: *ibid.*, 112–13
PL – life insurance companies, annual data: *ibid.*, 115. Quarterly data calculated by interpolation of annual data based upon quarterly investment transactions of 16 life insurance companies, *ibid.*, 118–19

NOTE: where annual or monthly publications are referred to, data are found in those and earlier issues.

Notes

CHAPTER ONE

1 These include flush and chemical toilets, piped hot and cold water, and installed bath or shower.
2 J.R. Mattila and W.R. Thompson, "Residential Service Construction: A Study of Induced Investment," *Review of Economics and Statistics*, 38 (November 1956), 466–73.
3 S. Klaman, *The Postwar Residential Mortgage Market*, National Bureau of Economic Research (Princeton, NJ, 1961), introduction by R. Goldsmith, xx.
4 Calculated from Central Mortgage and Housing Corporation, *Canadian Housing Statistics* (1969), 13 and 16.
5 Another factor responsible for this was the very strong demand for housing services.
6 J.S. Chung, *Housing and Mortgage Loans: Postwar Canadian Experience*, unpublished doctoral dissertation (University of Toronto, 1967).
7 This figure is based on CMHC estimates to 1968 updated to allow for an estimate of the excess of housing completions over demolitions.
8 J. Duesenberry, *Business Cycles and Economic Growth*, (New York, 1958), 135.
9 Another major distinction is that between low income subsidized and non-subsidized housing.
10 There are exceptions to this, especially with the development of high rise and row condominiums.
11 Figures are based on data in Central Mortgage and Housing Corporation *Canadian Housing Statistics* (1957), 4Q, 19, and *Canadian Housing Statistics* (1969), 75–99.
12 Central Mortgage and Housing Corporation, *Canadian Housing Statistics* (1969), 60.
13 Calculated from *ibid.*, 18.
14 If we assume that one half of other housing starts were financed without mortgage credit, then financial institutions supplied approximately 90 per cent of the private mortgage credit for new construction and 70 per cent of all mortgage credit for new residential construction; and CMHC supplied 22 per cent of all mortgage credit.
15 Royal Commission on Banking and Finance, *Report* (Ottawa, 1964), 269.
16 J.M. Guttentag, "The Behavior of Residential Mortgage Yields Since 1951," in J.M. Guttentag and P. Cagan (eds.), *Essays on Interest Rates, Vol. I*, National Bureau of Economic Research (New York, 1969), 30–60; J.V. Poapst, *The Residential Mortgage Market*, a working paper prepared for the Royal Commission on Banking and Finance (Ottawa, 1962), 122; G.W. McKinley, "Impact of Monetary and Fiscal Policy on Residential Capital Formation," in *1959 Conference on Savings and Residential Financing*, US Savings and Loan League (Chicago, 1959), 116–7.

17 An exception is that the government regulates the maximum loan to value ratio that various financial institutions can accept on conventional mortgages. However, this regulation can be easily circumvented by package arrangements with non-government regulated corporations.

18 Prior to 1954 a slightly different programme existed in which the government through CMHC made joint loans with financial institutions. Under this programme the government determined the rate to be charged.

CHAPTER TWO

1 For a survey of these interrelationships see J.S. Duesenberry, *Business Cycles and Economic Growth* (New York, 1958), 135–8.

2 This list is very similar to that suggested by L. Grebler and S. Maisel, "Determinants of Residential Construction: A Review of Present Knowledge," in *Impacts of Monetary Policy*, Commission on Money and Credit (Englewood Cliffs, NJ, 1963), 475–620.

3 This percentage has been increasing in recent years, being 6.3 per cent in 1968 and 8.0 per cent in 1969. Prior to 1967, the percentage was considerably under 3 per cent.

4 See chapter 3 for a derivation of this estimate.

5 This price may be expressed as a rent in the case of rental accommodation. The analysis for rental dwellings is analogous.

6 Even if wage rates are previously determined, increasing scarcity of skilled labour necessitates increasing overtime work at higher rates.

7 Approximately 80 per cent of housing starts in Canada are financed by mortgage credit. Central Mortgage and Housing Corporation, *Canadian Housing Statistics* (1970), 14.

8 For a discussion of Canadian and United States mortgage markets see S. Klaman, *The Postwar Residential Mortgage Market*, National Bureau of Economic Research (Princeton, NJ, 1961); J. Guttentag, "The Behaviour of Residential Mortgage Yields," in J. Guttentag and J. Cagan (eds.), *Essays on Interest Rates*, National Bureau of Economic Research (New York, 1969), 29–76, and J.V. Poapst, *The Residential Mortgage Market*, a working paper prepared for the Royal Commission on Banking and Finance (Ottawa, 1962).

9 The reasons for this are more fully discussed in J.V. Poapst, *Residential Mortgage Market*, 112, and J. Guttentag, *Essays on Interest Rates*, 29–60.

10 Despite the oversimplification, it is assumed that single-family units are owner-occupied and multiple-family units are renter-occupied. Multiple dwelling condominiums and renter-occupied single-family dwellings, while existing, are a relatively small proportion of the housing stock in each class.

11 It is interesting to note that periods in which existing home prices outpace prices on new construction coincide with periods of rising interest rates, suggesting that much of this difference may be explained by capitalizing the low interest mortgage finance associated with existing homes. This is discussed in more detail in chapters 3 and 4.

12 This assumes the mortgage factor (annual interest and principal payment required to retire the mortgage over the amortization period, as a percentage of the initial mortgage) is below the return on invested capital on an all-cash basis.

13 In addition to these factors the volume of construction depends upon such other factors as the developer owning non-revenue-producing land which he wants to con-

vert to a revenue producing use (especially if he can more than mortgage out on the building – i.e., if his final equity in the project will be less than his equity in the land), and having an organization which he wants to maintain for the future.
14 There appears to be a downward trend in the proportion of custom-built homes. However, an increase in the general demand for single-family dwellings will at least cause deviations from this trend.

CHAPTER THREE

1 L. Grebler and S. Maisel, "Determinants of Residential Construction: A Review of Present Knowledge," in *Impacts of Monetary Policy*, Commission on Money and Credit (Englewood Cliffs, NJ, 1963), 479, and R. Muth, "Demand for Non-Farm Housing" in A. Harberger (ed.), *Demand for Durable Goods* (Chicago, 1960), 46.
2 For a discussion of the relationship between population and housing see K. Buckley, "Urban Building and Real Estate Fluctuations in Canada," *Canadian Journal of Economics and Political Science*, 18 (February 1952), 52, and L. Grebler, D. Blank, and L. Winnick, *Capital Formation in Residential Real Estate: Trends and Prospects*, National Bureau of Economic Research (Princeton, NJ, Princeton University Press, 1956), 76, and W. Illing, *Housing Demand to 1970*, Economic Council of Canada Staff Study no. 4 (Ottawa, 1964).
3 This profile is based upon extremely broad generalizations.
4 For the characteristics of NHA new home borrowers see Central Mortgage and Housing Corporation, *Canadian Housing Statistics* (1970), 91–2.
5 W. Illing, *Housing Demand to 1970*, Economic Council of Canada Staff Study no. 4 (Ottawa, 1964), 40 and Central Mortgage and Housing Corporation, *Canadian Housing Statistics* (1967), 73.
6 Central Mortgage and Housing Corporation, *Canadian Housing Statistics* (1970), 94.
7 In 1951 only 13.3 per cent of households consisted of non-families. Central Mortgage and Housing Corporation, *Canadian Housing Statistics* (1970), 94.
8 Illing, *Housing Demand to 1970*, 4–8.
9 F. deLeeuw, "The Demand for Housing: A Review of Cross Section Evidence," *Review of Economics and Statistics* LIII (February 1971), 1–10; T.H. Lee, "Housing and Permanent Income: Tests Based on a Three Year Reinterview Survey," *ibid.*, L (November 1968), 480–90; M. Reid, *Housing and Income* (Chicago, 1962); Muth, "Demand for Non-Farm Housing," 29–96.
10 M. Reid, "Capital Formation in Residential Real Estate," *Journal of Political Economy* 66 (April 1958), 131–53; and *Housing and Income*. The dependent variable in these studies was per capita housing stock.
11 Muth, "Demand for Non-Farm Housing," 29–96; and "The Stock Demand Elasticities of Non-Farm Housing: Comment," *Review of Economics and Statistics* XLVII (November 1965), 417–19. The dependent variable in these studies was per capita housing stock.
12 See deLeeuw, "The Demand for Housing," 1–10, for an elaboration of these adjustments.
13 For an elaboration of this point see Lee, "Housing and Permanent Income," 488; A.R. Winger, "Housing and Income," *Western Economic Journal* 6 (July 1968), 227.
14 deLeeuw "The Demand for Housing," 1–10.
15 A.R. Winger, "Housing and Income," 226–32.

16 Lee, "Housing and Permanent Income," 480–90.
17 Muth, "Demand for Non-Farm Housing," 29–96.
18 His sample was based upon purchases of homes with Federal Housing Act mortgages. For a discussion of the bias adjustment see deLeeuw, "The Demand for Housing: A Review of Cross Section Evidence," 1–10.
19 R.S. Uhler, "Demand for Housing: An Inverse Probability Approach," *Review of Economics and Statistics* L (February 1968), 129–33. The dependent variable in this study was the value of owner-occupied housing.
20 T.H. Lee, "The Stock Demand Elasticities of Non-Farm Housing," *ibid.*, XLVI (February 1964), 82–9; "More on the Stock Demand Elasticities of Non-Farm Housing," *ibid.*, XLIX (November 1967), 640–42.
21 E. Oksanen, "Housing Demand in Canada, 1947–62; Some Preliminary Experimentation," *Canadian Journal of Economics and Political Science* XXXII (August 1966), 302–18; and "Estimation of Housing Demand Relationships in Canada," a paper presented at the Canadian Statistics Conference, Ottawa, 1967. The dependent variable in these studies was per family housing stock.
22 L.B. Smith, *Housing in Canada, Market Structure and Policy Performance*. Research monograph no. 2 in *Urban Canada: Problems and Prospects* (Ottawa, 1971), 32 and 41–63.
23 This re-estimation was done by T.H. Lee, "Housing and Permanent Income," 487.
24 R. Wood, "Credit Terms and the Demand for Residential Construction," in *Study of Mortgage Credit*, Committee on Banking and Currency, Subcommittee on Housing, US Senate, 85th congress, 2nd session, December 1958.
25 For a summary of a number of these studies see M. Dagenais, "Is the Demand for Housing Elastic? An Essay on Reconciliation of Econometric Analyses," mimeographed manuscript, Ecole des Haute Etudes (Montreal, 1969).
26 J. Duesenberry and H. Kisten, "The Role of Demand in the Economic Structure," in W.W. Leontief (ed.), *Studies in the Structure of the American Economy* (New York, 1953), 451–82.
27 E. Oksanen, "Housing Demand in Canada, 1947–62," 302–18.
28 M. Reid, "Capital Formation in Residential Real Estate," *Journal of Political Economy* 66 (April 1958), 131–53; and *Housing and Income*.
29 Lee, "Stock Demand Elasticities for Non-Farm Housing," 82–9.
30 Muth, "Demand for Non-Farm Housing," 29–96.
31 deLeeuw, "The Demand for Housing," 1–10.
32 J. Chung, "L'analyse de la demande de logements – propriétaires: l'expérience canadienne," *Actualité économique*, 4 (juin 1967), 66–86.
33 This relationship and developer failure to perceive or inability to adjust to turning points in this ratio explain the long cycle in residential construction.
34 This discussion assumes that a project is appraised at actual cost.
35 This discussion ignores any differential effects of the tax system and assumes the pre-tax and after-tax yields are proportional for all investments.
36 This assumes that alternative opportunities still yield 12 per cent.
37 This is calculated by taking the present value at the end of the tenth year of the forty $72,460 flows arising in years 11 to 50 – the discount rate being the market interest rate of 6 per cent – and finding the interest rate that would make the value at the end of year ten of the ten $63,408 payments equal to this amount. This interest rate is then the maximum the company could earn on its alternative investments without making this investment economically inferior. If all equity funds were assumed

to have the same opportunity cost, i.e., if the $72,460 flows were discounted at the same rate as the $63,408 flows were compounded, the break even yield would be lower.

38 This ignores the fact that equity funds will be required for the taxes payable on this investment during the period in which the investing company's taxable income exceeds its cash flow.

39 For an elaboration of this relationship see E.M. Fisher, *Urban Real Estate Markets: Characteristics and Financing*, National Bureau of Economic Research (New York, 1951), 69–75; and R. Wood, "Credit Terms and the Demand for Residential Construction," in *Study of Mortgage Credit*, Committee on Banking and Currency, Subcommittee on Housing, US Senate, 85th congress, 2nd session (December 1958), 39–45.

40 This was calculated from Central Mortgage and Housing Corporation, *Canadian Housing Statistics* (1970), 78 and 82.

41 Royal Commission on Banking and Finance, *Appendix Volume* (Ottawa, 1964), 100.

42 *Ibid.*, 100.

43 Of course there is no reason to assume families will not vary the proportion of their income spent on housing, so that all families within this income range $11,640 to $12,200 will not be priced out of the market by this increase in interest costs.

44 G. Break, *The Economic Impact of Federal Loan Insurance* (Washington, DC 1961), 60–2.

45 Lee, "The Stock Demand Elasticities of Non-Farm Housing," 82–9.

46 Other possible tax concessions such as allowing realty taxes and mortgage interest costs as deductions against personal income tax, as in the United States, would also increase housing demand.

47 R.F. Muth, "Urban Residential Land and Housing Markets," in H.S. Perloff and L. Wingo Jr. (eds.), *Issues in Urban Economics*, Resources for the Future (Baltimore, 1968), 285–331 (p. 286).

48 *Building the American City*, Report of the National Commission on Urban Problems, 91st congress, 1st session, house document no. 91-34 (Washington, DC 1968), 417–86.

49 Central Mortgage and Housing Corporation, *Canadian Housing Statistics* (1970), 70, 88, 89.

50 R.F. Muth, "The Derived Demand Curve for A Productive Factor and the Industry Supply Curve," *Oxford Economic Papers* 16 (July 1964), 221–34. Muth, using US data 1946 to 1960, obtained a similar elasticity of 0.75.

51 It should be noted in this respect that higher land costs will in the long run generate pressures for rezoning, changes in building regulations and increased research and development to enable higher utilization. These changes will increase the cost per unit of land but reduce the cost of land per dollar of construction. For an analysis of land prices see F.G. Adams, G. Milgram, R. Green, and C. Mansfield, "Undeveloped Land Prices During Urbanization: A Micro-Empirical Study Over Time," *Review of Economics and Statistics* L (May 1968), 248–58.

52 See, for example, H. Mohring, "Land Values and Measurement of Highway Benefits," *Journal of Political Economy* LXIX (June 1961), 236–49; F. Adams, G. Milgram, E. Green, and C. Mansfield, "Undeveloped Land Prices During Urbanization: A Micro-Empirical Study Over Time," *Review of Economics and Statistics* L (May 1968), 248–58; W. Alonzo, *Location and Land Use* (Cambridge, 1964); L. Wingo, *Transportation and Urban Land* (Washington, DC, 1961); R.N.S. Harris, G.S. Tolley, and

C. Harrell, "The Residence Site Choice," *Review of Economics and Statistics* L (May 1968), 241–7.

53 This assumes that real travel costs do not become imputed land costs, and the costs of public services are to a large extent borne by society and not the ultimate home purchaser.

54 Central Mortgage and Housing Corporation, *Canadian Housing Statistics* (1970), 88.

55 S. Behman and D. Codella, "Intermetropolitan-Area Differences in the Prices of new FHA-insured Homes," a paper presented to the Western Economic Association meetings, (Davis, California, August 1970), concludes that on-site labour in the US has also been reduced over time.

56 For an elaboration, see *Building the American City*, 431–45.

57 Y. Dubé, J. Howes, D.L. McQueen, *Housing and Social Capital*, Royal Commission on Canada's Economic Prospects (Ottawa 1957), 44.

58 For a discussion of the role of labour in construction see H.C. Goldenberg and J.H.G. Crispo (eds.) *Construction Labour Relations* (Toronto, 1968). For the impact of unions in construction see especially the essays by F. Wildgen, "Economic Aspects: Work, Income and Cost Stabilization," 26–97; G.W. Bertram, "The Structure and Performance of Collective Bargaining Systems," 416–519; and G.W. Bertram, "Wage Structure and Wage Changes," 520–86.

59 Central Mortgage and Housing Corporation, *Canadian Housing Statistics* (1970), 84, and (1964), p. 70. These data overstate the variation in concentration between periods because the scale of NHA building increased over time.

CHAPTER FOUR

1 This section draws heavily on previous studies by the author: L.B. Smith "A Model of the Canadian Housing and Mortgage Markets," *Journal of Political Economy* 77 (October 1969), 795–816; "A Bi-sectoral Housing Market Model," *Canadian Journal of Economics* 2 (November 1969), 557–69; *Housing and Mortgage Markets in Canada*, Bank of Canada Staff Study no. 6 (Ottawa, 1970); and *Housing in Canada: Market Structure and Policy Performance*, research monograph no. 2 in *Urban Canada: Problems and Prospects* (Ottawa, 1971), 41–53.

2 Central Mortgage and Housing Corporation, *Canadian Housing Statistics* (1970), 94.

3 See K. Buckley, "Urban Building and Real Estate Fluctuations in Canada," *Canadian Journal of Economics and Political Science* 18 (February 1952), 41–62, and L. Grebler, D. Blank, and L. Winnick, *Capital Formation in Residential Real Estate: Trends and Prospects*, National Bureau of Economic Research (Princeton, NJ, 1956).

4 In addition to the unavailability of this variable there are some theoretical reasons for deleting vacancies when constructing a national model. The basic problem may be seen by assuming internal migration from rural to urban areas. If the migrating family abandons, even temporarily, its rural dwelling and "doubles up" in an urban area, there is an increase in housing demand (since the migrating family now demands a dwelling of its own in an urban area) and an increase in vacancies (in rural areas). An increase in vacancies therefore does not necessarily indicate a lessening of unsatisfied housing demand on a national basis.

5 Where RSS_1 is the residual sum of squares associated with a regression of the dependent variable upon the intercept, Q1, Q2, Q3; and RSS_2 is the residual sum of squares associated with the final regression,

$$R^2 = \frac{(\text{RSS}_1 - \text{RSS}_2)}{\text{RSS}_1}.$$

6 Equation 5 was respecified to remove the per family deflator. This eliminates heteroscedasticity that would otherwise be built in because the "true" relationship is

$$\text{SH} = s'\left(\text{SH}_{t-1}, \sum_{i=0}^{n} \beta_i \text{HS}_{t-i}\right).$$

The per family specification is required for proper scaling of the housing stock variable in the price equation.

7 S. Almon, "The Distributed Lag between Capital Appropriations and Expenditures," *Econometrica* 33 (January 1965), 178–96. The actual regression using second (z_2) and third (z_3) degree Almon variables created on housing starts is

$$\text{SH} = 1.000 \; \text{SH}_{t-1} + 3.33 \; z_2 - 2.44 \; z_3.$$
$$\quad\;\;(776.94) \quad\;\;(4.30) \quad\; 3.73)$$

8 The average construction period was calculated by assuming that housing starts are uniformly distributed within each quarter. Thus, there is an average one-half quarter lag for housing stock changes (which arise from completions) behind housing starts.

9 J. Durbin and G.S. Watson, "Testing for Serial Correlation in Least Squares Regressions," *Biometrika* 37 (1950), and 38 (1951).

10 M. Nerlove and K.F. Wallis, "Use of the Durbin-Watson Statistics in Inappropriate Situations," *Econometrica* 34 (January 1966), 235–8.

11 C. Hildreth and J.Y. Lu, *Demand Relations with Autocorrelated Disturbances* (East Lansing, Michigan, 1960), Michigan Agricultural Experiment Station Technical Bulletin 276.

12 H. Theil and A.L. Nagar, "Testing the Independence of Regression Disturbances," *Journal of the American Statistical Association* 56 (December 1961), 793–806.

13 This implies an average constant dollar (1957 dollars) CMHC direct loan of $12,500 per unit. The actual average current dollar loan was $11,756 per unit, which suggests some private market offsets to CMHC direct lending. This is discussed more fully in chapter 9.

14 The zero-to-three-year government bond rate (R03) was used as a proxy for the cost of bridge or temporary financing because a direct measure of this variable is not available in Canada.

15 An 11 per cent federal sales tax was imposed on building materials in 1963, taking effect as follows: 4 per cent after June 1963, 8 per cent after April 1964, and 11 per cent after January 1965.

16 For a discussion of this point see G.L. Perry, *Unemployment, Money Wage Rates and Inflation* (Cambridge, Mass., 1966), 30–1; and C.L. Schultze and J.L. Tryon, "Wages and Prices," in J. Duesenberry, G. Fromm, L.R. Klein, and E. Kuh (eds.), *The Brookings Quarterly Econometric Model of the United States* (Chicago, 1965), 326–7.

17 A somewhat different specification for this equation has been suggested by J. Helliwell, "A Bunch of Price Equations," mimeographed manuscript, Bank of Canada (Ottawa, 1970), 5. He suggests creating a synthetic cost variable (RCC) as a weighted average of the index of the average hourly earnings in construction (WC) and the index of the cost of building materials (BM) such that RCC = 0.375 WC + 0.625 BM with

each index on the base 1961 = 100. His estimated equation in terms of percentage change (%CH) of annual changes in quarterly form is

$$\%\text{CH (CLC)} = -0.84 + 5.23 \ (\ln \text{INRC} - \widehat{\ln \text{INRC}})_{t-1} + 8.49 \ (\ln \text{IRC} - \widehat{\ln \text{IRC}})_{t-1}$$
$$(1.69) \quad (3.30) \qquad\qquad\qquad\qquad (3.57)$$

$$+ 0.57 \ \%\text{CH (RCC)} + 0.13 \ \%\text{CH (L)} + 0.012 \ \%\text{CH (R03)}$$
$$(5.05) \qquad\qquad (3.32) \qquad\qquad (1.58)$$

$1Q'55 - 4Q'68$, SEE $= 1.75$, $R^2 = 0.73$, DW $= 1.71$.

18 The specification of equation 14 has been greatly simplified by assuming that the supply of residential land is a constant. In fact the supply of usable residential land increases with the availability of transportation, water, electricity and other services and the proclamation of zoning regulations. However, most of these increases in the supply of usable land have been anticipated by developers and speculators and therefore the timing would be difficult to specify even if such data existed.

19 This abstracts from the growing trend toward owner-occupied multiple dwellings in the form of high-rise condominiums. During our estimation period condominium construction was an insignificant portion of new construction.

20 See note 6 in this chapter.

21 The actual regressions using second (z_2) and third (z_3) degree Almon variables created on single housing starts (HSS) in the owner-occupied stock regression and on multiple housing starts (HSM) in the rental stock regressions are

$$\text{SHO} = 0.9989 \ \text{SHO}_{t-1} + 3.75 \ z_2 - 2.69 \ z_3, \text{ and}$$
$$(1172.57) \qquad\qquad (5.85) \quad\ (4.75)$$

$$\text{SHR} = 0.9998 \ \text{SHR}_{t-1} + 3.97 \ z_2 - 3.09 \ z_3.$$
$$(809.86) \qquad\qquad (4.54) \quad\ (3.80)$$

22 The average construction period was calculated after adjusting the lagged start coefficients so that all housing starts give rise to housing completions.

23 If prices and rents in period t depend upon the demand for and supply of housing stock in t, increased land costs in t will have little or no effect on prices and rents in t. To the extent that increased costs reduce construction in t, they will restrain the increase in housing stock in $t + 1$ thereby raising prices and rents in $t + 1$. However, unless prices and rents immediately react strongly to changes in the rate of growth of new housing units and unless the elasticity of demand for housing with respect to prices and rents is considerably less than 1, the profitability of such construction falls.

24 Central Mortgage and Housing Corporation *Canadian Housing Statistics* (1970) 96.

25 By comparison in 1970, only 4.9 per cent of dwellings were without the use of a flush toilet, 8.1 per cent were without an installed bath or shower, and 5.4 per cent were without hot running water. CMHC, *ibid.*, 96.

26 The increase in downpayment requirements is so low because these payments were unusually high in 1957 (the base year). However, even beginning in 1958 when they were lowered, the annual average increase in downpayment requirements was only 2.7 per cent. Monthly gross debt service rose sharply after 1968 primarily because of rising interest costs. Between 1957 and 1970 the average ratio of gross debt service to income of borrowers rose from 18.5 per cent to 20.9 per cent. Much of this increase was due to the high downpayments in 1957. In 1958 when downpayments fell, the ratio

rose to 19.9 per cent. Central Mortgage and Housing Corporation, *Canadian Housing Statistics* (1965), 63; (1971), 82.

27 Over the longer 1951–70 period the average cost of new NHA financed bungalows rose 87 per cent compared to an estimated increase of 188 per cent in family incomes in large urban centres.

28 C. Barber, "Canada's Post-war Monetary Policy, 1945–54," *Canadian Journal of Economics and Political Science* 23 (August 1957), 355.

29 R.C. McIvor and J. Panabaker, "Canada's Post-war Monetary Policy, 1946–52, *ibid.*," 20 (May 1954), 211–2.

30 Central Mortgage and Housing Corporation, *Annual Reports* (1946), 8; (1947), 18; 1950, 4; and 1951, p. 3.

31 Bank of Canada, *Annual Report* (1950), 13.

32 Central Mortgage and Housing Corporation *Annual Report* (1949), 5–6; (1950), 3.

33 *Ibid.*, (1951), 3.

34 The relationship between availability of funds, as represented by the average mortgage-average bond yield differential (RM–RB), and housing starts may be seen by comparing the top and bottom graphs in Figure 6, and lagging housing starts 1 to 2 quarters. This comparison indicates a very strong similarity in the movement of the yield differential and housing starts between 1953 and 1963, and to a lesser degree in 1967 and 1968. In the 1964 to 1966 period the rise in housing starts corresponds with gradually declining mortgage costs, and high rates of growth of non-bank financial institution mortgage lending activity.

35 Y. Dubé, J. Howes, and D.L. McQueen, *Housing and Social Capital*, Royal Commission on Canada's Economic Prospects (Ottawa, 1957), 44; and Central Mortgage and Housing Corporation, *Annual Report* (1951), 3; and (1952), 4–5.

36 Net corporate new issues declined by an average of $15 million a quarter from mid-1953 to mid-1955, bank loans declined by $60 million from October 1953 to April 1955, while bank assets increased by $1068 million in this period; the government was a net redeemer of $301 million in government bonds in 1954 and $223 million in the first half of 1955, including Canada Savings Bonds, and $818 million excluding Canada Savings Bonds.

37 Net new corporate bond issues rose from a seasonally adjusted $75 million a quarter in mid-1955 to almost $300 million in the last quarter of 1956, and remained at high but slightly declining levels through 1957. Provincial and municipal net bond issues rose from $435 million in 1955 to $763 million in 1956 and $771 million in 1957. The government became a net borrower of funds in the last half of 1955, for the first time since mid-1953, and demand for bank loans increased rapidly, necessitating chartered bank sales of government securities of $1570 million in the last half of 1955 and 1956 in order to protect their reserve position.

38 For an institutional description of this availability effect see Central Mortgage and Housing Corporation, *Annual Report* (1956), 7.

39 Royal Commission on Banking and Finance, *Report* (Ottawa, 1964), 412.

40 H.S. Gordon, *The Economists vs the Bank of Canada* (Toronto, 1961), 17.

41 L.H. Officer and L.B. Smith, "Stabilization Policy in the Postwar Period," in L.H. Officer and L.B. Smith (eds.), *Canadian Economic Problems and Policies* (Toronto, 1970), 32–4.

42 *Ibid.*, 34–6.

43 *Ibid.*, 37–8.

44 Bank of Canada, *Annual Report* (1966), 4–6.
45 *Ibid.*, (1967), 9–10.
46 See J. Carr and L.B. Smith, "Money Supply, Interest Rates and the Yield Curve," *Journal of Money, Credit and Banking* IV (August 1972), 582–94.
47 Confirmation of this can be seen from numerous speeches of the Governor of the Bank of Canada and the *Annual Reports* of the Bank of Canada. See in particular L. Rasminsky, "Interest Rates and Inflation," a statement before the House of Commons Standing Committee on Finance, Trade and Economic Affairs (July 3, 1969), and Bank of Canada *Annual Report* (1968), 7.
48 For one calculation of real interest rates in Canada see Carr and Smith, "Money Supply, Interest Rates and the Yield Curve," 582–94.

APPENDIX TO CHAPTER FOUR

1 M. Nerlove and K.F. Wallis, "Use of the Durbin-Watson Statistic in Inappropriate Situations," *Econometrica* 34 (January 1966), 235–8.
2 C. Hildreth and J.Y. Lu, *Demand Relations with Auto-Correlated Disturbances*, Technical Bulletin 276 (East Lansing, Michigan, 1960).
3 This equation was estimated using second and third degree Almon variables created on housing starts.
4 This equation was estimated using second and third degree Almon variables created on single dwelling unit housing starts.
5 This equation was estimated using second and third degree Almon variables created on multiple dwelling unit housing starts.
6 H. Theil and A.L. Nagar, "Testing the Independence of Regression Disturbances," *Journal of the American Statistical Association* 56 (December 1961), 793–806.

CHAPTER FIVE

1 Royal Commission on Banking and Finance *Report* (Ottawa, 1964) 269.
2 On July 15, 1970 and 1971, an A.E. LePage Limited survey of mortgage rates reported in the Toronto *Globe and Mail* (July 17, 1971), 82 indicated the following rates by category.

	1970	1971
NHA: CMHC	9½ %	8¾ %
approved lenders – single dwellings	9¾–10	9¼–9½
– apartment and townhouses	10¼–10¾	9½
Conventional: single dwelling	10½	9½
apartments and townhouses	10¾+	9¾–10
industrial and commercial – major leases	10½–11	9½–9¾
– multiple tenancy	10¾–11¼	9¾–10
hotel and motel	12+	10+
residential second mortgages	14+	12–13

3 See J.V. Poapst, *The Residential Mortgage Market*, a working paper prepared for

the Royal Commission on Banking and Finance (Ottawa, 1962), 159–60.

4 Some of these arrangements are discussed in "Life Insurance Companies becoming Landowners," *Financial Times* (January 18, 1971), 9.

5 J. Guttentag, "The Behaviour of Residential Mortgage Yields Since 1951," in J. Guttentag and P. Cagan (eds.), *Essays on Interest Rates Vol. 1*, National Bureau of Economic Research (New York, 1969), 29–76.

6 For a discussion of the importance of non-price lending terms see S. Klaman, *The Postwar Residential Mortgage Market*, National Bureau of Economic Research (Princeton, NJ, Princeton University Press, 1961), 75–8, and L. Grebler, D. Blank, and L. Winnick, *Capital Formation in Residential Real Estate: Trends and Prospects*, National Bureau of Economic Research (Princeton, NJ, 1956), 223.

7 For more detail see S. Klaman, *The Postwar Residential Mortgage Market*, National Bureau of Economic Research (Princeton, NJ, 1961), 144–79, and J. O'Leary, "Effects of Monetary Policies on the Residential Mortgage Market," in *Study of Mortgage Credit*, Committee on Banking and Currency, Subcommittee on Housing, US Senate (December 1958), 85th congress, 2nd session, 236.

8 A variant of this argument was advanced by Guttentag, "The Behaviour of Residential Mortgage Yields Since 1951," 45.

9 This point has been stressed by Poapst, *The Residential Mortgage Market*, 122; G.W. McKinley, "Impact of Monetary and Fiscal Policy on Residential Capital Formation," *1959 Conference on Savings and Residential Finance* (Chicago, 1959), 116; Klaman, *The Postwar Residential Mortgage Market*, 78; and Guttentag, "The Behaviour of Residential Mortgage Yields Since 1951," 51.

10 Poapst, *The Residential Mortgage Market*, 125.

11 Grebler, Blank, and Winnick, *Capital Formation in Residential Real Estate*, 222.

12 Guttentag, "The Behaviour of Residential Mortgage Yields Since 1951," 51.

13 Grebler, Blank, and Winnick, *Capital Formation in Residential Real Estate: Trends and Prospects*, 223; and Klaman, *The Postwar Residential Mortgage Market*, 75–8.

14 Klaman, the Postwar Residential Mortgage Market, 77–8; and R. Muth "Interest Rates, Contract Terms and the Allocation of Mortgage Funds," *Journal of Finance* 17 (March 1962), 64.

15 Guttentag, "The Behaviour of Residential Mortgage Yields Since 1951," 42.

16 These mortgage repayment proportions are the average of each institution's gross annual decrease in mortgages outstanding less its sales of NHA mortgages, divided by its average mortgage holdings during the year. The data are found in Central Mortgage and Housing Corporation, *Economic Research Bulletin*, no. 77(R) (Ottawa, 1971), Tables 9 and 10, and Appendix B.

17 These figures compare with an estimate of 36.2 per cent for 1952 to 1961 for the trust and mortgage loan companies by the University of Western Ontario, *Role of Trust and Loan Companies in the Canadian Economy*, a study prepared for the Trust and Loan Company Association of Canada (Toronto, 1962), 125, and 11 per cent for life insurance companies over the same period by the Canadian Life Insurance Officers' Association, *Submission to the Royal Commission on Banking and Finance* (Ottawa 1962), 44.

18 L.D. Meredith, "Liquidity: A Growing Attribute of Mortgage Loan Portfolios," *Journal of Finance* 5 (December 1950), 317.

19 Royal Commission on Banking and Finance, *Report* (Ottawa, 1964), 269.

20 J. Guttentag, "Credit Availability, Interest Rates and Monetary Policy," *Southern Economic Journal* 27 (January 1960), 220, and J. Guttentag, "Federal National Mort-

gage Association," in Commission on Money and Credit, *Federal Credit Agencies* (Englewood Cliffs, NJ, 1962), 133.
21 L. Winnick, "Burden of Residential Mortgage Debt," *Journal of Finance* 11 (March 1956), 178.
22 The Canadian Life Insurance Officers' Association, *Submission to the Royal Commission on Banking and Finance*, 66, stresses this point.
23 These figures are derived from Central Mortgage and Housing Corporation, *Economic Research Bulletin* no. 77(R) (Ottawa, 1971), and Central Mortgage and Housing Corporation, *Canadian Housing Statistics* (1970), 14, 22–25, and 62–3.
24 W.C. Hood, *Financing Economic Activity in Canada*, Royal Commission on Canada's Economic Prospects (Ottawa, 1958), 303.
25 The participation percentages in this section are very approximate and are estimated from data in Central Mortgage and Housing Corporation, *Supplement to Economic Research Bulletin* no. 77(R) (Ottawa, 1971), and Central Mortgage and Housing Corporation, *Canadian Housing Statistics* (1970), 62–3.
26 Royal Commission on Banking and Finance, *Appendix Volume* (Ottawa, 1964), 25–8 and 41–3; and Royal Commission on Banking and Finance, *Report* (Ottawa, 1964), 29.
27 Dominion Bureau of Statistics, *Income, Liquid Assets, and Indebtedness of Non-Farm Families*, 1958, 41–3.
28 Poapst, *The Residential Mortgage Market*, 96.
29 *Ibid.*, 93.
30 Bank of Canada, *Statistical Summary* (1969), 104–5.
31 Royal Commission on Banking and Finance, *Report* (Ottawa, 1964), 161; and V. Salyzyn, "The Competition for Personal Savings Deposits in Canada," *Canadian Journal of Economics and Political Science* 32 (August 1966), 327–37.
32 For a history of CMHC see Central Mortgage and Housing Corporation, *Housing in Canada 1946–1970: Supplement to the 25th Annual Report* (Ottawa, 1970).
33 For an outline of government housing programmes see Central Mortgage and Housing Corporation, *Submission to the Royal Commission on Banking and Finance* (Ottawa 1962), and L.B. Smith "Postwar Canadian Housing Policy in Theory and Practice," *Land Economics* 44 (August 1968), 339–49.
34 A pooled guarantee fund system was established to guarantee any institution's losses up to an amount of a maximum of 15 per cent of the institution's aggregate joint loans with the government. For a discussion of this programme see J. Gillies, "Some Financial Aspects of the Canadian Government Housing Programme: History and Prospective Developments," *Journal of Finance* 8 (March 1953), 24, and J.V. Poapst "The National Housing Act, 1954," *Canadian Journal of Economics and Political Science* 22 (May 1956), 237.
35 The introduction of a tax on life insurance company earnings and an increasing rate of inflation both reduce the desirability of mortgage investments vis-à-vis equities. Because Canada did not have a capital gains tax during this period the relative before tax yield on capital appreciating assets increased with the introduction of a tax on income. In addition, capital cost allowance available on real estate investments reduces the effective tax rate for investors initially. Because increasing rates of inflation are not immediately reflected in higher nominal interest rates, equities, which should experience capital appreciation, usually become relatively more desirable with an increasing rate of inflation.

36 Canadian Bankers' Association, *Submission to the Royal Commission on Banking and Finance* (Ottawa 1963), 26.

CHAPTER SIX

1 This approach draws heavily on the work of J. Tobin, "Liquidity Preference as Behaviour Towards Risk," *Review of Economic Studies* XXV (February 1958), 65–86; H. Markowitz, "Portfolio Selection," *Journal of Finance* VII (March 1952), 77–91; and *Portfolio Selection, Efficient Diversification of Investment* (New York, 1959). J.R. Hicks, "Liquidity," *Economic Journal* LXXII (December 1962), 787–802; W.F. Sharpe, "Capital Asset Prices: A Theory of Market Equilibrium Under Conditions of Risk," *Journal of Finance* XIX (September 1964), 425–42; J. Lintner, "Valuation of Risk Assets and the Selection of Risky Investments in Stock Portfolios and Capital Budgets," *Review of Economics and Statistics* XLVII (February 1965), 13–37; D. Farrar, *Investment Decisions Under Uncertainty* (Englewood Cliffs, NJ, 1962).

2 The subscript p refers to the characteristics of the entire portfolio. μ_p is the expected return and σ^2_p the variance in the expected return for the entire portfolio, while μ and σ^2 are the expected return and variance in this return for an individual security.

3 The expected yield on a portfolio consisting of n securities is $\mu_p = \sum_{i=1}^{n} \mu_i x_i$ where μ_i is the expected yield on security i and x_i is the amount of security i in the portfolio. The variance of the expected yield is $\sigma^2_p = \sum_{i=1}^{n} \sum_{j=1}^{n} x_i x_j \sigma_{ij}$ where σ_{ij} is the covariance of the expected yield on x_i and x_j as estimated by the investor. See Tobin, "Liquidity Preference as Behaviour Towards Risk," 82; and H. Markowitz, *Portfolio Selection: Efficient Diversification of Investment* (New York, 1959), 156.

4 J.R. Hicks, "Liquidity," *Economic Journal* 72 (December 1962), 796–802; and Sharpe, "Capital Asset Prices: A Theory of Market Equilibrium under Conditions of Risk," 431–2 show that an investment opportunity curve between expected return (μ_p) and expected standard deviation in that return (σ_p) must be a straight line or concave toward the northwest. Markowitz, *Portfolio Selection: Efficient Diversification of Investment*, 153 shows there is no difference in properties between an expected return-variance curve and an expected return-standard deviation curve, except that the straight line segment in the $\mu_p - \sigma_p$ curve becomes concave toward the northwest in the $\mu_p - \sigma^2_p$ curve.

5 Scale effects are likely to arise because increases in portfolio size often alter the relative liquidity required in a portfolio and change institutional attitudes toward risk taking, shifting their marginal rates of substitution between σ^2_p and μ_p. Also, as size increases, relative acquisition and servicing costs of various securities may change, altering the net yield associated with these investments.

6 Since money is included as an asset, this refers to any change in interest rates.

7 See K. Brunner and A. Meltzer, "The Place of Financial Intermediaries in the Transmission of Monetary Policy," *American Economic Review: Proceedings* LIII (May 1963), 374, and W. Baumol, "Stocks, Flows and Monetary Theory," *Quarterly Journal of Economics* LXXVI (February 1962), 53.

8 For an elaboration of this and some of its implications see J. Tobin and W. Brain-

ard, "Financial Intermediaries and the Effectiveness of Monetary Controls," *American Economic Review: Proceedings* LIII (May 1963), 383; F. deLeeuw, "A Model of Financial Behaviour," in J. Duesenberry, G. Fromm, L.R. Klein, and E. Kuh (eds.), *Brookings Quarterly Econometric Model of the United States*, (Chicago, 1965), 469–70; and J. Duesenberry: "The Portfolio Approach to the Demand for Money and Other Assets," *Review of Economics and Statistics, Supplement* XLV (February 1963), 12.

9 Duesenberry, "The Portfolio Approach to the Demand for Money and Other Assets," 11–12, and deLeeuw, "A Model of Financial Behaviour," 470.

10 If gross flows are not positive, the institution can approach portfolio balance by liquidating some of its holdings of its excess securities, since the gross outflow makes liquidation of some security investments imperative.

11 A larger degree of portfolio imbalance is only temporarily maintained because portfolio balance will eventually be restored out of current flows. However, at any given time, until balance is restored, the degree of imbalance will exceed that which would have existed had some stock liquidation also occurred.

12 If two securities, bonds and mortgages, exist, with yields RB and RM respectively in period t, and which have some long-run normal yield differential, N, in the Keynesian sense, then mortgages are a relatively desirable investment in a period when RM − RB > N, and bonds are relatively desirable when RM − RB < N. N may be thought of as equal to

$$\sum_{i=0}^{n} a(i)(\text{RM}_{t-i} - \text{RB}_{t-i}).$$

13 This ignores the difference in compound interest which arises if interest yields possess a trend and systematically vary so as to cause the same security to be purchased first in every set of yield fluctuations, i.e., if bond yields always lead mortgage yields and there is an upward trend in interest rates, bonds are purchased in the period before mortgages, causing the institution to have an average holding of lower yielding bonds of slightly over 50 per cent. This, however, can be compensated for. Similarly, if the institution's desired portfolio differs from 50 per cent mortgages and 50 per cent bonds, then its optimum investment pattern must be altered but will still consist of investing more heavily in the relatively attractive security.

14 Canadian Life Insurance Officers' Association, *Submission to the Royal Commission on Banking and Finance* (Toronto, 1962), 39–41.

15 For a discussion of similar US experience see L. Kendall, "Trends in the Mortgage Market," in *1959 Conference on Savings and Residential Financing*, US Savings and Loan League (Chicago, 1959), 107; J. O'Leary, "Postwar Trends in the Sources and Uses of Capital Funds, 1947–1957," in *Study of Mortgage Credit*, Committee on Banking and Currency, Subcommittee on Housing, US Senate (December 1958), 85th congress, 2nd session, 228; and J. O'Leary, "Effects of Monetary Policies on the Mortgage Market," *Journal of Finance* 13 (May 1958), 179.

16 Royal Commission on Banking and Finance, *Report* (Ottawa, 1964), 237.

17 W.C. Hood and O.W. Main, "The Role of the Canadian Life Insurance Companies in the Postwar Capital Market," *Canadian Journal of Economics and Political Science* 22 (November 1956) 467.

18 This figure is derived from all life insurance company asset holdings in the Bank of Canada, *Statistical Survey, 1969 Supplement*, 115. Central Mortgage and Housing Corporation, *Canadian Housing Statistics* (1970) 62 shows this proportion for all

life insurance companies to be 51.8 per cent. For 16 life insurance companies whose net premium income in 1969 was 80.1 per cent of all premium income, these publications show the proportion at 50.8 per cent and 50.6 per cent respectively.

19 Canadian Life Insurance Officers' Association, *Submission to the Royal Commission on Banking and Finance* (Toronto, 1962), 77. Between 1951 and 1960 the investment expenses associated with mortgage investments declined 60 basis points from 1.02 per cent to 0.42 per cent while the expenses associated with bond investments remained unchanged at 0.09 per cent.

20 Net yield differentials are slightly smaller because of greater selection and management costs associated with non-government securities.

21 Canadian Life Insurance Officers' Association, *Submission to the Royal Commission on Banking and Finance* (Toronto, 1962), 63; and Hood and Main, "The Role of Canadian Life Insurance Companies in the Postwar Capital Market," 478.

22 For a discussion of the bond price support programme see the Bank of Canada, *Report of the Governor 1948* (Ottawa, 1948), 11; and Bank of Canada, *Report of the Governor 1950* (Ottawa, 1950), 13.

23 Trust Companies' Association of Canada, *Submission to the Royal Commission on Banking and Finance* (Ottawa, 1962), 34.

24 Canadian Life Insurance Officers' Association, *Submission to the Royal Commission on Banking and Finance* (Toronto 1962), 105.

25 This is especially true in the case of mortgages on the security of single dwellings or small multiple dwellings. In the case of large mortgages on commercial, industrial, or apartment complexes local orientation is of little importance.

26 Because they face an income line with the same slope as trust companies but have lower liquidity requirements which increases the slope of their indifference curves if asset A in Figure 8 is assumed to be mortgages, (i.e., their marginal rate of substitution of bonds for mortgages is larger) mortgage loan companies devote a larger proportion of their investment portfolios to mortgages than do trust companies.

27 Trust companies remain competitive on these loans by writing their mortgages with a longer amortization period than their term to maturity. They also endeavour to refinance these mortgages upon maturity.

28 For a discussion of a similar experience in the United States see J. Guttentag, "Federal National Mortgage Association," in Commission on Money and Credit, *Federal Credit Agencies* (Englewood Cliffs, NJ, Prentice-Hall 1962), 130.

29 Dominion Mortgage and Investment Dealer's Association, *Submission to the Royal Commission on Banking and Finance* (Ottawa, 1962), 3 and 32.

30 An important indirect influence the banks have upon the mortgage market arises from their short-term construction lending activities. Short-term or interim mortgage financing is required since mortgage disbursements are made in stages over the building cycle as certain specified stages of construction are reached and, therefore, a need for financing exists prior to each draw. The importance of this financing is greater than the following table indicates because these figures are "as at" December 31, which is a relatively slow time for construction, because the value of construction dependent upon a construction loan is several times the amount of the loan, and because these loans have a rapid turnover.

Another indirect influence the banks have on the mortgage market centres upon the lines of credit they provide trust and mortgage loan companies, since they affect the proportion of funds these companies can devote to relatively illiquid investments.

CHARTERED BANKS INTERIM LOANS TO
CONSTRUCTION CONTRACTORS AS AT DECEMBER 31

Year	Millions of $	Year	Millions of $	Year	Millions of $
1946	71.7	1955	278.3	1964	455.9
1947	85.7	1956	312.2	1965	506.8
1948	93.8	1957	253.5	1966	461.9
1949	100.3	1958	261.9	1967	461.6
1950	126.7	1959	308.2	1968	513.9
1951	132.6	1960	309.0	1969	565.7
1952	140.7	1961	315.6		
1953	162.7	1962	364.4		
1954	187.3	1963	396.6		

Source: Bank of Canada, *Statistical Summary, 1969 Supplement*, 36-7 and earlier issues.

31 Canadian Bankers' Association, *Submission to the Royal Commission on Banking and Finance* (Ottawa, 1963), 26.
32 For this classification see Central Mortgage and Housing Corporation, *Canadian Housing Statistics* (1970), 62.

CHAPTER SEVEN

1 Parts of this section draw heavily upon and are extensions of L.B. Smith and G.R. Sparks, "The Interest Sensitivity of Canadian Mortgage Flows," *Canadian Journal of Economics* 3 (August 1970), 407–21; L.B. Smith and G.R. Sparks, *Institutional Mortgage Lending in Canada, 1954-1968: An Econometric Analysis*, Bank of Canada Staff Research Studies no. 9 (Ottawa, 1973); and L.B. Smith, *Housing and Mortgage Markets in Canada*, Bank of Canada Staff Research Studies no. 6 (Ottawa, 1970), 23–42.
2 For other examples of this approach see F. deLeeuw, "A Model of Financial Behaviour," in J. Duesenberry, G. Fromm, L. Klein, and E. Kuh (eds.), *Brookings Quarterly Econometric Model of the United States* (Chicago, 1965), 465–529; S. Goldfeld *Commercial Bank Behaviour and Economic Activity* (Amsterdam, 1966), and L.B. Smith and G.R. Sparks, "Specification and Estimation of Financial Stock Adjustment Models with Special Reference to Life Insurance Company Mortgage Investment," *International Economic Review* 12 (February 1971), 14–26.
3 For a discussion of the forward commitment process see S. Klaman, *The Postwar Residential Mortgage Market*, National Bureau of Economic Research (Princeton, NJ, 1961), 143–6.
4 For an estimate of the lag patterns for life insurance companies and a discussion of the problems involved see L.B. Smith and G.R. Sparks, "Specification and Estimation of Financial Stock Adjustment Models with Special Reference to Life Insurance Company Mortgage Investment," *International Economic Review* 12 (February 1971), 14–26, and *Institutional Mortgage Lending*, 17–34.
5 For an estimate of the importance of this see *ibid.*, 14–26.
6 J.E. Pesando, "The Interest Sensitivity of Canadian Mortgage Flows: A Comment," *Canadian Journal of Economics* 4 (August 1971), 401–3.
7 J.E. Pesando, "A Model of Life Insurance Company Portfolio Behaviour," unpublished Ph.D. thesis, University of Toronto (1971).
8 The extent of the bias introduced by this assumption is unclear, but does not appear to be very large. For an indication of the bias for life insurance companies over

different time periods see Smith and Sparks, "Specification and Estimation of Financial Stock Adjustment Models with Special Reference to Life Insurance Company Mortgage Investment," 14–26; and Smith and Sparks, *Institutional Mortgage Lending*, 17–60.

9 If $\alpha = 1$ the gap between COM* and COM*$_{t-1}$ is COM–COM$_{t-1}$ which is a function of the change in the size of the institution during the period, and is likely to be relatively small.

10 Bank of Canada, *Statistical Summary, 1969 Supplement*, 103.

11 S. Almon, "The Distributed Lag Between Capital Appropriations and Expenditures," *Econometrica*, 33 (January 1965), 178–96.

12 Since mortgage loan companies have quite substantial and volatile short-term borrowings from other financial institutions, and since these borrowings are reflected in their asset positions but not in their debenture and deposit liabilities, it seems more reasonable to express their portfolio targets in terms of deposit and debenture liabilities than in terms of total assets.

13 M. Nerlove and K. Wallis, "The Use of the Durbin-Watson Statistics in Inappropriate Situations," *Econometrica* 34 (January 1966), 235–8.

14 C. Hildreth and J.Y. Lu, *Demand Relations with Autocorrelated Disturbances*, Technical Bulletin 276 (East Lansing, Michigan, 1960).

15 This is derived from equation (21.1a).

16 These mortgage repayment proportions are one quarter of the average of each non-bank institution's gross annual decrease in mortgages outstanding after adjusting for sales of NHA mortgages, divided by its average mortgage holdings during the year during the estimation period. Because the banks entered the period with no mortgage holdings, their proportion was assumed to be just below the proportion for life insurance companies. The data are found in Central Mortgage and Housing Corporation, *Economic Research Bulletin*, no. 77(R) (Ottawa, 1971).

17 If the Hildreth-Lu transformation estimates of these coefficients are used for these calculations, the speeds of adjustment become 0.184 for the chartered banks, 0.297 for the life insurance companies using equation (21.1b), and 0.193 using equation (21.1d), 0.166 for the trust companies, and 0.272 for the mortgage loan companies.

18 These results are obtained by dividing the adjusted stock adjustment coefficient $(\gamma - \delta\theta)$ into the coefficient on the total asset variable for each institution.

19 Parts of this section draw upon Smith and Sparks, "The Interest Sensitivity of Canadian Mortgage Flows," 416–18; and Smith, *Housing and Mortgage Markets in Canada*, 38–42.

20 An important determinant of the asset size of deposit taking institutions, the ease or convenience of dealing with an institution (its accessibility, hours of operation, etc.), has been ignored because of difficulties in specification and data collection.

21 For consistency the RCH and R1GIC variables should be included in the chartered bank regression. These variables were insignificant when entered, possibly because their effects were being captured by the R03 and RLT variables.

22 Non-price lending terms are ignored here although they should properly enter the supply function. They are similarly omitted in the demand function.

23 See for example P. Hendershott, "Recent Developments in the Financial Sector of Econometric Models," *Journal of Finance*, 41–66; and D. Huang, "The Short Run Flows of Non-Farm Residential Mortgage Credit," *Econometrica* 34 (April 1966), 433–59.

24 Deposit and debenture liabilities were used in the case of mortgage loan companies.

25 The regression results are virtually identical, except for the coefficients on the ALTM and MLTM variables which vary to reflect the difference in the magnitude of these variables, when the weights used for each institution's asset and mortgage holdings were taken from the total mortgage approval regressions (Table XXI) and from the total residential mortgage approval regressions (Table XXII).

26 The data are found in Central Mortgage and Housing Corporation, *Economic Research Bulletin*, no. 77(R).

27 For a discussion of the mortgage approval and mortgage disbursement relationship see Smith and Sparks, "Specification and Estimation of Financial Stock Adjustment Models with Special Reference to Life Insurance Company Mortgage Investment," 20, and *Institutional Mortgage Lending*, 17–34.

28 The estimated equations using second (z_2) and third (z_3) degree Almon variables created on each institution's mortgage approvals are shown below.

	Dependent variable	z_2	z_3
Life insurance companies	$M - 0.979 \, M_{t-1}$	2.67 (3.53)	-1.72 (2.27)
Trust companies	$M - 0.956 \, M_{t-1}$	2.84 (5.14)	-1.90 (3.46)
Mortgage loan companies	$M - 0.967 \, M_{t-1}$	3.61 (5.97)	-2.62 (4.36)
Chartered banks	$M - 0.980 \, M_{t-1}$	5.35 (9.83)	-4.39 (8.15)

CHAPTER EIGHT

1 Privately financed housing starts were determined by subtracting CMHC housing starts, calculated from the housing start equation (equation 9 in chapter 4), from total housing starts.

2 L.B. Smith, *Housing and Mortgage Markets in Canada*, Bank of Canada Staff Research Studies no. 6 (Ottawa, 1970), 89. This study also presents an investment in residential construction equation over the same estimation period for the disaggregated housing model as follows:

$$\text{IRC} = 45.02 + 6.56 \text{ HSS} + 3.00 \text{ HSS}_{t-1} + 2.00 \text{ HSS}_{t-2} + 2.89 \text{ HSM}$$
$$(2.42) \quad (14.55) \quad (6.84) \quad (4.34) \quad (4.69)$$

$$+ 1.19 \text{ HSM}_{t-1} + 1.15 \text{ HSM}_{t-2} + 1.64 \text{ HSM}_{t-3}$$
$$(1.59) \quad (1.78) \quad (3.18)$$

$R^2 = 0.94$, DW $= 1.44$.

3 This view can be found in M. Colean, "A More Effective Mortgage Insurance Corporation" in *Study of Mortgage Credit*, Committee on Banking and Currency, Subcommittee on Housing, US Senate, 85th congress, 2nd session (December 1958), 295; L. Grebler, "The Role of Residential Capital Formation in Postwar Business Cycles," US Savings and Loan League, *Conference on Savings and Residential Finance, 1959 Proceedings* (Chicago 1959), 71; S. Klaman, "The Availability of Residential Mortgage Credit" in *Study of Mortgage Credit*, 198; A.M. Schaff, "Federal Mortgage Interest

Rate Policy and the Supply of FHA–VA Credit," *Review of Economics and Statistics* XL (November 1958), 284–5; and W.L. Smith, "Impact of Monetary Policy on Residential Construction, 1948–1958," in *Study of Mortgage Credit*, 248–53.

4 For an alternative way of stating part of the argument see W. Alberts, "Business Cycles, Residential Construction Cycles and the Mortgage Market," *Journal of Political Economy* 70 (July 1962), 263–81.

5 For an institutional discussion of the relationship between the conventional mortgage rate and other market rates see J. Guttentag, "The Behaviour of Residential Mortgage Yields since 1951," in J. Guttentag and P. Cagan (eds.), *Essays on Interest Rates*, Vol. 1, National Bureau of Economic Research (New York, 1969), 29–76; J.V. Poapst, *The Residential Mortgage Market*, a working paper prepared for the Royal Commission on Banking and Finance (Ottawa, 1962), 122; S. Klaman, *The Postwar Residential Mortgage Market*, National Bureau of Economic Research (Princeton, NJ, 1961), 75.

6 See also L.B. Smith, "On the Economic Implications of the Yield Ceiling on Government Insured Mortgages," *Canadian Journal of Economics and Political Science* XXXIII (August 1967), 420–31.

7 These figures are based on 1970 tax schedules.

8 For a discussion of these effects and approach see L.B. Smith, "Effects of the White Paper on the Demand for and Price of Real Estate," *Report of the Proceedings of the Twenty Second Tax Conference*, Canadian Tax Foundation (Toronto 1970), 374–83.

9 An additional implication of the tax system is the preference it may provide for different forms of housing. One bias in favour of home ownership in Canada is the failure to include imputed rents as taxable income. In the United States this bias is carried much further by allowing mortgage interest and realty tax payments as deductions from taxable income for income tax purposes.

CHAPTER NINE

1 Parts of this chapter are based upon L.B. Smith, *Housing in Canada: Market Structure and Policy Performance* Research Monograph no. 2 in *Urban Canada: Problems and Prospects* (Ottawa, 1971), 70–83; and L.B. Smith, "Postwar Canadian Housing Policy in Theory and Practice," *Land Economics*, XLIV (August 1968), 171–9.

2 For a discussion of the objectives and history of direct housing programmes see Central Mortgage and Housing Corporation, *Submission to the Royal Commission on Banking and Finance* (Ottawa, 1962). For a discussion of this programme see also J.V. Poapst, *The Residential Mortgage Market*, a working paper prepared for the Royal Commission on Banking and Finance (Ottawa, 1962), 171–8; and J. Gillies, "Some Financial Aspects of the Canadian Government Housing Program: A History and Prospective Developments," *Journal of Finance* 8 (March 1953), 24.

3 For a discussion of the effects of the tied NHA rate see Smith, "Postwar Canadian Housing Policy in Theory and Practice," 344.

4 Between 1946 and 1954 the proportionate increase in NHA mortgage holdings was accompanied by an equivalent increase in conventional mortgage holdings.

5 Since this discussion is restricted to the relative desirability of alternative forms of mortgage investment scale effects may be ignored.

6 Canadian Life Insurance Officers' Association, *Submission to the Royal Commission on Banking and Finance* (Ottawa, 1962), 77.

7 Y. Dubé, J. Howes, and D.L. McQueen, *Housing and Social Capital*, Royal Commission on Canada's Economic Prospects (Ottawa, 1957), 44.
8 For details see Central Mortgage and Housing Corporation, *Canadian Housing Statistics* (1959), 9 and *ibid.*, 26.
9 For the US experience see L. Grebler, "Stabilizing Residential Construction, A Review of the Post War Period," *American Economic Review* XXXIX (September 1949), 902.
10 L.B. Smith, "The Postwar Residential Mortgage Market and the Role of Government" unpublished PhD thesis, Harvard University (1966), 219.
11 Some qualification is required here to account for secondary effects. To the extent that increasing residential construction activity raises construction costs (equation 11 in chapter 4), and rising construction costs restrain new construction, some secondary upward price effects arise. However, to the extent that increased availability leads to more construction and housing stock, this exerts downward pressure on prices.
12 To completely specify the availability effects in each sector the RC–RB variable should also be included in the NHA equation. However, multicollinearity prevented this.
13 Although it is not significantly higher than in the NHA housing start regression, the coefficient of the RNHA–RB variable in the conventional housing start regression seems a little too high relative to the coefficient of this variable in the NHA regression.
14 The 1954 rate change increased the cost of NHA credit to borrowers and reduced the yield to lenders as a result of the removal of the federal yield subsidy. Although it is not clear whether these adjustments represent a net increase or decrease in the NHA rate, they clearly represent a reduction in lender yields and hence the direction of their availability effects is clear.
15 Royal Commission on Banking and Finance, *Appendix to the Report of the Royal Commission on Banking and Finance* (Ottawa, 1964), 100.
16 This does not include a special bonus provision introduced in December, 1949 and withdrawn in February, 1951 as part of the adjustment in downpayment requirements.
17 An exception to this is the very large increase in the loan maximum for apartment units to $18,000 per unit in February, 1968.
18 For this view see the Royal Commission on Banking and Finance, *Report* (Ottawa, Queen's Printer, 1964), 273; Poapst, *The Residential Mortgage Market*, 100; and Central Mortgage and Housing Corporation, *Submission to the Royal Commission on Banking and Finance* (Ottawa 1962), 4.
19 This value compares with the average loan per dwelling unit in current dollars in 1957 of $10,250 and in 1967 of $15,547 for single detached dwellings, and of $6724 in 1957 and $12,511 in 1967 for multiple dwelling units. The vast majority of CMHC direct lending during the estimation period was for single detached dwellings.
20 This conclusion is confined to section 40 lending since over 90 per cent of CMHC direct lending during the estimation period occurred under this section.
21 In the long run this reduction will be mitigated by additional savings and investment flows arising from increased expenditures generated by this government lending. However, in the short run, it is likely that only a small percentage of these flows will go into those institutions most directly involved in mortgage lending.
22 For another statement of this view see S. Maisel, "The Relationship of Residential Financing and Expenditures on Residential Construction," *Conference on Savings and Residential Finance, 1965 Proceedings*, US Savings and Loan League (Chicago, 1965), 132.

www.ingramcontent.com/pod-product-compliance
Lightning Source LLC
Chambersburg PA
CBHW051351070526
44584CB00025B/3725